TOTAL CONFINEMENT

CALIFORNIA SERIES IN PUBLIC ANTHROPOLOGY

The California Series in Public Anthropology emphasizes
the anthropologist's role as an engaged intellectual. It continues
anthropology's commitment to being an ethnographic witness, to
describing, in human terms, how life is lived beyond the borders
of many readers' experiences. But it also adds a commitment,
through ethnography, to reframing the terms of public debate—
transforming received, accepted understandings of
social issues with new insights, new framings.

SERIES EDITOR: Robert Borofsky (Hawaii Pacific University)

CONTRIBUTING EDITORS: Philippe Bourgois (UC San Francisco),
Paul Farmer (Partners in Health), Rayna Rapp (New York University),
and Nancy Scheper-Hughes (UC Berkeley)

UNIVERSITY OF CALIFORNIA PRESS EDITOR: Naomi Schneider

1. *Twice Dead: Organ Transplants and the Reinvention of Death*,
   by Margaret Lock

2. *Birthing the Nation: Strategies of Palestinian Women in Israel*,
   by Rhoda Ann Kanaaneh (with a Foreword by Hannan Ashrawi)

3. *Annihilating Difference: The Anthropology of Genocide*,
   edited by Alexander Laban Hinton (with a Foreword by Kenneth Roth)

4. *Pathologies of Power: Structural Violence and the Assault on Health
   and Human Rights*, by Paul Farmer (with a Foreword by Amartya Sen)

5. *Buddha Is Hiding: Refugees, Citizenship, and the New America*,
   by Aihwa Ong

6. *Chechnya: The Making of a War-Torn Society*, by Valery Tishkov

7. *Total Confinement: Madness and Reason in the Maximum Security Prison*,
   by Lorna A. Rhodes

8. *Paradise in Ashes: A Guatemalan Journey of Courage, Terror, and Hope*,
   by Beatriz Manz

TOTAL CONFINEMENT

Madness and Reason
in the Maximum Security Prison

Lorna A. Rhodes

University of California Press   Berkeley   Los Angeles   London

University of California Press
Berkeley and Los Angeles, California

University of California Press, Ltd.
London, England

Library of Congress Cataloging-in-Publication Data

Rhodes, Lorna A. (Lorna Amarasingham)
    Total confinement : madness and reason in the
maximum security prison / Lorna A. Rhodes.
        p.   cm.—(California series in public
anthropology ; 7)
    Includes bibliographical references and index.
    ISBN 0-520-22987-8 (alk. paper).
—ISBN 0-520-24076-6 (pbk. : alk. paper)
    1. Solitary confinement—United States.
2. Prisoners—Mental health—United States.
3. Imprisonment—United States.   4. Prisons—
United States.   I. Title.
HV9471.R473   2004
365'.66—dc21   2003050138

Manufactured in the United States of America
10   09   08   07   06   05   04
10   9   8   7   6   5   4   3   2   1

The paper used in this publication meets the
minimum requirements of ANSI/NISO z39.48-1992
(R 1997) (*Permanence of Paper*).♾

For Lilamani

CONTENTS

This book is based on participation in dozens of situations and conversations and on over one hundred interviews conducted by me and others. The observations and interactions described here took place over a number of years in seven prisons and in several other correctional settings. Names and identifying features have been changed. In addition, some of the descriptions of individuals and scenes contain elements taken from more than one person, situation, or prison. They accurately reflect specific events and conversations, but rearranged or conflated to preserve confidentiality. With the exception of events in the last chapter, almost everything described is based on more than one, and sometimes many, instances. Quotations are from tape-recorded interviews or from notes made at the time of interactions; they have been edited for length and style. In the interest of confidentiality, I use generic terms such as "prison worker," "mental health worker," and "custody supervisor" to designate individuals with a variety of job titles. This book is about all-male institutions, and the masculine pronoun is used throughout to refer to prisoners.

My interest in prisons began when a colleague invited me to join a small group of mental health professionals on a visit to a nearby state prison. Two moments during that carefully arranged event have remained with me over the ensuing years. One was a discussion with several officers who worked in a maximum security psychiatric unit. They were blunt about how poorly, in their view, psychiatric care fit into custodial containment. Behind the immediate content of what they said, I had a sense of pent-up narrative energy: these prison workers clearly had more to tell than the format of our visit could contain. The second moment was when our tour took us to the outer gate of the prison's "supermaximum" or "control" unit. Our little knot of academics stood awkwardly in front of the double gates, able to see nothing more than an empty hallway and the edge of a heavy steel door. We had little idea what lay beyond, and we were clearly to be allowed no further.

This book is the result of my engagement as an anthropologist with the maximum security prisons I was so briefly introduced to that day. The visit was an early step in the Correctional Mental Health Collaboration, an association between the University of Washington and the Washington State Department of Corrections that began in 1993 and ended in 2002. This relationship between my university and the prison system made it possible for me to enter prisons and to carry out the ethnographic work on which this account is based. I was familiar with how public psychiatry is practiced, and knew that many thousands of people who once would have been hospitalized are now incarcerated. Realizing that I was seeing an extension and replacement of the state hospital I had studied earlier, I wondered how psychiatrically impaired inmates and the standard diagnostic system were assimilated into the prison context. What powered the intensity so evident in the way the officers we met described the mental health setting in which they worked? At the time of that first visit, however, I knew almost nothing of the existence of control prisons. When I did eventually enter these facilities, which are designed specifically to isolate prisoners from one another, it became clear that prison "mental health" exists in a dynamic relationship to the management of those prisoners designated "the worst of the worst" and assigned to super maximum security housing. I began to explore the links and tensions between madness (psychiatric and otherwise) and reason (the presumed rationality of people and systems) as they are contained and expressed in conditions of total confinement.

This is a work of ethnography spread across several maximum security facilities. I draw on the whole period of university involvement with the corrections department, but especially on three years of intensive research that occurred after I had become somewhat familiar with how control and psychiatric units are related within a larger institutional system. Sometimes I indicate my membership in a close-knit team of generous colleagues with whom I visited prisons, organized interview sessions, and met with officials. More often, this account reflects my own ethnographic work, carried out while visiting prisons on my own. I interviewed maximum security inmates formally in visiting booths and talked with them informally at cellfront. I talked with uniformed staff, mental health staff, administrators, and officials, and attended numerous prison events and meetings. The collaborative project that most contributed to this book was our three-year study of the state's control units, for which we interviewed almost ninety randomly chosen maximum security prisoners as well as forty staff members at three facilities.

Much of the material in this book is in the form of conversations, some with me, and others in which people speak primarily with one another. These conversations form layers of commentary on the experience of being imprisoned and how that experience is interpreted, on the conflictual

and difficult nature of prison work, and on the fraught relationship between punishing and caring for those excluded from ordinary social life.
When the custody officers in the psychiatric unit complained about
conflicts with the mental health staff, they were not just grousing about
difficult work. They were describing unresolved questions about control,
rehabilitation, and individual choice that bear—often painfully—on the
practices that sustain confinement. As I got to know prison staff and prisoners, it became increasingly clear that what is the stuff of classroom debate elsewhere was the content of their everyday lives. During the past
twenty-five years of prison proliferation, the historical prison has become
a potent academic metaphor for power, domination, and the problemat-
ics of governmental order. Prisoners and prison workers who struggle over
the interpretation of behavior engage long-standing and deeply rooted
dilemmas about what it means to be a human—and a social—being.

The intensive prison expansion of the last quarter of the twentieth century produced an institutional complex of almost unimaginable size and
complexity. Although prison growth has recently slowed, the prison complex remains a massive—if partially hidden—presence that matters to our
public life in a myriad of both obvious and subtle ways. Large-scale incarceration has its most obvious effects on those directly involved as prisoners, workers, and their families and communities. Perhaps less clear are
the ways in which the growth of imprisonment as an almost reflexive response to social problems affects our priorities for public life and is reflected
in a pervasive media imagery of violence in the service of the law.

This book appears at a moment when debate on prisons seems to be
shifting, with increased questioning of the effects of sentencing laws, prison
construction, and other aspects of the boom in incarceration. Such questioning has begun to take into account the increasing imprisonment of
the mentally ill and the contradictory expectations that result. While the
effort to meld psychiatry into custodial containment is extremely difficult
at the local level, it is—relatively speaking—fairly transparent to critical
analysis. It is not yet clear, however, to what extent control units—the specialized maximum security facilities I describe here—will be subject to the
same level of debate that is overtaking prison building in general. These
facilities are less accessible to public scrutiny, and apply a sophisticated
technology to processes of social ejection with deep historical roots and
broad implications for the national psyche. Although these expensive pris-

ons are profound in their effects on inmates and workers and useless for other purposes, they have the momentum of a compelling and exclusionary cultural logic. My aim is to allow the conundrums that unfold daily within prison walls to enter into a larger conversation about these institutional practices and the ways they immerse us in certain confounding aspects of our national life.

INTRODUCTION

> I don't know if you can get your point across except by
> bringing the public in and sticking them in one of those
> little cages for a week or two.

JEREMY ROLAND*, CONTROL UNIT PRISONER

Waiting on my side of a visiting booth in a maximum security unit, I am looking through a clear, thick plastic window into a small, bare room identical to the one in which I am sitting. But unlike the ordinary wooden door I just closed behind me, the door into the room on the other side is solid steel with a small hinged slot, or cuffport, at waist height. As it opens, two blue-uniformed officers hand in a dark-haired young man in a white jumpsuit, hands cuffed behind his back. The door closes behind him with a heavy clank. In one smooth motion the prisoner takes a step inside and backs his hands through the cuffport so that one of the officers can free them from the cuffs.

After Jeremy Roland settles onto the metal stool on his side of the window and I place my tape recorder microphone up against the small speaker in the wall on my side, he tells me that he knows this situation would seem odd to an outsider.[1] "Seeing someone come in here with handcuffs and backing up to the door probably seems very strange to you, but I've been doing it for a few years now. It's like putting on your shoes and walking out of your house." But his grandmother will be coming soon for what he knows will be the last time, and he is sorry that he will have to meet her in one of these booths. He doesn't want her to see him here under maximum custody restrictions. "I still get embarrassed in front of visitors

*All names given for prisoners in this book are pseudonyms.

and being handcuffed. Not so much embarrassed as I am ashamed . . . I'm gonna have a real hard time with it." I notice that the window between us is covered with smudges right at eye level where previous visitors have tried to press their hands together through the plastic pane.

Jeremy has a life sentence. He came to prison at twenty after his third "strike"; his worst offense was an assault during a robbery in which no one was killed. "Everything that was most important to me then is least important to me now," he says. "And everything that was least important is most important to me now. [My third strike] woke me up. I wish it had happened ten years ago. I wish so much. But it's too late. They've thrown away the key." He talks about the other prisoners who are here with him on this unit where he is confined to a solitary cell for twenty-three hours a day. Some seem to be deranged, "sick individuals" who "make everyone miserable, day in and day out" by pounding on their sinks and doors. It seems to him that no sooner does one leave than another takes his place. Others are murderers who have done "brutal things"—"I know some horrible people [who] commit horrible crimes . . . You've got some pretty bad prisoners in here, just awful."

Once he gets past the "little trouble" that brought him to this unit, Jeremy likely will do his time in the "general population," where the vast majority of prisoners live. But like many who live or work in prisons, he frames his description of his environment with two figures who, like bookends, mark the limits of comprehension: one "sick" and the other "bad."

Jeremy is typical of many prisoners and staff in his description of the disturbing—but far from uniform—effects of intensive confinement. My introduction to a prisoner Jeremy would have called "sick" occurred one day during the first year of our project when I visited a psychiatric unit for seriously mentally ill inmates. A small group of staff took me to the end of a long cell-lined hallway. Thomas Vincent had lived there for several years, and his delusions, odd behavior, and attacks on staff had diminished in response to the care he received. But his sentence expired the next day, and two days earlier his condition had deteriorated dramatically. Now, he was "locked down" in his small room behind his heavy door with its small window. He had destroyed most of his property, including his clothes, and had wrapped his naked body in threads unraveled from a sheet. Before I quickly glanced away, I saw his frightened eyes and the gleam of dozens of white strings wound around his tense body. He looked as though he wanted to jump out of his skin.

One of the unit's counselors was rather awkwardly cradling a pair of shoes, which he held up in front of the window so that Vincent could see them. Setting them carefully on the floor in front of the cell, he explained to me that he wanted to reassure the prisoner that the things that had been removed from his cell were still available. After we had walked back down the tier, we gathered in a little knot near the unit's control booth. The staff explained that they could not, of course, keep Vincent where he was, and they had no obligation other than to let him go from the gate of their prison into the surrounding semi-rural landscape. They had scheduled a commitment hearing with a state hospital and planned to argue that his psychosis and history of assault made him a danger to both himself and others. What, I asked, if that doesn't work? Then they would drive him to a nearby city and drop him off outside the emergency room of a public hospital.[2]

A prison mental health worker described the facility that Vincent seems reluctant to leave as a "black box within a black box" into which the public and even other prisons want men like him to disappear.[3] Vincent may well have arrived there from another maximum security setting, psychotic and banging on his cell like the inmates Jeremy described. Now he had nowhere to go, no reason to step into those shoes outside his door.

During that same first year I went for the first time into the kind of maximum security unit in which I interviewed Roland. The unit had a circular design, with a control booth in the center and rows of cells around the periphery. Standing next to the control booth with the two prison workers who were escorting me, at first I barely noticed the man exercising in a small indoor yard in front of the tiers. The prisoner, Jamal Nelson, was facing the wall and swinging his arms out in gradually widening circles, an exercise that made sense given the lack of any exercise equipment in the little space. But gradually we became aware that he was calmly and rhythmically swinging one arm closer and closer to the wall, a bloodstain spreading as his hand hit the concrete. "Let's go," said one of my companions sharply, "before we give him any more attention." As we left, I saw that two officers had moved quickly into the yard to stop him.

The "box" of the prison presents a smooth surface to the outside world, which is of course how it works as a place of disappearance. But inside, it has distinct internal separations. The two prisoners I have just described were in the different, though equally controlled, environments designated for the system's "problem children." Vincent had a diagnosis of chronic mental illness; the staff of the treatment unit felt he needed attention in the form of medication, reassurance, and, they hoped, some sort of continuing treatment. Nelson was considered disturbed, though more ambiguously; those keeping him felt that he was playing for "attention" and that attention was harmful to him. They believed that he needed to be maintained—maybe permanently—in a condition offering the barest of human contact.

Maximum security prisons have in common extreme forms of control that go well beyond that effected by ordinary prison discipline. Confined to these units are the prisoners called—in the shorthand of psychiatry—the "mad" and the "bad." At the heart of this book is the paradox represented in my sketches of Vincent and Nelson: the tighter control becomes, the more problematic are the effects it precipitates. Often situations like these are approached in terms of whether and how individuals choose their own behavior. To what extent are these men in control of themselves? Are these strange behaviors signs of underlying disturbances—"madness" in one of its many forms—in those subjected to intensive confinement? Or are they willful, character-based attempts to exert a minimal, if counterproductive, resistance? A second way to frame these questions, however, is to shift to the level of the institutional mechanisms of control. What assumptions about dangerousness, self-control, and individual choice are contained in, and signaled by, measures of extreme confinement? What conundrums are encountered both by those who are the object of these measures and by those who enforce them? These questions point us less toward the inmate as a disturbed individual and more toward his position in and his responses to the social world formed around him by the conditions in which he is held. It is primarily this second kind of question that I explore in this book.

Reflecting on the path that sent him to prison, Roland says that he has "made some mistakes in [his] life, some bad choices" for which he deserves punishment, though he protests that the punishment itself is excessive. He mourns the rational actor he could have been and wants to be now. "So here I sit," he says sadly. Vincent clearly cannot make rational choices and has been given a kind of partial exemption, but he is in a larger context that has abandoned him. Nelson's strange act is ambiguous; is it a calculated bid for attention? He has lived in a control unit for years without a resolution to this question. Within the larger issue of control, then, we find that the behavior of these prisoners is understood in terms of their capacity to reason, an understanding that in turn determines where they live and the attitudes they encounter in prison staff. Both the "horrible" prisoners described by Roland and the "attention-seeking" Nelson, as well as Roland himself, are being treated as rational actors. They are believed capable of choosing not to be where they are. Vincent, on the other hand, is treated as irrational and therefore unable to control his behavior.

The issue of whether and how prisoners make rational decisions is embedded in a larger question: what of the institution itself? The kind of control exercised in these maximum security settings is technologically sophisticated and planned down to the smallest detail. The myriad elements of housing design, placement, and daily routine shaping these prisoners' situations rest on the assumption that rational practices underlie the operation of "the system." But what, really, is this rationality of the system? Perhaps—as suggested by the history of modern forms of punishment— it lies in an institutional regime of order designed to contain and correct the disordered products of society. Perhaps, as many prison workers and some prisoners believe, it arises "naturally" from the connection between the project of containment and our innate capacity to reason. Punishment, in this view, simply aligns human nature with laws that reflect that nature back to us. But perhaps the institution carries a secret: that it is, under these surface appearances, profoundly irrational. Roland's sentence, with its wastefulness of life and incredible cost, Vincent's impending ejection, delusional and assaultive, to "the streets," the interpretation offered for Nelson's self-destruction—all suggest that the "system" itself may be mad. These prisoners are entangled in institutional contradictions within which they become—and suffer for becoming—the extremes and exceptions that mark the limits of the rational.

How these limits are situated—that is, what happens to prisoners deemed more or less capable of reason—depends on an opposition fundamental to prisons. On the one hand, punishment in the form of a harsh environment is presumed to teach a lesson; on the other, treatment offers a partial alternative to that environment. I explore here how these alternatives are worked out—or struggled through—in practice. I do not treat these categories for sorting prisoners as given; in fact, the reader should suspend judgment as to whether and in what sense individuals fit into them. Instead I treat the process of sorting as one element in the shifting institutional terrain within which prisoners and staff alike must somehow make sense of intensive confinement.

Several things are at stake in trying to connect everyday events in prisons with certain fundamental assumptions about how people do, do not, will not, or cannot choose their behavior. The first is that these assumptions have been central in driving the recent growth of prisons and underpinning the proliferation of maximum security facilities within prisons. The human situations represented in these brief stories and throughout this book happen every day all over the United States. They involve an extraordinarily large number of people—prisoners, prison workers, and others—in wasteful and damaging forms of institutional life. We have evolved a public discourse in which paying attention to these situations is taken as a sign of indifference to the suffering of those who have been harmed by others and of lack of common sense in the face of obvious social dangers. But attention to the effects of prisons on individuals and of large-scale imprisonment on the country does not require us to turn away from the effects of crime or to minimize the fact that some people need to be prevented from harming others.[4] In fact, much in the current situation increases the likelihood of future harm. Conversely, while some prison workers are harsh or worse, presuming that all are harsh not only misrepresents the many who are not, but also keeps us from a more nuanced understanding of the work they are being asked to do. It will become clear in this book that many (though certainly not all) in corrections realize and are puzzled or frustrated by the contradictions they experience. Exploring the internal logic of the prison can make it clearer what these contradictions are and open possibilities for questioning our approach to them.

The second thing at stake in understanding prisons is that, perhaps more than most institutions, they raise the question of whether there is any "give" or hope in the "system." In posing the issue of rationality I am not proposing some sort of structural approach that works from within the terms already provided—for example, to argue that more study would enable a more accurate system of inmate classification. Rather, I take these premises that are important within the prison and explore their persistent and perversely troublesome effects. Psychiatry and custody, for example, are mutually dependent and at the same time speak irreconcilable languages. At their points of intersection people are necessarily forced to articulate and reflect on what they do, and it is at these moments that possibilities for change emerge. Even a very local effort such as the one I describe in the last chapter—however tentative and necessarily enmeshed in the terms it resists—can be seen as an indicator that seemingly monolithic systems have openings.

The third thing at stake has to do with the fact that current theoretical debates in anthropology and many other disciplines make heavy use of the historical prison to draw connections between power—particularly the power of the state—and the conditions in which the modern sense of self or personhood is formed. The usefulness of these debates for understanding the contemporary prison has been little explored, nor has the social world inside the prison been approached for what it might have to say to them.[5] This book reflects my desire to stay alert to how conversation on these matters can cut both ways. Recognizing the implications of certain historical echoes, such as the mutual shaping of architecture and modern state power, helps to illuminate the encrusted layers of practice within institutions. It suggests, also, that it is not just the perversity of human nature that gives these institutions their unintended consequences. At the same time, those who live inside the actual practices of confinement—staff and prisoners—offer an embedded commentary that can illuminate theoretical difficulties being excavated elsewhere.

Finally, the contemporary prison has developed a new technology—in the form of the control prison—for the creation of a potentially absolute social exclusion. Historically, and in many prison systems in the United States, this exclusion is correlated with and profoundly linked to race. The current proliferation and expansion of the technology suggests that it is being enlisted to manage other projects of separation and isolation as well. When these projects of exclusion are framed in entirely individualistic and non-rehabilitative terms, they confront us with disturbing questions about what it means to be a human—a social—being. I believe this is the issue most deeply at stake in the contemporary prison. I approach it here, not at the level of national policy where it has been well described, but at the level of local practice where it is enacted in daily assertions of authority and resistance.

Prison is a big "black hole" we pour resources into.

PRISON MENTAL HEALTH WORKER

Even those who haunt our dominant institutions and
their systems of value are haunted too by things they
sometimes have names for and sometimes do not.

AVERY GORDON, *Ghostly Matters*, pp. 4–5

Prisons create by their very nature sets of opposing and aligned positions,
at the least consisting of prisoners, correctional workers, and the "public."
To these one must add the many auxiliary industries and workers arrayed
around prison systems, the legal and human rights organizations that help
prisoners, and the media. In addition, scholarly interest in prisons goes
back deep into the nineteenth century and has generated an enormous literature across many disciplines and perspectives. All these positions, of
course, have genealogies that are in turn subject to much exploration and
debate. I present here a brief and simplified overview of this territory and
of how it is related to my purpose. Before doing that, however, I need to
mention that the writer on prisons is faced with certain unavoidable points
of complicity with her subject.

One of these is that crime, criminals, and "prison life" are—and have
been at least since the nineteenth century—a source of public fascination
and debate. Looming cellblocks, stone-faced guards, dangerous and deranged felons: these familiar tropes tell us in advance what to expect of
prison. Allen Feldman writes of what he calls "cultural anesthesia": the fact
that we are bombarded with images representing all kinds of violence but
are also able, by means of these same images, to evade the disturbing phys-
icality and immediacy of violence itself.[6] Many aspects of the contemporary representation of crime and punishment carry the danger of this kind
of anesthesia. One consequence is that prison becomes an "abstract site"
in the public imagination precisely through the fetishizing of its concrete
details.[7] An element in this dynamic, of course, is the captivating relationship between watching and being watched that pervades prisons. This
relationship inevitably molds description (witness mine of the three prisoners I just described) and thus perpetuates itself even as one attempts to
evade it. Although I do not pretend to resolve this dilemma, I choose to

emphasize the social contexts in which what people said had meaning and to refrain from using a case study format to describe prisoners.

One officer who read an earlier version of this book told me that he had at first felt concern about how I would describe officers, wondering, as he put it, "Is she on our side?" This is a field in which several vocabularies represent positions that are in a state of chronic tension with one another. Often, two or three highly charged words refer to the same thing, and words from one or another "side" are offensive to the others. Thus the people who watch over prisoners are "officers" to themselves, "guards" in the media and to prison critics, and "guards," "police," or "cops" to prisoners. Prisoners are "prisoners," "inmates," or "convicts" to themselves, "inmates" or—the currently favored term—"offenders" to correctional workers.[8] Similar conflictual terms and positions exist among perspectives on prison as a whole: "corrections" and the "prison industrial complex" refer to, but certainly do not live in, the same world. I attempt to represent rather than resolve these difficulties, choosing words reflective of the various contexts I describe and juxtaposing multiple perspectives. The effect may be disconcerting to those accustomed to staying within one of these vocabularies, but my aim is to evoke a sense of movement from the space of one discourse to another.

Prisons as Industry

The expansion of the prison system that began in the early 1980s has resulted in the highest rate of incarceration in the world. Today in the United States over two million people are in prison. Half of these prisoners are African Americans and three-fourths are people of color.[9] The incarceration of women, three-fourths women of color, expanded dramatically during the period of prison growth.[10] The prison complex is immensely costly, draining money from other arenas of public life; in 2000 state and local incarceration costs came to almost $40 billion.[11]

Critics of the prison industrial complex point out that prisons do many things that depend upon but are only indirectly connected to those they confine. In many parts of the country prisons have become a substitute for traditional industries, offering middle-class, union-protected wages to rural people facing globalization and diminishing employment opportunities.[12] Here—in often factory-like conditions—former factory, mill, and agricultural workers are given over to the containment of unemployed urban youths and of some of their more demoralized neighbors. Prisons create new markets for law enforcement technology, provide cheap labor for corporations, add to the census of depopulated rural counties, disenfranchise poor and minority people, and lower official unemployment statistics.[13] Recent works that refer to a "prison nation" and a national lockdown point to the fact that the prison complex is grounded in these wider economic and political developments.[14] By "disappearing" large numbers of poor, mostly minority people as well as many who are seriously mentally ill, prisons exercise a kind of social magic that produces "multiple invisibilities."[15] From this perspective what happens to individual prisoners once they fall from public view is an almost incidental—though devastating—effect of incarceration as an industry.[16]

The decade of the 1990s saw the greatest prison population increase in U.S. history. However, a recent slowing of prison expansion suggests that fiscal realities and changing public and political concerns are beginning to shift the pattern. Since 2000 a number of states have reduced their prison populations and placed construction plans on hold; there is evidence that state governments, correctional officials, and many citizens are questioning the large-scale imprisonment of nonviolent offenders over the past twenty years.[17] This is, perhaps, an indication that the moment is right for efforts to unpack the consequences of prison growth. At the same time, however, the fading of the boom in the absence of any significant reduction in the overall prison population may simply serve to show the strength of its systemic social and economic underpinnings. Criminal justice policies that disproportionately affect minorities, the use of prison construction to manage rural unemployment, and the multiple industries geared to corrections may be extremely resistant to change. And the strong attribution of individual "choice" to prisoners—so central to the current politics of incarceration—remains thoroughly embedded in a larger discourse of economic and social autonomy that shows no signs of losing its grip on the public imagination.

Corrections

"Corrections"—the governmental system that operates prisons—is a bureaucracy centered on the management of large numbers of people. It is a world of policies, documents, meetings, acronyms, and all the other governmental practices that make up such management. As in other organizations, one can spend a good deal of time in administrative meetings without getting much flavor of what it is, exactly, that is being managed. This "paper" side of the prison system has grown in size and impact as the result of an increasingly professional and managerial focus within corrections.[18] Centralized management overlays a second organizational hierarchy, the older paramilitary structure—called "custody"—composed of officers and the sergeants, lieutenants, and captains who make up their "chain of command" in each prison.[19] The prisons themselves are administered by superintendents (wardens) and managers who must both support and control the uniformed staff. In addition, a multitude of other workers also enter the prisons each day. Among these are the psychologists and other mental health workers who staff mental health units and work as outpatient staff in other parts of the prisons.

At the seams of this system two, three, or more of these lines of authority intersect, each of them operating on assumptions that are in part opaque to the others.[20] In this book the main intersection I describe is between custodial (security) and mental health staff. Two related but sometimes conflicting discourses meet at this juncture, one centered on projects of discipline founded in notions of rationality and the other on projects of restoration aimed toward normal subjectivity.[21] The degree of harmony or friction among those who occupy these positions varies greatly over time and from one prison to another. My interest here, however, is how the issues themselves are embedded in a larger vernacular logic. This logic manifests itself in everyday practice as a struggle over which individuals should be forced to take responsibility for their actions and reflects the contradictions of a Euro-American individualism that is widely shared and deeply implicated in the historical origins of both prisons and psychiatry.

Correctional management at the local level is far from static. Administrators and officials come and go, expectations of staff change (for example, a formerly all-male officer corps now includes women), vocabularies change, and management tools (such as total quality management and computerized tracking systems) are imported. Evidence for this kind of change appears in this book in a number of places: the presence of female staff is commonplace, some of my examples come from relatively new training classes for officers, and people from different "eras" speak openly about differences between past and present practices and expectations. These changes always take place, however, in the context of security requirements and the time-tested authority structure that enforces them.

Line staff, the mainstay of the prison's round-the-clock operation, spoke with me of their ways of understanding prisoners, their responses to the governmental practices they are taught, and the emotional toll of what they do. Like many who have studied prisons, I found most correctional workers to be decent people doing difficult work. This is not to minimize the potential for brutality; there is ample evidence of abusive behavior by prison workers. Ted Conover, a journalist who spent a year working as a guard at Sing Sing, notes that on this point the officers he worked with adopted a "siege mentality . . . a closing of ranks" that prevented them from acknowledging "the obvious, that among the many good officers there are a few bad ones."[22] While removing abusive officers is clearly important, it does not address the larger systemic issues that impinge on all workers and prisoners and, as I show, contribute to the circularity of some of their responses to one another. Prisons have complementary but in some ways quite similar effects on inmates, officers, and prison workers in general, a point that has some potential for undermining stereotypical depictions.

The fact that I worked in Washington State prisons influences this account in several ways that I am aware of and probably in some ways that I am not. Clearly the fact of our work in the system and the help we received from correctional officials, administrators, and line staff suggest an openness that may not be present elsewhere.[23] Further, because of the relatively small size of Washington State, its largely white prison population, and its progressive history, some of what I describe here may not be typical of other states. Much critical literature on prisons examines the massive incarceration of African Americans, control prisons of up to several thousand beds, and the systematic use of permanent preventive detention; none of these issues characterizes Washington State. Finally, changes in Washington's prisons during the period of our work and our involvement in specific projects of change likely influenced the reflective tone of some of my material.

A former prisoner writes, "Most Americans remain ignorant . . . that they live in a country that holds hostage behind bars another populous country of their fellow citizens."[24] In this other country there is tremendous variation among prisoners and among the environments in which they live. One reason I began with my conversation with Jeremy Roland is that although he was a maximum custody inmate at the time, he represents the many inmates who pass through that status quickly and whose lives in prison do not revolve around the kind of difficulties that I describe in this book. The term "general population" is used in prisons to refer to the ordinary conditions under which most prisoners live and to which Roland would return.

General population inmates are not personally restrained and move about the prison (at specific times) to jobs and other activities. They eat together in large dining halls, share two- to four-man cells in crowded living units, and exercise in large communal yards A prisoner living in general population writes of Stateville in Illinois:

> If you expect the usual tale of constant violence, brutal guards, gang rapes, daily escape efforts, turmoil . . . you will be deeply disappointed. Prison life . . . is not a daily round of threats, fights, plots, and "shanks" (prison made knives)—though you have to be constantly careful to avoid situations or behavior that might lead to violence . . . For me, and many like me in prison, violence is not the major problem; the major problem is monotony . . . boredom, time-slowing boredom, interrupted by occasional bursts of fear and anger, is the governing reality of life in prison.[25]

For the purpose of understanding the contexts I describe here, the most important feature of general population is that it requires prisoners to manage themselves in groups within a complex, overcrowded system. Assignment to special maximum security units occurs in a larger context of pressures for conformity, jam-packed quarters, intergroup tensions, and various kinds of victimization. Large living units can be dangerous for prisoners with psychiatric problems or other vulnerabilities; even fairly minor aberrant behavior may cause an inmate to be rejected or injured by his peers.[26] Once confined to a special unit, some inmates regard general population as a sort of Promised Land where they can have access to their property, sit in the sun, yard with other inmates (in prison, "yard" is a verb as well as a noun). Others, however, find the intense social life on regular living units more deadly than a lonely special unit cell.[27] Both prisoners and staff negotiate an environment in which the difficult, boring, or dangerous conditions of the prison as a whole are in ongoing tension with—and the only alternative to—the isolation and stasis of intensive confinement.

THINKING THROUGH PRISONS

I became aware, over and over again, of how tenaciously
the past searches for its expression in the present.
ANTHONY GIDDENS (QUOTING A THERAPIST),
IN BECK, GIDDENS, AND LASH, *Reflexive Modernity*, p. 72

Instead of dividing the world into good and bad
exercises of power, Foucault prefers the question . . .
"What happens?"
JOHN RANSOM, *Foucault's Discipline*, p. 42

In movies and in accounts by prisoners and visitors, being "inside" for the first time is a stock scene, the sound of clanging steel gates (always closing behind one) the classic rendering of confinement's threshold. I was somewhat prepared for this, the moment when one imagines never coming out again. But when I stood inside the control unit during Nelson's yard, I was distracted by something else: the historical specificity of the unit's design. I was standing at the center of a circular prison almost identical to the now-famous "Inspection House" designed by the English philosopher Jeremy Bentham in the 1790s. The fact that we watched from the center as a prisoner responded—negatively—to our gaze was a perverse twist on Bentham's belief that with his new panoptical design the prisoner would internalize the inspector's gaze and thereby instill a positive discipline in himself.[28]

Throughout the writing of this book I have grappled with the question of what to do about history. The architecture, practices, and conflicts I describe here all reach back to specific historical moments: the birth of the modern prison in Bentham's utilitarian philosophy of punishment; the intermeshing of psychiatric and penal theories about the individual in the nineteenth century; the prison slavery of Reconstruction; the layers and layers of reform that promised to bring order to the penal systems of Europe and America. Hundreds of works document the development of the modern prison and the histories of specific prisons. After a long tussle with this material I have realized, with the help of Avery Gordon's wonderful *Ghostly Matters*, that what I want to convey is less the comprehensive historical detail—impossible in any case—than a sense of echo. What assailed me in that first control unit visit was the sort of echo that Gordon calls a haunting—a moment when history offers itself to us as a presence rather than a collection of facts. Contemporary prisons are indeed haunted in this sense, holding as they do a history of disappearances. And they are pervaded by past efforts and failures, often taking up where some long-forgotten plan left off. I have incorporated history into this book in small bits that point to its effects and in notes pointing to additional sources. I want these occasional digressions to show the temporal depth and resonance of certain practices and to suggest a contact with the past "in which [we] touch the . . . shadows of ourselves and our society."[29]

For me, as for many others, the prison is haunted not only by its actual history, however that is understood, but also by the interpretation of it provided by Michel Foucault in *Discipline and Punish*. Taking as his central image Bentham's dream of an all-pervasive surveillance, Foucault describes the nineteenth-century prison as a force for the creation of modern forms of subjectivity. I do not see my project as an "application" of Foucault to prisons—an absurd exercise in any case—but rather as an inevitable immersion in the issues of power, knowledge, and self-governance with which he was concerned. I have chosen not to belabor the connections, but the reader familiar with Foucault's work will see that in each chapter I am working with a set of problems for which he suggests some ways of asking questions. The attempt to differentiate madness and reason constituted, for Foucault, the historical genesis of the modern project of incarceration. It is an attempt that still haunts the contemporary prison.

Each chapter of this book considers how—in several permutations within the maximum security prison—social exclusion is entangled with questions about what makes for a rational, self-regulating human being. Part I centers on control units and explores the individualism and emphasis on choice that underpin their operation. In chapter 1 I describe the physical space of these units and the practices of containment that manage the prisoners who live in them. Drawing on interview material and other sources to touch first on how prisoners describe the effects of isolation, I then turn to two pervasive forms of reaction to this environment. Despite and because of intensive control, prisoners in these units use their body wastes as weapons and engage in episodes of violence. I explore the extreme forms of social distancing, contamination, and shaming that thus emerge at the cell door and consider how an emphasis on control over the body works to secrete its opposite. The conversations I enter into in this chapter are a point of entry to the ways in which contemporary control units fall away from the "rehabilitative ideal" toward a warehousing approach that—despite its physical resemblance to earlier prison experiments—does not rest on any gloss of self-transformation.

In chapter 2, I turn to how notions of individual choice and rational management intersect to form the background and underpinning to control. I describe how training in the use of restraints suggests problematic connections between enforcement and the law and examine ways in which prisoners and staff articulate their expectations of autonomy under conditions in which it is both valued and constrained. Ending this chapter with an exploration of how electrical technologies of control collapse choice into obedience, I lay the groundwork for understanding the contrast between responses to those prisoners who appear to have a capacity for reason and those who do not.

Part 2 is about the relationship between treatment for mentally ill prisoners and the custodial orientation of prison operation. Chapter 3 centers on the issue of irrational behavior and the psychiatric treatment designed to contain it. I approach this in two ways. First, I ask how "the mentally ill" precipitate out of the general prison population through screening and diagnostic practices that create a partial and temporary exemption from discipline for those who cannot take responsibility for their actions. Second, I explore how mental health unit staff understand and manage their charges by using metaphors of parenting and the logic of behaviorism. These approaches to the mentally ill are connected, as I show, to techniques of encirclement that attend to inmates' language as well as their behavior.

Chapter 4 is about how the relationship between custody and treatment is negotiated by uniformed and mental health staff. Classification hearings and the *Diagnostic and Statistical Manual of Mental Disorders* are elements in this negotiation, which involves alignments and conflicts between custodial power and psychiatric knowledge. I describe how the division of psychiatric disorders into the major mental illnesses and the character disorders is taken up by, and reflected in, a division of labor between psychiatric and custodial staff. Here, in contrast to the previous chapter, I emphasize the permeable and contested boundary between these two aspects of the prison and the conundrums that form around the interpretation of behavior.

In Part 3 I turn to the question of long-term confinement and describe an attempt, in one control unit, to challenge the assumptions underlying it. In chapter 5 I return to the control unit to consider prisoners who come to represent ongoing danger within and outside the system. I describe how prison workers are taught to anticipate manipulation and how prisoners, in turn, struggle against the suspicion of lying. Here the diagnostic manual interjects a theory of character that supports a utilitarian view of language and reinforces a sense of "fit" between long-term prisoners and the environment in which they are contained. This chapter ends by pointing to the relationship between characterological interpretations of prisoners' language, public representations of the danger represented by criminals, and the warehouse prison.

Finally, chapter 6 is about a control unit involved in a process of change. I describe how staff instituted new practices such as regular and direct contact between administrators and prisoners. These attempts to shift toward a more humane practice interrupt the contradictions of control discussed in the first chapter and show staff trying to address the most fundamental issue raised by the maximum security prison: its capacity to produce extremes of isolation and exclusion from the human.

PART ONE   CONDITIONS OF CONTROL

Chapter I | CONTROLLING TROUBLES

These people are taught we're the enemy, that this is the
worst of the worst.

CONTROL UNIT INMATE, OF OFFICERS

He is definitely a very dangerous person, capable of
probably doing anything that he has ever been accused
of, whether founded or unfounded. He is very dangerous,
very smart.

CONTROL UNIT OFFICER, OF AN INMATE

The control unit sits alone on the prison grounds, built partly underground
and surrounded by its own razor-wire fence. My companion, a quiet man
who works in a different section of the prison, leads the way through the
double gate in the fence, through a set of heavy metal doors, along a clean,
bright hallway, and past several small offices. Finally we emerge into the
circular interior. A glassed-in control booth sits in its center, slightly ele-
vated, a row of video monitors visible above the booth officer's head.
Around the perimeter are two tiers of tightly secured cells. Each has a narrow window on its outside wall, frosted to prevent prisoners from seeing
out. Looking down a tier, as in Figure 1, one sees rows of cells with their
steel doors, small windows and cuffports hinged to open outward. The interior space of the unit is divided into sections of these cells—called
"pods"—separated from one another and from the control booth by
shatterproof clear walls and locked doors. This clean, shadowless interior,
almost devoid of natural light, gives the fleeting impression that it is empty
except for the uniformed staff working the booth.

An officer takes us for a brief and gingerly walk along one of the tiers,
where we can see through the little windows into the 8 x 10 cells. Most
of the prisoners wear only their underwear. Some sleep on their concrete
beds, or simply lie on them staring into space; others pace restlessly back
and forth. Some gaze at us silently; others yell up and down the tiers to

Figure 1. Control unit tiers. From the perspective of someone facing the cells, the doors that seal the pods are to the left and right and the control booth is to the rear. Photo by Allan R. Adams.

one another. Echoing in the hard-edged interior, their shouts are a blur of rage-saturated sound. The atmosphere is dense as an inmate calls out to us from his cell. He's got a "nine mil" in his cell, he says through the window, and he's gonna kill himself if they don't let him out. The officer asks him what he means. He raises a clenched fist and waves his muscled, tattooed arm in our faces: *This* is my nine mil. The noise around us escalates, though I can't make out the words. My companions explain that this man's neighbors are egging him on. Eventually, they say, he will do something to himself because, the officer tells me, "The guy next to him will talk him into it."

On our way into the unit we walked past big carts stacked with plastic meal trays. Since the inmates are not allowed to have anything sharp, all the food is soft or bite-size; today each tray has a grapefruit cut into quarters. Two officers deliver lunch to each pod, carrying the trays to the inmates one at a time. One officer opens the cuffport and stands carefully to one side while the other, who is dressed in a waterproof jumpsuit, quickly pushes in the tray. The officers stay clear because sometimes inmates stab them through the opening or hurl feces or urine at them. On the upper tier of cells one door has been covered with plastic to keep the man inside from throwing as the officers walk by.

Like all control prisons, this one is based on a "lockdown" system that keeps prisoners in their cells twenty-three or more hours a day. Booth officers operate a twenty-four-hour computerized system that runs the unit's mechanized doors and gates, trains video monitors into every corner of the building, and makes it possible to listen in on cells and tiers (Figure 2). An inmate can leave his cell only under escort after allowing himself to be cuffed through the cuffport. The two officers who bring him out may add leg and waist chains, or a tether that hooks onto his cuffs. One on each side, they lead him to a brief shower or to solitary exercise in a small, walled-in yard.[1] An ad from a correctional trade journal (Figure 3) reflects the concerns of those who design these units. Offering the "highest reliability," it promises a seamless electronic control that works in tandem with architecture to completely encompass the space of the prison. Each panel of the illustration shows an aspect of this control: the centralized system that manages the internal doors, the tight, possibly electrified perimeter, the computer screen that can display not only the space itself but the history and photograph of every inmate, and the impressive electronics. Thus the prisoner who is controlled by visible and routinized forms of bodily restraint is also contained within a pervasive and efficient surveillance. The intent is to ensure that all "complexities" remain in the hands of management; in reality, as we have just glimpsed and as the ad itself seems to acknowledge, this focus on control occurs in the face of "possibilities" that challenge the order imposed by these technologies.

The United States has over sixty maximum security prisons like this one. They have many names: maximum security units, supermaximum

Figure 2. Control booth. Photo by Allan R. Adams.

prisons, special housing units, or intensive management units (the term in Washington State). I will use the generic "control prison" or "control unit." Control prisons are freestanding institutions, while control units, which are more common, are special sections of larger prisons. These facilities are routinely described by correctional officials and in the press as housing "the worst of the worst" and thus serving as "prisons within prisons."[2]

To meet with prisoners, I leave the main part of the unit and circle around the back to a row of visiting booths like the one in which I talked to Jeremy Roland. Two officers bring a man about twenty years old whose shaved head and muscular shoulders give him an air of being ready for anything. In prison on life without parole, he is polite and enthusiastic as he tells me "what it is like in here."

> This is real confined in here. Talk about antisocial [not a term I had mentioned to him], they try to *make* people antisocial! But there's no way to keep your mind going in here. I've been in [the control unit] two years.

Figure 3. Correctional trade journal advertisement: "The Best Design Implementation."

It gets boring. I wake up about lunchtime, work out for three or four hours, pace, write letters. There's a big part of the day with nothing to do. Anger does build up. I don't know how to put it into words. Most of us have an anger problem, but we have no security to express it. We don't trust the guards, and if we go to psych we have to keep our guard up. Anger just boils up.

Eager for conversation, he has scarcely paused for breath when the officers come to return him to his cell, bringing another man who is in his late twenties. He too speaks rapidly and intently, as though he feels we are running out of time before we start.

> Petty things build up in here, the *police* [officers] sometimes go overboard . . . You can't do nothing that can make an impact . . . The police are running around and playing games, little games to mess with me. Stress builds. It's true, I've slipped at times. I want to try not to assault, try not to throw piss or shit.

These prisoners convey a sense of pressure in their speech and bodies. When at one point the second man jumps up to act out an incident of trouble with officers, he seems almost too big for the room containing him. But a third man who talks with me that day sits quietly on the other side of the glass and apologizes, in a voice almost too low to hear through the scratchy speaker in the wall, "I haven't talked to anyone in a long time." Haltingly he speaks of difficulty sleeping and distress caused by other inmates on the tier. One young prisoner, describing later what he had seen during a control unit stay, says of prisoners like this, "A lot of the guys have nothing to live for and just give up."

The officers in the control unit spend most of their time working in pairs to escort prisoners to and from their brief yards and showers. When not in protective jumpsuits, they wear uniforms decorated with state insignia and indications of rank. They carry no guns, only a radio to call for help and a heavy set of keys; handcuffs dangle from their belts.[3] Their shifts are often hectic; during brief breaks they retreat to the sergeant's office to sit around a table with cans of soda and coffee in Styrofoam cups. Here an older man, retired from the military, confides that he finds the paramilitary structure of the prison disappointing. I assume at first that he is criticizing it for being lax, but it turns out that what he objects to is the difficulty he feels in being heard by his superiors. A younger officer, big circles under his eyes, says he sometimes works two shifts in a row, then goes home to take care of the children while his wife comes in for her shift in a different part of the prison. As the room empties, a heavyset woman who has been sitting silently at the end of the table turns to me and says, "I hate this job. It's made me hard. Here there's two answers, yes and no, and it's usually no. You think, 'This person's being awfully nice, what do they want?' You forget that people out there might just be *nice*."

Some officers describe working in a control unit as a challenging, dangerous assignment. Prisoners, they say, have "all the time in the world" to watch them, notice their weaknesses, and plan attacks against them.

[Other prison units] are a cakewalk compared to this. You see every type of emergency response in here. Most people won't work here. I like it, the excitement, the action. You're respected for working here. And it's interesting, you *do* things. But at times it can get to you—there aren't too many jobs like this.

But others insist that because lockdown conditions in fact require little spontaneous decision making the danger is overblown. One man who no longer worked in a control unit said,

There are a lot of people [there who] have a kind of cowboy mentality. But it's not a difficult job. It's one of the most secure places to work. [Out here in population] you can't treat the inmates poorly and get away with it because they'll come after you. So [the control unit's] a very easy place to work because everything's routine.

Regardless of whether they see the control unit as dangerous, many believe that prison work requires a specialized emotional stance. "You've got to have a little bit of compassion but you cannot become involved," said one officer of his wary approach to inmates. Asked if they like their work, officers shrug and say, "Well, it pays the bills."[4]

As we leave the control unit, my escort talks about the changes he's seen in the many years he has worked in prisons. He is proud of the way the prison system has "tightened up" and become more "progressive" since the widespread prison uprisings of the 1970s and early '80s. Then, he says, "this place was a pit." Now, in contrast, "*we're* gonna control the institution. It's gotten less violent." He believes that better management, more professional staff—and, not least, the existence of the unit we've just visited—have moved the prison away from the chaos of earlier years. The administrator of the control unit later explained,

We need to contain the bigger disruptions. It's a very necessary unit. It has a positive effect with the general population and it has the negative deterrence of [taking the prisoner out of] the general population. There's less

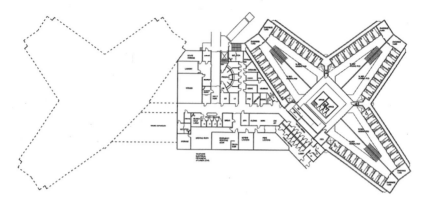

Figure 4. Architect's preliminary plan for a control prison. Reproduced with the permission of KMB Justice Facilities Group.

privileges, and it's a more sterile environment. It's a negative effect, but it's a positive effect from our standpoint of basic security and the safety of the staff and the other inmates . . . You have to be able to remove people from the population.

American prisons have always had a "hole," a special area for solitary confinement or "segregation." Traditional forms of "seg" consist simply of fairly brief periods of isolation and deprivation of privileges. A prisoner who was placed in segregation at Alcatraz in the late 1950s describes a dark, dank cell, out of sight of inmates and guards, in which he lost all track of time.[5] Control units, by contrast, are a product of the rationalized management my companion pointed to when he said that prisons have become "more progressive"; they are tightly organized, brightly lit, and maximally visible in every corner (Figure 4). Many observers note that the current belief in the "negative/positive" effect of these facilities began at the federal prison in Marion, Illinois, in 1983. There a week of violence led to a prolonged emergency lockdown, a "large scale-experiment in solitary confinement," that continues to this day.[6] As the number of people being incarcerated rose dramatically in the 1980s and '90s, prison systems all over the country began using isolation to "tighten up" on their inmates.[7] This high-tech, sharply individualized form of custody is labor-intensive— an endless round of escorts, meals, mail deliveries, and cell searches. But administrators like my companion, charged with keeping order in less restrictive settings, argue that it is worth the price to keep the "worst" prisoners locked down where they can do no harm.

This project of exclusion, however, produces troubles of its own. One is that a mechanized, almost seamless, containment of prisoners' bodies exacerbates or produces extreme states of mind. Raging, depressed, or hallucinating men "knot up" within the tiny confines of their cells. A second, paradoxical, effect is that tight control over the body precipitates extreme uses of the body itself. These resist containment despite the multiple steel doors and scripted practices designed to manage them; a piece of plastic taped over a cell door becomes the last defense against a prisoner's body waste. Thus the routine work that creates the intensive order of the control unit is not enough; additional work—physical, emotional, and intellectual—is necessitated by that very order. This chapter is a consideration of how, through practices that yield more trouble the tighter their hold, the prison tends to secrete the very things it most tries to eliminate.[8]

ISOLATION IS THE WORST THING

There's no way you can know what it's like for us in here.

> CONTROL UNIT INMATE QUOTED IN
> HUMAN RIGHTS WATCH, *Cold Storage*, p. 1

Isolation is the worst thing we do to people.

> PRISON OFFICIAL

The natural man can be maintained while the social man
withers away.

> MICHAEL IGNATIEFF,
> *The Needs of Strangers*, pp. 50-51

Go into your bathroom, say the prisoners, and lock the door. Now try to imagine the passage of hours . . . days . . . years. One prisoner gave this typical description:

> It's pretty much like not living. You're locked in a cell twenty-three hours a day . . . That's it. Sit in the house, watch TV, listen to the radio if you have those . . . It's boredom, a real intense boredom. No outside air . . . you can't see out the windows. They don't treat you bad, but it's just that everything is so impersonal. It's like dealing with automatons.

Most control units operate on a "level" or step system in which prisoners spend an initial period in a bare cell with almost nothing to do; in some cases only a Bible or Koran is available. If they can "do good," they gradually gain a radio, television, and limited access to books, magazines, and writing materials. One young prisoner in his first thirty days on the "program"—as it is called by inmates and staff—said:

> Your lights are on all day . . . it really kind of dulls all your senses . . . It makes you numb. You get easily mad. You feel that everything they do is just to make you mad . . . It's terrible in here. I think they go out of their way to turn this into hell.

Confined to their small, densely walled cells (Figure 5) along the periphery of the unit, prisoners are both physically and psychologically distant from the officers who move briskly down the tiers or stand in the center looking out at them with the grave disengagement of the police. Inside the cells, the concrete walls are painted a dull gray and contain nothing but a built-in bed and desk and a metal combination sink and toilet. A light fixture high on the wall is covered with tamper-proof clear plastic and left partially on twenty-four hours a day. One day, standing outside an empty cell with a group of prison workers, I ventured a request, and an administrator signaled the booth officer to close the door on me. Once I was inside, it slid shut with a massive clang, far louder than the same sound heard from the outside. The small room felt completely airless. The administrator looked in at me through the little window in the door and said firmly, mimicking the frequent response to a prisoner's requests: "*No.*"

The administrator captured with this "no" the essence of the captivity I so fleetingly experienced. Prisoners depend on the staff to bring them everything—food, toilet paper, books, and letters from home. They depend on the scheduling and discipline of the staff for their brief showers and yards. As many officers put it, "We bring them breakfast in bed, we take them to recess, we take them to showers . . . We're responsible for their well-being." Well-being is here so minimally defined, and the lack of contact with other people so complete, that this dependency—which officers complain makes them feel like servants—can turn almost any inmate request into a "bid for attention." Officers and prisoners agree on the deadening effects of an atmosphere in which there is so little room for

Figure 5. Control unit cell interior. Photo by Allan R. Adams.

maneuver. One officer said, "There's probably very few more negative places in this world. If nothing happened it was a great day." Many prisoners describe a contracted, thickly enclosed world.

> They put you in an environment where you can't talk to anybody else, you can't have any contact . . . unless you yell or scream . . . The only thing you get to hear is the keys jingling . . . And that type of psychological imbalance you place upon somebody is very detrimental . . . Because when you're subjected to these types of things and you are without the elements of life . . . if you're without those things, it'll make you go crazy. You end up talking to yourself . . . It's part of their psychological war that they inflict upon us

in order to get us to conform and to do what they want. But they don't realize that they're actually doing more harm to us . . . There's no correction here. There is no rehabilitation here . . . If you take a dog and put him in a corner . . . sooner or later this dog is going to come out biting, snapping.

Using an animal idiom pervasive in these units (dogs, in particular, will recur in this account), this man points to the extreme effects of conditions of isolation and sensory distortion. In a state of derealization in which all forms of contact become attenuated, "you end up talking to yourself." Like many who critique these units for producing sensory deprivation, this inmate suggests that one consequence is the "snapping and biting" of a cornered animal.[9]

Derek Janson, a prisoner to whom I will return in later chapters, wrote "Just One More Beautiful Day in Your Captivity" after living for many years in a control unit.

So smile
And don't let them see you sweat.
Sweat? . . . Shit, how about
Pure unadulterated hatred oozing
From every core of your being
And smelling the stink that comes off your dark thoughts
When all you can think of
Is dying, yeah dying
Like a rabid animal in a cage
Because you find yourself spending
One more endless day in this
Cold fucking cage that tries
To steal the very life from your soul
And you are no longer capable
Of even shedding a tear.

And all around you is a rag tag
Assemblage of dysfunctional miscreants
And pathetic deviants who can't muster
The social or mental capacity of a
Skid row wino who's spent the past
Decade sucking sterno juice over a
Bottle of Mad Dog 20/20

And just as you think you've found
A moment of peace within your
Dreams . . . You are awakened by
The maddening screams of a delusional
Psychotic who's just thrown
A handful of shit from his cage
Only to land in front of yours.

Yeah smile
Because when the skeletons come rising out
Of your closets to haunt your poor
Misguided ass
I'll still be standing righteous within
The valves of my own soul
Even after your cages have claimed my bones.

Yeah . . . smile
Because this is just one more
Beautiful day in your captivity.

Janson describes himself engulfed by a numbing anger and hatred behind a "smile" of compliance, his social isolation manifested in a virulent aversion to weaker prisoners and a burning sense of injustice. Many prisoners speak similarly of the "dark thoughts" that haunt them in isolation. For some, all contact and stimulation become aversive. Some cover their windows, living for weeks in the dark. Others become too apathetic to respond even when moved to other units and provided with more stimulation. One young man who had been taken out of a control unit and sent to a psychiatric facility said, "I'm kind of institutionalized. I'm afraid to be around other people. The [control unit] kinda wears and tears on you. Sometimes you get really depressed, you have no contact at all." "A lot of the guys," said another inmate, "don't care about anything and just want to die."[10]

Though prisoners in control units are in solitary cells and cannot see one another, they can talk by shouting back and forth to their neighbors or across the tiers. Some of these conversations are about everyday events (the television news, for instance) or express anger toward the prison system, officers, or other inmates. In this sense control unit confinement is not entirely "solitary"; rather it fosters distorted forms of sociality patched together from the little contact that is available. But for many prisoners, particularly those who experience tenuous mental states, these shouted conversations create a disturbing echo-chamber effect. One man complains, "They tell shit to each other all night long. There's no peace in the place." In one unit we spoke briefly with a frantic prisoner, identified by officers as mentally ill, who said, " I gotta get outta this place—it's a jellybowl, and it makes you worse! It's an isolation tank, and these walls, there's nothing painted (on them) and they capture the voices, and you keep hearing things . . . It angers you."[11]

Despite the need for contact, many prisoners also undergo an expansion of personal space and an inability to tolerate others. One officer explained:

> [Inmates] spend so much time in single cells they get very paranoid. We have an inmate [who] went to a regular unit, but he only lasted a day. He asked to come back here. He said, I can't stand it, people come up and *talk* to me. His personal space has gotten larger than usual.

An inmate made the same point:

> When I get out I am going to have to go to a four-people cell. That's going to be a lot of anxiety . . . I'm trying to do my yoga right now so I won't be so tense when I get out there. Plus I've got some people out there I know from the streets and I know they're going to give me a hug. But I won't be able to do it because it's embedded in my mind that when people touch me it has a negative effect, you know, that every time somebody touches me it's a cop.

As this comment suggests, many prisoners look for ways to keep themselves going in solitary; working out, reading, letter writing, meditation, and yoga were mentioned by inmates we interviewed. One said of the control unit, "It's given me solitude and either I went nuts or I got my mind right. I took the opportunity to try and get my mind right." A survival guide published by the American Friends Service Committee contains advice from prisoners held in California. "The mind and body needs to continually be fully active," one prisoner suggests, outlining a rigorous reading, writing, and exercise regimen. Another insists, "Only my body is being held captive."[12] Some prisoners come to define strength itself in terms of resistance.

> If you're not strong-minded, this place will tear you down. I'm walking around here like a caged animal—it makes you feel so inadequate, so inferior, so *less than*. The thing that keeps me sane is knowing I'm strong-minded.

But although some prisoners are able to muster emotional and intellectual strength against captivity, often these measures described by "survivors" are simply no match for the intensity of this form of confinement. Unable to "stonewall the boredom devil," in the words of one California inmate, prisoners go to extreme lengths to fill the void with human attention in whatever form it is available.[13]

> Behavior problems get the most attention. Like if you kick the door, they respond, or you can get your needs [for contact] met by going on a hunger strike. Then they label you a manipulator.

> Holding trays [refusing to return meal trays], things like that are the only way you can get the guards' attention. You try to talk to them, they don't really give a shit.

The extremes of behavior that are common in control units are almost unknown in the outside world, but these comments point to one way we can begin to comprehend them. In these settings it is not only prisoners' bodies that are tightly managed. Here attention itself—those moments when one human being notices and responds to another—is administered, "guarded," and applied sparingly. In this economy of attention, prisoners' oppositional use of their bodies expresses not only their diminished options for action but also the parsimonious way in which "trouble" comes to be defined in a setting that takes for granted the reduction of the self to its narrowest range.

A SURPLUS OF POWER

In the eighteenth century . . . as if with a blinding flash
of insight . . . architecture [was] discovered to be a service-
able weapon in the war against vice . . . A new role had

been found for it as a vessel of conscience and as pattern
giver to society.

ROBIN EVANS, *The Fabrication of Virtue*, p. 6

Our father God, we thank thee for this prison.

CHAPLAIN BLESSING A PRISON
ANNIVERSARY CELEBRATION

Prison workers and administrators sometimes fantasize about a facility so
automated that food would be delivered on a conveyor belt with absolutely
no human contact. Perhaps robots could even do some of the escorting.
A more humane vision of the perfect prison, called "Self-Sufficient Isolation," was described in *Corrections Forum* in 1995. The author, Andrei
Moskowitz, suggests that prisoners be kept alone in small, simple apart-
ments. An accompanying drawing shows a solitary man sitting at a desk
in a freestanding unit complete with books, a kitchen, and woodworking
tools (Figure 6a). A second, unpublished drawing by Moskowitz indicates
that these units would be placed in a suburb-like configuration with a substantial yard around each one (Figure 6b). By "mustering discipline in complete isolation"—pictured as the constructive colonization of a small but
complete domain—prisoners thus housed would "master their projects"
in preparation for life in the outside world.[14]

The dream of the perfect prison has deep historical roots. In the early
nineteenth century, America's first prison-building boom was based on a
fervent belief that incarceration could produce an almost magical cellular
individualism. New "silent system" prisons kept inmates in either partial
or total isolation and enforced complete silence; at Cherry Hill in Philadelphia, for example, inmates labored alone in their cells and wore hoods
during exercise periods. These prisons were based on the theory that regimen and architecture could be combined into a force for moral regener-
ation, acting on those within to "soften the mind" and make "each individual . . . the instrument of his own punishment."[15] Alexis de Tocqueville's
trip to America in 1832 was for the purpose of visiting these institutions,
which were regarded as models for penal systems elsewhere. In *On the Penitentiary System in the United States* he and his friend Gustave de Beaumont
reported enthusiastically that "the solitary cell of the criminal is for some
days full of terrible phantoms . . . [but] when he has fallen into a dejec-
tion of mind, and has sought in labor a relief . . . from that moment he is

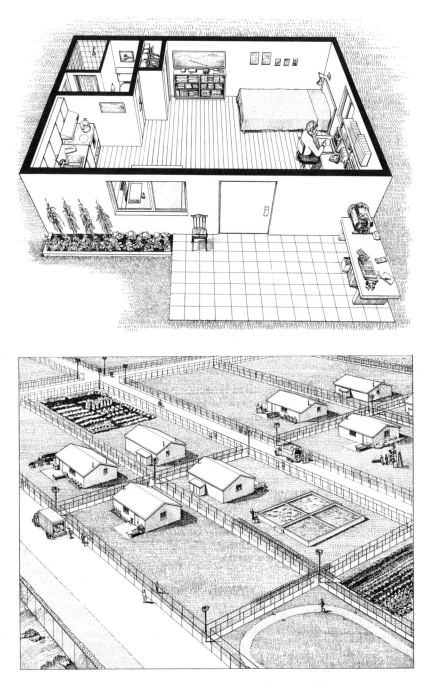

Figure 6. "Self-Sufficient Isolation" by Andrei Moskowitz. (a) Interior of housing unit. (b) Exterior view. Reproduced with the permission of Andrei Moskowitz.

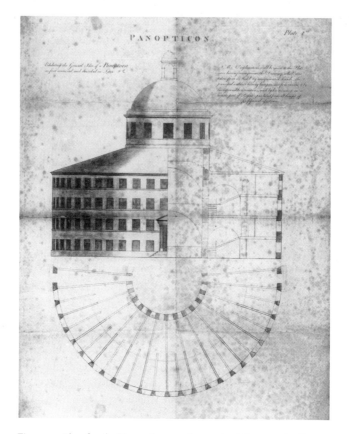

Figure 7. Plan for the Panopticon, or Inspection House, 1787 (Bentham 115/43). The Critchef Panopticon shown here is an early version of Bentham's plan drawn by an engraver. The cells are around the periphery with the governor's quarters in the center. Reproduced with the permission of Special Collections, University College, London.

tamed and forever submissive to the rules of the prison."[16] Informing this method for taming the criminal was Jeremy Bentham's late eighteenth-century plan to make his utilitarian philosophy the foundation of punishment (Figure 7). Individuals could be changed by architecture—or so went the theory—because human nature dictated a predictably self-regulating response to the imposition of painful consequences for bad behavior. The discipline and loneliness of an organized form of solitary confinement could be trusted to make work and repentance less painful

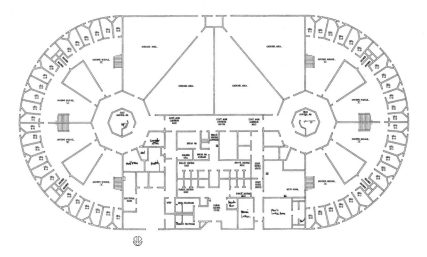

Figure 8. Architect's plan for an oval control prison. Reproduced with the permission of KMB Justice Facilities Group.

than the alternatives. Just as in "self-sufficient isolation" two hundred years later, a "useful individual" would be the product, not of contact with other people, but of a deliberately controlled material environment.[17]

The silent era was short-lived: expensive to build and maintain, the early prisons soon gave way to overcrowded and often chaotic facilities in which there was little room for solitude.[18] As a number of recent critics of the control prison have pointed out, it is as though the silent prison lay dormant for almost two centuries—persisting mainly in architectural memory and the elaboration of forms of surveillance—only to resurface now in an eerie replica of the panopticon (Figure 8).[19]

One telling similarity between the early experiments and contemporary prisons is a preoccupation with a technologically elaborate efficiency. The designers of the silent era facilities, for example, came up with ingenious mechanical methods for delivering meals while keeping prisoners from seeing or hearing other human beings. In the contemporary prison, technological innovation is combined with bureaucratic management in a similar attempt to organize every detail of prisoners' lives and officers' behavior—to ensure, in other words, that "nothing" happens.

Consider, for instance, the lunch trays stacked on a cart at the control unit's gate. Each tray with its dull spoon and bland food has emerged from a tightly regulated food service to meet that need for sustenance in which every inmate is just like his fellows, while at the same time differentiating him, if necessary, according to whatever dietary specifics—diabetes, religious restrictions—make him individual. The trays are neatly labeled, the contents carefully prepared to make eating possible where weapons can be made out of anything. This system of meal delivery—like the systematic operation of the earlier prisons and like dozens of other elements of contemporary management—is simultaneously abstract and concrete, distant and proximate. On the one hand, it involves much classification, planning, and paperwork dedicated to the speedy accomplishment of complex tasks in which the inmate himself is simply a unit of operation; these tasks spring from an apparatus of control located elsewhere, in a multitude of policies, legal rulings, and governmental and institutional offices. On the other hand, this form of efficiency bears in on the most intimate details of daily life, especially on those closest to the body—eating, bathing, and physical activity. The dream here is that the more effective the prison becomes in materializing administrative plans—framed in one advertisement for food service as the implementation of a "security business, a social service business . . . even a political business"—the more efficiently it can provide for the natural man.[20]

Those who point to the similarity between control prisons and the silent system are struck by the observation of nineteenth-century critics that solitary confinement—particularly the form that involved no work—drove prisoners mad. Writing about England's most intense experimental prison of that era, Michael Ignatieff notes, "Men came apart in the loneliness and silence . . . every year at Pentonville between five and fifteen men were taken away to the asylum."[21] We can find in the failures of the silent prisons the equivalent of a disturbing message in a bottle, taking from this bitter history a warning not to continue. But seeing the design of these prisons as inherently madness-inducing follows those who originated the early prisons in giving the architecture itself a kind of automatic force. Tucked away in the last few pages of *On the Penitentiary System in the United States* is a different message. Beaumont and Tocqueville append to their report a transcript of their interview with Elam Lynds, the first warden of Sing Sing, in which they asked him, "Do you believe that [in the new prisons] bodily chastisement might be dispensed with?" He replied,

"I am convinced of the contrary . . . I consider it impossible to govern a large prison without a whip. Those who know human nature from books only, may say the contrary."[22]

As Lynds clearly knew, the bodily life that the prison regulates inevitably provides opportunities for prisoners—and, he might have added, staff—to interrupt the fusion of abstract order and material practice on which the operation depends. Some of the early prisons turned out to be "defective" because prisoners could hear one another through the walls.[23] In control units—staying for the moment with mealtime—prisoners describe having their food spat on or their meals withheld, being falsely accused of sharpening spoons into weapons, and being unable to eat on some days because stinging gas saturates the air. Officers describe prisoners who decline their food, refuse to return their trays, make shanks out of the dull plastic, or throw urine out the port as the tray is handed through. Because prison rules do not allow trays to be kept in cells for fear they will be fashioned into weapons, the tray itself, one of the few items exchanged at the cell door, becomes an opportunity. How is a desperate or lethargic prisoner to respond to the demand to return it? If he acquiesces, he shrinks into a debilitating visible anonymity, a tacit acknowledgment that he has been tamed or broken. If he refuses, a team of officers organized into the prison version of a SWAT team and encased in protective gear will forcibly extract him from his cell.[24]

An advertisement for food trays (Figure 9) suggests that mealtime in a prison requires special technologies to meet the unusual circumstances the trays, and perhaps those who deliver them, must endure. The text plays on a conflation between the toughness and "rugged durability" of the tray—"specifically designed to take punishment"—and the implied toughness of the prisoner serving time. Expressing a similar theme, officers explain that inmates' refusal to return trays is a matter of self-will. Regardless of whether the withheld tray results in a full cell entry, in their view it places the prisoner in the position of creating the action.

They won't return their tray because earlier somebody did something to them so now they are gonna . . . retaliate . . . Whether they hope we are going to suit up and come after them, so that they can get a blow in on that officer, or they are just doing it because you messed with them, so now they are gonna

Figure 9. Correctional trade journal advertisement: "The Toughest Tray on the Block."

mess with you . . . So they hold their tray and make the officer go through the whole mess . . . The officer suits all the way up . . . and then [the inmate] will cuff up, just to make [the officers] do all the work.

One officer, fresh from an "incident" involving a tray, described a tacit agreement to follow implicit rules of engagement.

He just had a conflict with a couple of officers. It was a personality conflict . . . so he just . . . instead of giving up his tray, he had us do the show of force to get his tray. [He wanted] everyone to stop what they were doing, "now focus on me, this is my statement. ". . . He went so far, and he can't back down now . . . Once you cross so many lines you can't back down . . . You've got to [do it]—everyone has their code. His statement was made by us coming in there, by us entering his cell.

These remarks describe struggles in which both sides are compelled to respond to the symbolic as well as the overt content of the gestures of antagonism that gather around their points of contact. The apparently trivial tray—the only thing the prisoner can get his hands on—takes on a charge of defiance. This is a "power struggle," as prison workers often say. But in what sense? The control prison is already structured around an intense form of power. These struggles indicate a certain "extra," a surplus generated at the point where the full force of institutional domination meets the oblique resistance of the prisoner. Both prisoners and officers can be seized by the possibility of engaging one another's attention in this way, as though this surplus power exerts a kind of uncanny hold on them.[25] Each side, obeying its respective "code," moves forward with a sense of inevitability to "make the statement" that affirms the boundary between them.

A control unit does produce a "tame" prisoner, in the sense that it is difficult for him to affect the world beyond his cell no matter what he does inside it.[26] The plan put forth by Bentham and the architects of the silent prisons was intended to make this taming effect reach all the way into the prisoner's mind and soul—to change him—though as Lynds admitted, the strategy did not necessarily work. The question of whether this is still the prison's purpose—and whether, if it happens, it constitutes rehabilitation or what prisoners call being "institutionalized"—haunts the contemporary prison and will come up repeatedly in this account.

SOMETHING SO DISGUSTING

Alone in his cell, the inmate is handed over to himself.

DARIO MELOSSI AND MASSIMO PAVARINI,
The Prison and the Factory, p. 238

It is impossible to spend much time with prison workers without hearing about prisoners' defiant or deranged use of their body products. Inmates throw feces, urine, blood, and semen at the staff; sometimes they smear feces around their cells and on themselves. Occasionally this behavior starts in general population, causing the inmate's transfer to a more specialized facility. More often, throwing starts in control units.

Written accounts by prisoners describe "shit throwing" as an effective weapon developed by those deprived of everything but their own bodies. Willie Turner, a death row inmate executed by the state of Virginia in 1995, wrote, "It was a normal thing in Isolation for prisoners to keep containers of feces around, in case an occasion for throwing it arose . . . Some guys doctored it with urine, eggs . . . and other stuff, so it would cover better."[27]

A story by Jarvis Jay Masters, who is incarcerated at San Quentin, illustrates how a prisoner who throws is doing so in relation both to prison staff and to his compatriots, in this case with an intensely negative response.

> Not long after I'd been relocated [to the maximum security unit] . . . the evening chow cart came rolling down the tier . . . When the cart was just a few cells away from mine, I saw a hand lunge out of an open port and fling a cup of urine and feces into the faces of the two guards serving the food. It took a few seconds before I could believe my eyes and nose. The guards stood there with faces dripping, their serving spatulas still in their hands. Then a maniacal laugh broke the silence.
>
> "Eat my shit! I saved that from yesterday when you punks didn't give me no shitwipe. Now both of you can just eat it."
>
> "You'll pay for this," one of the guards said calmly . . .
>
> "You did it now!" said Joe [a neighboring prisoner]. "They'll be back to beat the Rodney-King shit out of you, Walter!"
>
> ". . . I did that for you guys too . . ." [Walter responds]
>
> "You did that on your own," Joe yelled. ". . . So don't try to pull us into it."[28]

While one might initially assume that throwing indicates individual pathology or regression, Masters is typical of many prisoners who frame it as a distinctly *social* act. Even though it contaminates their own environment and brings down the rage of the guards, inmates describe shit throwing as a particularly satisfying form of resistance. One said, "We throw shit because they've searched the cell, taken away our *Playboys*, denied our yard. The guy in the next cell [to me] could throw ten feet; [the staff] had total respect for him." Here is one act capable of reversing—at least momentarily—the usual trajectory of contempt.

The prisoner quoted earlier who said that he was *trying* not to throw also suggests that in this context there is an element of attraction, even seductiveness, to this mining and manipulation of the body. It offers, among other possibly more perverse forms of pleasure, an opportunity to play with meaning. In a world where your food is thrown at you through a hole, where the head of your bed is next to your toilet, where toilet paper has to be requested, throwing shit *says* something.[29] One prisoner put it this way:

> [On that unit] the guards are right up front; they tell you they have it in for you. Their job is just throw-away-the-key. I was throwing shit and pissing on them. It's cold there, you're a piece of shit, you don't even [dare] look them in the eye.

This kind of scatological reference pervades the prison. A prisoner writes, "prisoners are human waste. The more forbidding the penitentiaries, the more like garbage they define us."[30] Shit, garbage, and scum—both the material kind and the prisoners defined as such—seem to threaten escape and the contamination of everything they touch.

This contamination produced at the point of overflow is emotional and social as well as literal. In *The Anatomy of Disgust,* William Miller writes about the capacity of disgust, the most visceral of emotions, to connect the gut to the social order: "*Me* . . . is not just defined by the limits of my skin . . . The closer *you* get to me without my consent . . . the more alarming, dangerous, disgusting you become, even without considering your hygiene. I understand your violation as a moral one . . . You are dangerous simply by being you and not me." It is this danger that throwers exploit. The prisoner who sees himself defined as a piece of shit hurls into the faces of his keepers the very aspect of himself that most intensely represents his contaminated status in their eyes. He spreads to them a kind of contagion, not only by contaminating them with "him" but by making them, at least momentarily, disgusting themselves.[31]

Custody workers find that the sheer fact of knowing about and observing this behavior alienates them from normal society and reinforces a sense of the separateness of the prison. Imagine coming to work and arriving at your assigned area to shouts and the smell of human waste, a murky fluid trickling from under the doors of the cells, and the weary admonition to "suit up, it's one of those days." A control unit officer says:

> Until you've stood there and had it dripping off your face you just don't know what it's like. I could tear down the door [to the cell] but all I get to do is write an infraction. It's tough. It's humiliating. The first thing I feel is anger: the cell door is there partly to protect *him* from *me*. Other staff will get me in the shower—the anger will be partly gone when I get back, but I still think of ones [in the past] who threw at me.

Disgust surrounding throwing is made the more intense—if that were possible—by the compelling medical aspects of contamination in institutions where HIV/AIDS and hepatitis are common. Signs everywhere in prisons warn about the danger of contact with body fluids and set out procedures for handling them. When a prison worker is attacked with body fluids—and particularly if the attack involves blood—his or her life is affected for months by tests and fear of infection. The issue is exacerbated by the fact that officers are not supposed to be aware of inmates' medical status (due to confidentiality rules) so that, from their point of view, all inmates must be considered equally dangerous. Any inmate is thus seen as having a powerful potential to make his infringement of workers' personal space permanent and deadly.

Thus the prisoner who throws has a weapon that makes the most of the connection between the intense emotions that surround body wastes and the creation and maintenance of social boundaries. That "alarming, dangerous" aspect of "you" is intensified by contact—or even the thought of contact—with the products of your body. But the products of the body are also heavily charged symbolic carriers of the fact that you are "other" than me; one way a social boundary can be sustained is through the projection of disgust onto those on the "other" side of it. Unlike those involved in the more rhetorical forms of projection that aim to keep relatively distant others in their place, prisoners and their keepers are constantly in one another's presence yet enjoined never to lose sight of the line between them. Under these circumstances it is not surprising that some prisoners enlist the most literal aspects of the body to invoke the tangle of wary contempt governing that boundary. The rage, humiliation, and fear described by prison workers in the face of shit throwing arise from loss of control and an unwilling enmeshment in the body of another, and not just any other but one already identified as abject, dirty- and possibly life-threatening.[32]

To my knowledge, prison workers do not get used to having shit thrown on them. When I mentioned how preoccupied some seemed with this topic, a prison psychiatrist asked rhetorically, "Has anyone ever thrown shit at *you?*" The impossibility of not reacting with disgust attests to the visceral qualities of both the situation and the emotion. But if they can personally stay out of the way, workers do adjust to the *idea*, and to cleaning up after these episodes. One officer said, "You get used to dodging turds." It is this routinization that threatens officers in the world outside the prison.

I recall sitting with another officer in her backyard, talking about her twenty-year career at the prison. In the pleasant early evening a litter of kittens tumbled at our feet as she reflected on how her work often seems remote from daily life. One day, she said, she was washing dishes while her husband sat behind her at the table in their kitchen. Caught up in telling him of the day's events at work, she began describing one prisoner who was smearing feces all over the walls of his cell. As she started going into detail she noticed a strange silence in the room; turning, she saw that her husband had gone pale. "How can you do this?" he asked. "How can you just stand there and chat about something so disgusting?" Her un-nerving effect on her husband caused this officer to notice the "harden-ing" or indifference that had crept up on her, and after this conversation she became more cautious about "bringing it home." In public discussions of these situations, prison workers are careful and formal in their language. A mental health worker described testifying in court about an inmate who was masturbating with feces; she had to describe his behavior, loudly, to a judge who was slightly deaf. She was embarrassed by the silence that fell over the room and uneasy about her public association with such extreme behavior. Just as prisoners can be seen as "pieces of shit," so those who clean up after them may fear the perception that they too are veering away from humanity toward dirt.[33]

On the inside, among themselves and when pulling in outsiders, prison workers make something else of this experience—a dismaying but also compelling mark of affiliation. During the early months of our work with prisons, workers told us tales of incorrigible shit-throwers and joked en-thusiastically about "feces art." I eventually realized that this is not a euphemism but a reference to drawings made by smearing; one inmate made drawings of Christmas trees on the walls of his cell. Experienced prison workers play on the aversive fascination of this kind of behavior when they communicate with those less familiar with the prison. In a course for new custody workers, veteran worker-volunteers set up mock scenes of challenging situations. One was particularly violent and included exuberant "inmates" who threw paper cups of water representing "cocktails" into the faces of the rookies. "Kill all the cops!" they shouted, banging furiously on the cell doors. "Come here, you assholes!" Once the students had attempted, awkwardly, to carry out instructions and quell the riot, the veteran teachers exhibited a mixture of enjoyment at their discomfort and concern that they might have gone too far in their attempt at realism. One of the officers said, with a touch of relish, "Officers get douched all the time. You haven't *lived* until someone throws shit all over you. And it's not nice turds either, they mix it up, it'll go all over you." However, once the scenes were over and the students back in their seats at the end of the day, an older instructor said gently, "Don't walk out of here unless you're OK. Stay and talk if you need to. We've all had this queasy feeling. Everything you heard, everything that came flying out of those cells is something we've lived through."

In these comments, seasoned prison workers say to the inexperienced: you can expect this, it happens all the time. They point to the way in which negative associations emanating from the prisoners' abject status concentrate themselves at the line that separates them from the workers, with the body as the highly charged medium of exchange at this border. But in addition—and the reason the instructors are so certain the exchange is ongoing—is that repetition is what sustains this bodily reiteration of social order. The line between the prisoner and everyone else cannot be demarcated once and for all. Instead it is repeated literally, as a dramatic extrusion and intrusion of "waste."[34]

We might see throwing as theatrical or spectacular, as some prisoners certainly do. It creates incidents and emergencies in which attention must be focused on the perpetrator and victim and in which, as in Jay Masters's description, both positions threaten to spread and reverse. But this kind of trouble is also chronic, involving prisoners and their keepers in a persistent round of dirtying and cleaning and keeping everyone engaged in this aversive corporeal "conversation." In this way the body that is the target of control, far from transferring acquiescence to the mind, turns onto itself; instead of being the solution to the project of achieving order, it becomes the problem.

The prisoner who throws manages for a moment to throw sand, so to speak, into the machinery of control prison operation. But one wonders—and prisoners and prison workers wonder—what kind of resistance this is. Is it something no sane adult could do? Or is it a willful—perhaps even *too* sane—deployment of the most obvious of weapons? This is a central question in the relationship between custodial and psychiatric responses to extreme behavior, a question that bears on the rationality and intentionality of the thrower and, ultimately, on what kind of attention he receives.

YOU'RE NOT GONNA WIN

Fighting is to prove you're not scared.

TEENAGE CONTROL UNIT PRISONER

He threatens to kill me . . . but the isolation wears on
him, it has to mess with his head.

OFFICER IN CONTROL UNIT, OF INMATE

They want to make me learn a lesson, they want to *make*
me learn. I'm real resistant to that.

CONTROL UNIT PRISONER

It is difficult for the visitor to a control unit to imagine what prisoners could do to gain the upper hand in this environment. But prison workers know that this effect is hard-won and most likely temporary.

One morning I visit a control unit that is—at first—strangely quiet. But there are many signs of recent trouble: scratches and graffiti on the walls, cells with fixtures torn out, a small office ripped apart. Graffiti smear the windows of the pods and yards. My companion is an administrator from another prison, here to learn what she needs to do to fortify her own units against this kind of damage. According to the officer who shows us around, it is peaceful now only because the inmates were up late; "This place has been rockin' and rollin'," she explains. As she talks, a prisoner wakes up and hears her voice ("They hate me right now," she adds) and starts banging out a loud drumbeat on the metal door of his cell. We study an empty cell, uninhabitable now because the sink fixtures were ripped out and used as weapons. This tenuous nature of normal prison discipline lies behind ads like the one for the "violent prisoner chair" (Figure 10). Prisoners with any freedom of movement at all have some capacity, however slight, to lash out. The restraint chair straps down all four limbs and, in some designs, the head as well. The ad promises a control that goes beyond architecture, something administrators faced with rebellious inmates may well be "waiting for." Such direct measures—chairs, four- or five-point restraints (with the prisoner lying down), pepper spray, and electronic forms of control—not only offer final resort in case of trouble, but also form the backdrop to a more general atmosphere of threat and counterthreat. Their mere presence—the threat of use—has weight. As one officer put it:

> The bottom line is that if he assaults the staff, you gas him, you go get him, and you bring him out of the cell. And you either stick him in the chair or you stick him in one of those holding cells with very little and you say, "When your behavior dictates that a staff member can open that cuffport without being afraid of being hit with something, we will give you something back."

One former control prisoner pointed out that because these units are "the end of the line . . . if you misbehave there, what are they gonna do to you, lock you up?" Once violence starts, the cycle of resistance and further punishment is hard to break. This man continued, "They do something, you do something to show 'em and before you know it years have passed by."

Riots like the one that destroyed the unit described above are relatively rare; they may be spontaneous but usually depend on leadership from dominant prisoners who urge or coerce others to join in as the situation escalates. One young inmate gave this description of what it was like to be in such an "incident."

> It gets really boring [in the control unit] . . . some guys who mostly just sleep come alive for riots, excitement, when the goon squad comes and someone gets gassed. A guy lit his cell on fire and it was a chain reaction, the whole place went up [not in fire, in riot]. A guy came out of his cell swinging, and the cops had gas and shields, the guys on the tier were breaking out glass, there was smoke rolling out of another house, they

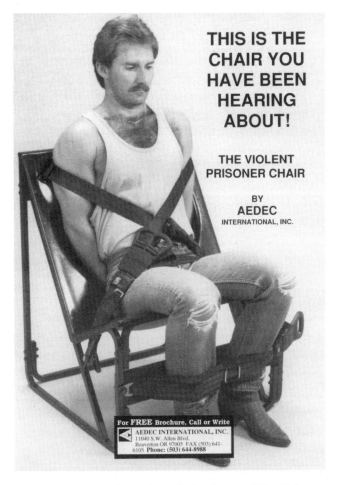

Figure 10. Correctional trade journal advertisement: "The Violent Prisoner Chair."

were kicking partitions, breaking concrete pieces off. Watching the excitement, it's entertaining, I like to see it . . . but it's stupid, you're not gonna win in this system.

Charlie Chase, a long-term prisoner in a Massachusetts control unit, draws heroic superman-like prisoners fighting with huge, gas-masked guards (Figure 11). This one seems to echo that long-ago remark by Warden Lynds, as well as the fascination and resignation expressed by the young man's "you're not gonna win." Here, heavy-set men have overwhelmed a bloodied prisoner whose body takes up almost no space compared to the blood-spattered shield in the foreground of the picture.[35]

As these examples suggest, violence by and upon individual inmates does occur in control units despite their architectural and managerial constraints. Inmates and staff can experience this environment as a battleground of malevolent intentions on both sides—the "little games to mess with me" a prisoner described earlier. Prisoners make weapons from any available material, stab officers through the cuff ports, or manage to wrest free and attack their escorts. A few openly express their determination to harm or kill specific officers. Officers in turn provoke or retaliate against inmates. An administrator said of cell extractions, "If they don't want to come out [of their cells] we'll get them—they're *coming* out. They can get hurt . . . Anytime we go in a cell, we assume they have a weapon."[36] A prisoner who had a long history of violent stand-offs with staff described his experience of hurting and being hurt:

> They said I tried to head-butt 'em, throw things through the cuff port. They throw your food at you, they turned off my water. They say weird things over the speakers . . . I was also being a jerk too.

Administrators charged with system-wide order insist that this kind of trouble inside control units cannot be separated from violence and other problems elsewhere in the prison. Many inmates come to these units because they are being separated and punished for fighting, attacking officers, or harming other prisoners. Administrators also believe that "the inmates that are coming into our system [now] are much more prone to violence . . . to a lack of respect for life in general" than those of past decades. Prisoners sometimes have a similar perspective, describing their own behavior in terms much like those of the administration. An inmate in his late teens said:

> This is pretty messed up. It is not a good place to be. But there is probably a need for [these units] because of the violent inmates that can't function well on the main line . . . I am here because we had a multiracial fight on the yard . . . We got into it. [Last time in solitary] I was pretty bad. Cussed at them. Threw everything I could . . . I guess it is kind of like us against

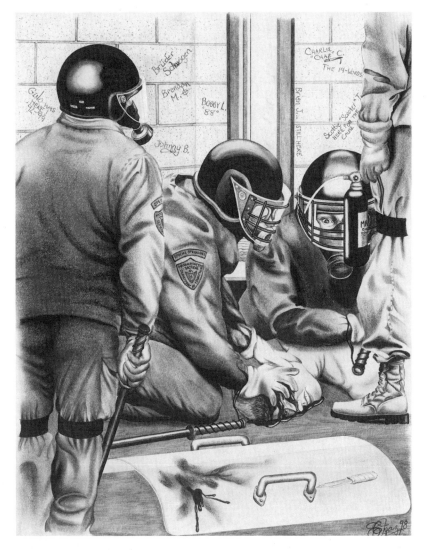

Figure 11. Untitled drawing of cell extraction by Charlie Chase. Reproduced with the permission of Charlie Chase and Bruce Porter. Previously published in Bruce Porter, "Is Solitary Confinement Driving Charlie Chase Crazy?" *New York Times Magazine*, November 8, 1998.

them, you know? I been doing this since a pretty early age. Been to a lot group homes and mental hospitals and stuff—ward of the state, and honestly, the state is not a very good guardian.

The formal system designed to move inmates out of control units is based on a behavioral model that rewards the avoidance of bad behavior. In order to move up the levels and, perhaps, back to general population, a prisoner must be able to impassively endure the indignities of this form of confinement: the constant noise at night, the raving man in the next cell, cold food, late mail delivery, a delayed yard. Some inmates are also on the receiving end of racial taunts, encouragement to commit suicide, or other predatory behavior directed at signs of weakness. One who had been transferred to a psychiatric unit said:

> I stayed in the [control unit] six months . . . I kept getting infracted because I was the only black on the tier and they would tease me, call me nigger, crazy . . . It got worse when I cried, when people died in my family . . . so I said, I'm gonna keep everyone up [making noise at night] . . . Plus, I couldn't have no radio because of infractions so I was only listening to them, what I heard and what they said.

A prisoner who had been kept for years in control units vented barely contained fury at those he regarded as weak:

> We've got to deal with these mentally ill inmates who rub shit on themselves and these PC [protective custody] cell warriors . . . they should put the rats and snitches in one pod, the mental patients in one pod—they stir up anxiety and stress. They [administrators] put them in [here] to *create* stress.

In these ways anger "just boils up," and an episode of loss of control can gain an inmate like this additional months or years in solitary.

Many prisoners come to feel that difficult conditions are designed to *test* their control, to "create stress" and "make us antisocial" in a purposeful effort to produce negative effects. These effects in turn confirm the reason for the attempt: to break them and make them "crazy." The man described earlier who perceived the control unit as a "jellybowl," and who seemed to be struggling with psychosis, said, "I don't know, man, I been tryin' to turn the other cheek, man, but it don't seem like nothing I can do to get out of here." Many prisoners believe that they can leave these units only by "turning the other cheek," that is, through self-control bordering on self-abnegation. A survival guide written by control prisoners at Pelican Bay offers this counsel:

> We have to accept things we don't like. Even certain amounts of disrespect will have to be tolerated . . . Let your wisdom, your discipline . . . guide your actions. Not! your anger, your hostility, or your dislikeful feelings for the wrong things they do to you.[37]

This writer points to what makes "discipline" problematic in this context: to control one's response to prison is to allow oneself to be disrespected. Some prisoners do not acquiesce: "I kept my humanity through my anger," said one. "Every time they opened the door I would fight . . . The [control unit] is to break a man's spirit, that's what it's about." And in fact both staff and prisoners express contempt for the "cell warrior"—the inmate who is full of bravado so long as he remains safely in his cell. The prisoner whose "alligator mouth gets his hummingbird ass in trouble" is seen as weak when he *doesn't* follow through on his rage. Thus the very "good behavior" that may reward a prisoner within the disciplinary logic of the system—control of anger and obedience to the rules—may work against him within a logic of masculine self-respect. One man explained:

> If I'm being good and they don't give me nothing, I can't take that kind of rejection . . . I just went off, spitting, urinating, tearing up my cell, the whole nine yards . . . If they feel like I'm gonna be a badass, why not be one? . . . They think they can control me, but I'm gonna be the one in control.

Like the men quoted earlier who try to bring people to them through "bad behavior," this prisoner attempts to locate *his* will at the center of the effects of his imprisonment.

Respect is a pervasive theme in prisoners' descriptions of their own violence, with seemingly small slights carrying a tremendous charge in the saturated atmosphere of the prison. The destruction of the unit I described earlier began when a powerful inmate was given a "level" that was later taken away from him. A younger prisoner who "followed" this man in rioting later explained how respect was central to this relationship.

We are respectful to the older guys [except for child-killers and rapists, he carefully adds]. Respect depends on how you carry yourself, and on your crime. I get respect because I have "life without" [i.e., he is a murderer]. The older con helps with kids who get out of line and teaches them respect.[38]

For this man, respect is the social glue allowing him to feel that he can "carry himself" well—and safely—among his peers. Many inmates suggest that they cannot afford injuries to the self-respect acquired in this way. James Gilligan, who worked for years in a Massachusetts maximum psychiatric facility, believes that the violence endemic to these institutions can be located in the threat that feelings of humiliation pose to the "coherence of the self."[39] He points out: "We find it hard to comprehend how a trivial incident could lead to violence . . . because such explanations violate our sense of . . . rationality . . . The secret [of violent men] is that they feel ashamed—deeply ashamed . . . over matters that are so trivial that their very triviality makes it even more shameful to feel ashamed about them."[40]

What "sets off" a prisoner may thus seem insignificant or irrational, but it is something he feels himself compelled to redress. Overt interpersonal conflict is one sign of this dynamic. "The guards," said one prisoner, "they fuck with you." Another spoke bitterly of "going off" after "behaving" for six months only to be refused the transfer to general population he felt he had been promised. "They say 'calm down,' which is hard . . . 'give us no infractions for six months' . . . it's almost like a test. They didn't recommend release [from the unit] and I snapped." Another, speaking about his level of intolerance for other inmates, said, "Prison has made me horrible. It's made me capable of being violent . . . I don't want to [be] when I think rationally, but I could. That comes from here."

A sense of exposure and shame—the threat of being "broken"—also becomes a pervasive pattern of feeling, apart from any particular incident of overt humiliation.[41] The prison environment could not be better designed to activate a sense of threat to the coherence of the self. Petty humiliations like withheld toilet paper, to which a "rational" person would not react with homicidal rage, are both the effect and the sign of a larger, more fundamental source of shame. Disrespect is chronically implicit in what Michael Ignatieff calls the "cold gray space of state confinement" because people who are indifferently provided with basic "needs" are defined *by the giving* as merely needful.[42] They may be maintained with water, stale air, the tasteless prison food cut into small pieces, a place to sleep, basic medical attention.[43] But when the administrator looked through the cell door at me and said "no," he was saying: most things you might *want* are not needs. "In the best of our prisons," writes Ignatieff, ". . . inmates are fed, clothed and housed in adequate fashion . . . Yet every waking hour . . . [they] still feel the silent contempt of authority in a glance, gesture or procedure." In these places the contempt of authority is not separate from the procedure, the feeding or cleaning; rather it is embedded in it. "Needs are met, but souls are dishonoured."[44]

Officers can sometimes be very clear about the surplus power generated at the cell door, insisting on the value of self-control in the face of provocation. A young sergeant remarked, "Inmates feed on making you mad, it's like negative energy. If you do get mad, you don't belong here." As with the prisoners, self-control involves "accepting what we don't like." "You get tired of dealing with the same crap every day. It does get to you [but] you try to tell yourself it's not personal. You say to yourself, Yeah, he's a butt-head, but just deal with his behavior." But some prison workers cannot or do not want to resist the excess of authority made available to them, using their position to launch aggression of their own—gratuitously, preemptively, or in retaliation, openly or covertly. To be "manly" and "not be a sissy" is to act. One officer said of his peers:

> The term "supercop" comes up—most of them won't give the inmate the time of day. They won't de-escalate a situation . . . they almost want to accelerate it. It makes them feel powerful and commanding . . . There was a time when I was the same way, I enjoyed suiting up. When an inmate would go off, you would rub your hands together and say, "We need to do something about this guy. It is very dangerous for us, and let's get her done."

It is in this context that supervisors may try to convey to officers that their own emotional control is a fundamental tool of their trade. Explaining the importance of a rule-oriented "security mindset," a correctional class teacher said to new officers: "Everyone gets stressed out in this work. You need to adhere to policies and procedures—violations come back to haunt us." Lapses in attention to detail or loss of emotional control may result in dangerous incidents that in turn produce a diffuse sense of unease and exposure. For many prison workers, whatever success they have in controlling their own behavior under these conditions becomes evidence that such control is possible, a point that underlies many officers' insistence that inmates, too, should be able to control themselves under difficult circumstances. This is one way in which the notion that we create our own behavior—that the will is at the center of rational action—becomes vital to the interpretation of events between prisoners and their keepers.[45]

THE "WORST OF THE WORST"

You either deal with it or you don't deal with it . . . I feel
I could act like a fool and do crazy shit and talk shit to
them all the time and smash my TV and break up the
cell. People get pretty determined sometimes. You can
tear the toilet off the wall if you're strong enough.

CONTROL UNIT PRISONER

It's the end of the line for inmates who threaten the
security of the staff, the security of the institution. This
is basically the end of the line and this is where you will
go and you will be [here] until you can get a straight
behavior.

CONTROL UNIT ADMINISTRATOR

HEARING OFFICER: Why are you still in the [control unit]?
PRISONER: Because I refuse to submit.

Control units are in a complex relationship to a larger institutional system for which they serve both practical and symbolic purposes. In some cases of misbehavior a prisoner undergoes a fairly brief—if thoroughly unpleasant—period of segregation followed by an uneventful reintegration into the general population. But many ambiguities attend the issue of "misbehavior." The placement of mentally ill inmates in control units and the development in some cases—whether the prisoner is regarded as mentally ill or not—of ongoing patterns of throwing and violence raise questions about the relationship between the ratcheting up of measures of control and a decreasing ability on the part of the prisoner to control himself. In addition, particularly out-of-control prisoners who are kept in these units until the end of their sentences emerge directly into their communities.

This raises troubling questions about what purpose such control really serves.

Those outside prisons assume that "the worst of the worst" refers to prisoners who have committed particularly heinous crimes. Control units do contain a greater proportion of prisoners with violent histories, younger prisoners with juvenile records, and, of course, prisoners who have harmed other inmates or prison staff. But others are in intensive confinement for their own protection or because they have accumulated a prescribed number of infractions. Mentally ill, disturbed, or persistently defiant inmates continue to accumulate sanctions while in maximum custody, thus adding to their time. Some prisoners may be placed in isolation preemptively, and some are kept there indefinitely regardless of their behavior.[46]

These differences among prisoners raise the question of what it means to "get a straight behavior," as the administrator quoted above said in defense of his unit. Those who manage these units offer arguments based on their own accountability as well as the inmates'. A control unit administrator explained, "We try our best and we're professional. We make the inmates accountable and so we keep them [here, in the control unit] for a long time . . . [because when we recommend release] we have to deal with the inmate in a revolving door process." Some argue bluntly for a primarily punitive and deterrent effect. The warden of a large facility in Minnesota, for example, said in response to inmate interviewers, "[Special housing units] serve a punitive purpose . . . They exist to deter people from acting out. I'm not going to apologize for that."[47] These comments point to fundamental issues that have attended imprisonment since the early 1800s: Is its purpose punishment, with or without a presumed deterrent effect? Or is it—perhaps instead, perhaps also—intended to change behavior? And in what sense do these purposes make for accountability?

In the rest of this book I explore the vexing consequences of these questions for those who must live within them. Maximum security confinement—in control units and in the mental health units that stand as their complementary doubles—entails difficulties in the interpretation of behavior. When a fairly brief stay in solitary confinement does result in better behavior, prisoners and staff may be in general agreement about how to interpret such change.[48] But the common sense that makes such agreement possible—shared notions of individual autonomy, rational action, and free choice—is also a source of unsettling complications. Disturbed mental states are addressed by imposing conditions that further disturb the mind. And the indeterminate "accountability" of long-term solitary confinement ultimately escapes behavioral explanation and is interpreted as a "choice to be bad" no longer subject to the possibility of re-inclusion.

The possibility that what they were creating with the silent prisons would look like slavery troubled the prison reformers of the early 1800s, many of whom were abolitionists.[49] As Angela Davis points out, the main thing differentiating the silent prisons from slavery was the rehabilitative model that inspired them. Softening the minds of prisoners for their own good was not a rationale for the enforced labor of the South either before or after the Civil War. In the control units I describe—geographically and politically far removed from the prison-farms of the South—most prison workers believe that the inmates ultimately control their own fate. Yet at the same time, as we've just seen, prisoners in these units can slip toward seeming nothing but bodies—beyond or unworthy of rehabilitation—to be managed by nothing more than a parsimonious economy of attention. This tension about the shape of accountability raises the question of what it means to allow the "social man" to wither on the other side of the bars while, at the same time, attributing to him an almost superhuman ability to exercise his will.

Chapter 2 | THE CHOICE TO BE BAD

It is the sincere hope of the Department that inmates
will conform their conduct to a minimum level of good
behavior and leave the [control unit] at less than full
occupancy; however, that choice will be up to the inmate.

MASSACHUSETTS PRISON MEDIA BOOKLET, QUOTED IN
MICHAEL JACOBSON-HARDY, *Behind the Razor Wire*, p. 94

It don't hurt to keep asking if they are tight, but if he
keeps complaining and you can see he can move, you're
gonna have to say, so be it.

SERGEANT INSTRUCTING OFFICER ON THE USE OF LEG IRONS

I joined the correctional training class during the week the students—new
officers with less than a year on the job—learned how to use restraints.
Sitting at long tables in a cavernous building just outside the perimeter of
the prison, we were each issued a cloth bag containing a set of handcuffs
and leg irons. The keys were passed out separately, and our instructors—
all veteran correctional workers—warned us firmly not to lose them. I discovered from the first exercise—using one hand to cuff the other—that it
took concentration to achieve the smooth, sliding effect that came so
effortlessly to those with experience. Soon we moved on to practice on
one another under the watchful eyes of our teachers. It was clear that it
would take some practice to be comfortable with this strangely intimate
procedure, which required us to stand awkwardly near the "inmate" and
hold his hands closely while maintaining a composed and watchful psychological distance.

It was also clear that the aggressive application of cuffs would be intrusive and painful, the "inmate" spoken to harshly, his arms jerked back, the
cuffs slapped against the bones of the wrist. The instructors devoted themselves to articulating the difference between careful practice and nasty ex-

cess. They urged the students to "issue verbal commands" such as "Put your hands behind your back," and to avoid "hauling and shoving." "Don't slap him with the cuff, put it up against him," they advised, demonstrating again and again. At the same time, they constantly referred to the fact of force involved in what we were learning. One instructor showed how easily an open cuff can be used as a weapon, and displayed a long scar on his arm where he had been "sliced" by an inmate who wrested the cuffs from him. Despite the cooperation that putting on cuffs fostered—since it is much easier if the subject makes his hands available—the instructors cautioned that this should not be encouraged. "Don't let 'em help you out," one explained. "There's always a possibility for violence in this work. That's the stress, that's what you take home with you every night."

Taking advantage of a moment when he thought himself unobserved, one student mimed "kneeing" his cuffed partner, who said in mock disapproval, "Well, *that* was unprofessional." The instructors didn't see this interaction, but they seemed to know it was there. They spoke constantly of the need for professionalism and the danger to the students of failure to understand the "changing face of corrections." "Be cautious," one had said to the class before we began practicing. "We don't need to be slamming restraints on people. That's a good way to lose your job . . . You might as well go to McDonald's and flip burgers." This was no idle threat. Low-paying jobs in the service economy are the likely alternative for these beginners, the youngest of them barely out of high school and the oldest recently unemployed or retired from the military. The instructors hoped that the professional identity and sense of career opportunity they tried to instill would fortify the students against the "bad habits" they might learn from older corrections workers (called by one instructor "the old style dinosaurs, the knuckle-dragging officers") and protect the department from grievances and lawsuits. One instructor, after warning the students that their superintendent would not come to their defense in court, said of the purpose of the class, "You want to get into the least force and *know* how to use the least force."

The members of this class confront a fundamental difficulty in the work of the prison: the relationship between legitimate and illegitimate force. What does it mean to use the least force? What are these students being asked to know? Here new officers encounter ambiguities surrounding legitimacy itself, tensions that are inherent in the very "lawfulness" with which they are being entrusted.[1] Further, producing a docile and obedient inmate requires that the prisoner's *will* be brought into direct contact with the will of the officer. This moment of contact—evident in the disconcerting intimacy attending the application of cuffs—is fraught with the uncertain relationship between will and obedience. It raises the question of whether what one is *made* to do can—or should—become what one *chooses* to do. And this question, in turn, is entwined with the issue of whether the officer who does the making enacts his or her own will or is simply the efficient instrument of a larger, institutional power. As the class on restraints illustrates, these issues are embedded in the everyday practices that constitute the "system" as reasonable and prisoners as rational actors within it.

The students had started the day with a lesson on "containment" in which they were told that "prisons would be only warehouses" without the "mission of instilling boundaries in the inmates' minds." Harking back to the original mission of the nineteenth-century prison—to "fix the shape of experience" in order to shape the inmate's consciousness—this comment expresses a common-sense assumption about how institutional constraint is related to individual choice.[2] At one level the class on restraints trains students to internalize a fairly mechanical behavior, which is presented to them simply as a skill. But within this lesson is another: that it is possible to exercise rational self-regulation in response to disciplinary shaping. This lesson starts with the students themselves, as instructors make clear to them that they can choose *how* they apply cuffs. Their choices—what they communicate with the gesture itself—have consequences for them and for the inmates. This teaching is extended to inmates, who are described making choices in response to the controls applied to them. For both, these choices matter because, once internalized, they become the "force" of habit.

As the bags of restraints were being handed out, one instructor mentioned Derek Janson as an example of a strong and willful prisoner who, to his knowledge, required three, rather than two, escorting officers. "I wish I could show you the video we have of him [participating in a riot]," he said. This invocation of a dangerous individual served to highlight the attention to detail being demanded of the students. But it also called up the link between choice and consequence; just as Janson suffers the consequence of the control unit for his intransigence, so will the students suffer for carelessness. Learning to cuff a willing or recalcitrant prisoner foreshadows numerous other situations in which desire and obedience must be engaged by the practices that make up prison discipline. These situations are interpreted through a cluster of interconnected ideas about responsibility, accountability, conscience, and consequences that make it possible to see the individual as someone who possesses a will.

Another, deeper issue underlies this question of how the will of the prisoner is to be met by the constraints that prison workers seek to impose. Even in the artificial situation of the classroom, fascination and unease surrounded the fact that in a prison the use of force explicitly backs up legal order. Although prisons are an extension of the law and their charges defined by having broken it, part of the work of the class was to instill a sense of the legitimacy of intensive coercion in the service of social regulation. Tom Wicker, who visited the Attica prison during the inmate uprising of 1971, describes the point at which the sense of social order he had always taken for granted—along with the law implicitly underpinning it—suddenly revealed its fragility. As he crossed into the area where the insurgent inmates had gained control, he was "acutely conscious . . . that he was leaving behind the arrangements and instruments by which his civilization undertook to guarantee him order and safety—the law with its regulations, officers and guns. At the moment he stepped from under their protection, he realized not only how much he ordinarily assumed their presence . . . but also how much, even in civilization, law seemed to assume in the same unspoken manner, its dependence, at bottom, upon guns."[3]

The phrase "to enforce the law" says more than we sometimes hear: that the law depends for its perpetuation on the possibility of force. Though force may need only to be threatened, the consistent display of its potential deployment is what creates the appearance of a guarantee of order. This potential exists behind or at the bottom of the law as it operates in the present. But it is also implicit in the larger sense that the law rests on moments—now seemingly forgotten—when it was originally produced by the exercise of force. Popular fascination with the outlaw often centers on the possibility that someone outside the current regime of law could escape its guarantee of order and, by the use of force alone, establish a new regime based on his own, currently illegitimate, desires. This bottom where law and force meet is, as Wicker notes, generally unspoken; rather, "the law is the law" as it deploys its arrangements and instruments against the outlaw.[4]

Prison workers are thus asked to stand on a middle ground that is inherently unstable. The issue in the class is how students will use, and ultimately how they will interpret their ability to use, the extreme power over other individuals being vested in them by this handing out and handling of the instruments of control.[5] The correctional class instructors teach their students a standardized response to the potential violence of the inmates, a response that merely threatens—or, they hope, need only gesture toward—the activation of more literal varieties of enforcement. This response is intended to convey that enforcement will be extended into the indefinite future. Some officers habitually open and close the set of cuffs they carry on their belts, emanating, as they walk, the little ratcheting sound made by the spring. One of the class instructors noted that at the minimum security prison where she worked, she was careful not to play with her cuffs. "My guys [who are on their way out of prison] hope not to keep hearing that sound." The sound of cuffs drives home the claims of authority, but its constant repetition suggests how that authority is—and, in one way or another, must be—constantly reiterated.

Just as an officer faced with a complaint about tight leg irons might say, "So be it," so the contradictions of control can be muted—perhaps, like the prisoner, temporarily suppressed—by these routines of containment. But these are contradictions that cannot be resolved.[6] Prison work takes place right at the unstable edge of legitimacy; the terms in which it is understood—individuality and choice—require ongoing attention in order to retain their meaning under conditions of coercion. In control units where confinement is reduced to its barest elements, and in the more extreme electronic forms of restraint, the relationship between the practices that contain and the terms in which they are understood is brought into sharp relief. It is in these situations that prisoners and staff engage most intensely the connections among the prisoner's will, the quasi-legal system that governs him, and the instruments at hand to ensure that he complies.

A CHOICE, AND NOT A CHOICE

The only freedom which has a claim on modern attention
is the freedom to choose.

MICHAEL IGNATIEFF, *The Needs of Strangers*, p. 63

Willing seems to me to be above all something complicated, something that is a unity only as a word.

FRIEDRICH NIETZSCHE, *Beyond Good and Evil*

[In close custody] the things that you have to do to be the heroic type definitely [do] not fit in society. It's a different world. Crazy tough guy, whatever . . . After a while, institutionalized is what they call it. After a while, it adapts to your character.

CONTROL UNIT INMATE

Many conversations in prison are about how the prisoners have *chosen* to do what they do. "You did the crime, you do the time," the officers say to the inmates. The specifics of the crime are not the point; what this remark means is that the prisoner alone is accountable for his current situation. No one else (for example, the officer) should have to suffer. In a context of incessant friction between an imposed order and the needs and desires of those who feel its constraint, the question of how time can be done is ever present. How will you, as prisoner, officer, or administrator, do your part in relation to the doing of time? With the power to act on one's own behalf far more available on one side of the bars than the other, choice is the currency that negotiates the resulting dynamic of domination and abjection. How and whether a person can be in possession of his or her own actions when compelled by a regime of force is a pervasive issue for both inmates and staff.[7]

A prison official defending the growth of control units provides a particularly pure statement of the notion that self-generated action is the material on which prison does its work. In order to show that solitary confinement is not harmful, this writer goes back to a study of men who served time at Alcatraz from 1934 to 1963 under conditions of isolation and deprivation of privileges.

Few resumed their troublemaking ways . . . even a year or two on the Rock was sufficient to help prisoners "get the message.". . . Interviews with inmates who succeeded . . . clearly indicate that these men came away from a penal setting in which they had been given plenty of time—and with very few distractions—to think about their future prospects. [They were] men with strong personalities who made decisions based on rational choice. They were not out-of-control automatons being buffeted about by powerful, unconscious, psychological forces and early childhood experiences or by social disadvantages over which they had no control. This study clearly indicates that the Alcatraz inmates had the time and the inclination . . . to start calculating the costs and benefits of both past and future misconduct.[8]

Here "men" "make decisions" based on "rational choice" that involve "calculating the costs and benefits of both past and future misconduct." The choice-making individual with a strong personality is sharply contrasted with out-of-control automatons at the mercy of psychological and social forces (here clearly caricatured as a liberal fantasy).[9] Just as the architecture of control units echoes the historical moment when the modern prison was invented, this statement echoes the assumptions about the purpose of confinement that accompanied that invention. For the prison to do its work of control, a self capable of responding to and eventually internalizing that control must be assumed for the prisoner. This self is represented as a kind of charmed circle of autonomy and potential self-regulation; the man with a strong personality both owns himself *and* is responsive to circumstances that impose reflection and change on that self.[10]

Some inmates in control units constitute themselves as the obverse of the successful inmate described by this writer, yet explain their position in terms of a similar juxtaposition of rational calculation and force of circumstance. Tony Hollister, who was around thirty years old and described himself as an "old-style convict,"—had this conversation with me after I asked him about the frequency with which the staff talked of inmates' choices.

HOLLISTER: I have a choice, and I don't have a choice. I am one of them people that believes that no matter what the situation, I have a choice in everything. OK, [another inmate] is bad-mouthing me. He is telling me, "Fuck you, come in and do something about it." Right then and there I have a choice to go in there and beat him up and go to the hole . . . or ignore him and suffer greater consequences than going to hole.

LAR: So, what are those consequences?

HOLLISTER: The consequences would be . . . [my cellmates] would [say], "He is weak. He has no heart. He doesn't stand up for himself." [But if I go to the hole] when I get out it's all about "Ain't gonna say nothing to you. We got respect for you."

LAR: So, you benefit . . .

HOLLISTER: Hugely.

LAR: From coming in here, showing that you can do that . . .

HOLLISTER: That you *will*, not that you can.

Another inmate, seeming to stand firmly on his position as an independent subject and an outlaw, said that he saw no way out of the control unit because "Personally speaking, I'm beyond rehabilitation. I mean, I'm gonna do what I want to do when I want to do it, and anybody who gets in my way or says differently is gonna be dead. I'm doin' the rest of my life in prison, I really have nothing to lose."

This statement—so firm in its representation of extreme masculine autonomy—raises the question of how someone comes to position himself in this way. The prisoner himself seemed to realize this. In the next breath he said, "I've been doing this [prison] my whole life, since I was a kid . . . You can say I'm institutionalized. Yeah, I consider this home, it's all I know." On the one hand this man explains himself as an outlaw in full possession of free will, while on the other he can see himself as made or constituted by his "home" or position. This juxtaposition can be framed—as it is by the official defending solitary confinement—in terms of political differences over how much weight to give environmental influences in the emergence of certain kinds of behavior. But it points us to a more fundamental question about these differences: what are the contexts in which certain ideas about self and self-responsibility become useful? What *work* is done, in the kind of practice that engages this man, by regarding himself in such full—not to say murderous—possession of individuality and autonomy?

Consider a prisoner I met in a prison psychiatric unit. He was a thin young man who gestured occasionally with slender hands, one of which was missing the thumb. Describing the moment when he mutilated himself, he said, "I made 'em carry me to the hole." Several years after the event, he was still triumphant. "I *made* 'em cut off my thumb." He had been able to dissociate from his body and assert his will—his "making"— retaining a sense that he was in control of what happened to him and not simply an abject other to "them." This man's sense of transcendent self-possession—of being able to literally write his own sense of individual power on his body—allowed him to see the bloody mess he made in instrumental terms. While he made use of his own body for this purpose, the purpose itself seems similar to that expressed by those prisoners whose energy is directed toward the bodies of others. These men find themselves engaged in the performance of an autonomy that both resists the domination of the prison and fiercely engages its terms.

These conversations show how belief in the reality of individual choice can be framed in terms that seem to gain intensity in response to institutional situations. At the same time, this insistence on disengaged and autonomous action coexists with reflection on the shaping effects of the constraints it attempts to deny. Derek Janson, who wrote the "Beautiful Day" poem presented in chapter 1 and whose reputation as one of the "worst of the worst" served as a teaching tool, is an example of how notions of autonomy can create an almost mythic aura around a self-sufficient prisoner. Janson is considered by prison officials too dangerous for general population because of his repeated escape attempts and reputation as a leader. He has been confined in control units for almost ten years. A sturdy man with large green eyes and a broad smile, Janson has the extraordinary pallor of one who is never exposed to the sun. He says of himself:

I'm guilty of the crime I committed . . . I knew the consequences of being arrested for aggravated murder. That's life without parole or death. I'm not one that pushes the blame on other people. But to be continuously warehoused in a [control unit] . . . I guess their feeling is, I'm a dangerous man. And . . . I *am* a dangerous man in a lot of aspects. Anybody in here can be dangerous. [But] I've never had an assault charge, a fight, or nothing in a general population.

Janson does not regard all the prison staff as the same—"There are guards that will treat you like a human being, you can approach and tell them what's on your mind"—and many of them have heard his vivid descriptions of what it is like to be locked in indefinite solitary:

You go through days where you think, I like living, but if this is all I have to look forward to, I'd kind of like to die . . . You've got two choices. You can either kill yourself . . . or you can let it turn you into an unfeeling, uncaring person . . . After many years in here, you get the feeling that this is all I have to look forward to, this cell right here . . . This loss of hope, that's what starts building what I call that monster inside of you.[11]

A few years before this conversation Janson participated in a riot that seriously damaged the facility where he is held. Since then, however, he has received no infractions and has earned the respect of the staff. Officers and counselors say that he is patient and honest. They know that at another prison he was forced to undergo a body cavity search that left him in a rage over the assault on his masculinity. As he describes it:

> They told me, if you don't bend over and let this PA stick his finger in your ass to see if you've got hacksaw blades secreted in your anus, we'll do it by force. So the next thing you know I've got a stun gun here . . . shocking me . . . just because I'm not going to bend over and spread my ass cheeks for you . . . So now I've got [an] electric shield laid on top of me . . . So, of course, in the end they went ahead and had the PA do his rectal exam. No contraband. They knew that to begin with. They use body cavity searches against the most rebellious, [saying] "We're gonna degrade you to where you don't want to break the rules." The only way I can feel like I'm living and I'm a man is to fight [them] for what I have.

The staff notes that Janson has "his own sense of honor." If he is angry, he will try to keep those who haven't hurt him out of harm's way: one officer said that he sometimes tells her, "They wronged me, don't open the cuffport today." The officers and administrators of this unit do not believe that Janson should be kept indefinitely. An officer who had left the unit said, "[He] is the perfect example of how the system can really screw a guy over . . . They will not give him a chance. If we are going to play fair, let's play fair. I just don't want no part of it no more." Janson, too proud to ask for help directly, nevertheless expressed frustration, even desperation. "I can't do another eighteen months [in here]," staff members reported him as saying. "I will kill someone. I will kill myself." Disturbed by the failure of "the system" to reward his good behavior, and by his eloquent distress, workers on this unit have responded by pressing for a transfer to another state prison system where he can start over in general population.

One day I went with two prison workers to talk with Janson. We walked out on the tier to his cell, where they opened the port, cuffed him up, and then waited, holding the tether attached to the cuffs, for the booth officer to open the door. When the door opened Janson quipped, "Just another day in paradise," as the two correctional counselors fell into place beside him. They were careful with the routine, but their manner was casual. The four of us went to a glassed-in room visible to the booth officer, and arranged ourselves at the built-in metal table and stools that are its only furniture. On one side the tabletop has two iron rings to which Janson's hands were carefully cuffed; his legs were put into irons and chained to the table. The three men settled themselves and began talking about how long Janson had been locked up.

FIRST
COUNSELOR: You may be an escape risk, but you've done what we've asked. Nobody who knows you blames you [for trying to escape]. You've done some bad things in your life, but as a person we respect you.

JANSON: I don't see how I've gotten this reputation.

SECOND
COUNSELOR: You've done some notorious things. These young inmates are looking up to you, talking about you, saying that you're a leader . . .

JANSON: [The authorities] don't see the things I've prevented. (*He goes on to describe talking kids out of trouble, suggesting, for instance, that it won't help them to throw feces on officers.*) I'm not doing it for y'all. I don't think a kid should bury himself like me.

SECOND
COUNSELOR: I don't think you would hurt us.

JANSON: You've always been professional.

FIRST
COUNSELOR: I don't always give [what you/prisoners] want.

JANSON: Sure! But there's very limited ways we can [express] ourselves in here.

SECOND
COUNSELOR: . . . and you need to be heard.

JANSON: I deserve punishment, but sometimes it's personal. At [the other prison] they made things so personal. You can't do that to a man. They know what they did.

SECOND
COUNSELOR: What ends up happening is [inmates like you] get built up into mythic proportions. No one knows how to deal with a myth. They [the officials who could let him out of the control unit] just defer, defer, defer . . . What frightens people is the successful repeat attempts. And you're very methodical.

LAR: What do you think happens about this mythic character?

SECOND
COUNSELOR: There's some charismatic thing

FIRST COUNSELOR:	Some staff members can say, I've done . . . [whatever] with Janson (*that is, they use dealing with him to bolster their own reputations*).
JANSON:	The whole purpose is to hurt me. They're trying to make a name for theirself and they make you so mad you stop thinking about consequences. I have two choices. I can go crazy or occupy myself, burn off energy with exercise or reading. There's days in here I think, what's the purpose of my life?
FIRST COUNSELOR:	There's days I can tell you're pissed off and frustrated.
JANSON:	If I stop fighting I'll die. You get these bad thoughts in your head, and you have to ask yourself, would I really want to do that? I try to put my mind on something else. I have these thoughts that I don't care whether I live or die.

The staff on this unit understands Janson's desire for escape. They also believe, as one officer said, that if they stood between him and freedom, "he would kill someone without a thought." They and he are in agreement that it is their job to prevent this eventuality. But they are not afraid of him day-to-day because they see in him the embodiment of a comprehensible and rational response to his situation. Janson has been on the receiving end of an enforcement he sees as illegitimate, an intensely symbolic and raw form of power. His stance—I'll die if I stop fighting—makes sense to the staff as an attempt to hold on to himself under conditions that—in his and their view—rob him of manhood as well as freedom. Janson and the staff use the available elements—choice, honor, manhood—to produce a sense of autonomy despite the rigid outlines of their situation. This doesn't make the staff see him as someone who would be safe to release from prison. It doesn't make him less angry about his situation or his long years in solitary less disturbing. But within what would seem, from the outside, an extraordinarily narrow range of movement, keepers and kept have found a bit of "give." Thus, for example, Janson wrote of one of his drawings (Figure 12) "It's mostly meant to get a laugh, yet on the flip side it is a serious picture of my unbreakable spirit."

In some cases both prisoners and staff believe that the situation of confinement offers the possibility of intervention in the process of self-

Figure 12. Untitled drawing by "Derek Janson." Courtesy of artist.

making. Some prisoners describe how being backed to the wall breaks them down and forces them to reconstitute themselves on different terms. Carl Tuttle, also in his late twenties, has a gentle face, sad eyes, and a spectacular but faded warrior tattooed on his arm. He has been out of detention or prison for only a few months since the age of ten. Recently, he spent months in a control unit where he experienced sensory distortion and intense anger, entering into a "war" with the staff. As he describes it:

> In isolation . . . I was losing it. They basically broke me. They broke me.
> They had me to the point where I wasn't getting anywhere fighting 'em
> back. I . . . had to stop . . . The only thing you can do, you can go crazy
> or you can get your mind in a positive direction and it's hard to do. They
> force you to take a [cognitive change] course . . . [it's about] facing life

head-on, accepting yourself. I'm sitting here thinking, OK even if there is one thing in this course that I can get out of it then it's worth it. So I got a lot out of it. And, you know, I started looking at other things like that, it's catching. I started educating myself a little bit.

Courses like the one Tuttle was given are workbooks of text and written assignments that prisoners complete in their cells. The idea of self-direction, of picking oneself up from the depths, is a frequent theme in these materials.[12] One such book contains this passage:

> Men in prison have the opportunity to become their "best self." It is important that you find the man you were meant to be . . . A baby is a blank slate. What do you wish had been written on you as a baby? . . . Society puts imprints on the baby. What imprints were put on you? Think about it. We have a choice for our circumstances. What choices have you made? . . . Look around you at this moment. It is hard . . . to look around and not realize that there were definite choices you made that cause these circumstances to visit you . . . What exact choices got you here in this mess?

Here two ways of seeing the self exist side by side in the space of a page or two of instructions for control unit prisoners. The inmate was a blank slate, on which a dysfunctional self was inscribed. *And* in the mess created by that self, he can choose to look for his true self, his best self. The true self can be found only if he can see himself not as merely inscribed but as having chosen.

Tuttle describes his experience, somewhat differently from Janson, as an internal process that gives him the hope of becoming a positive agent on his own behalf—a possibility fostered by the choice he was forced to make between "going nuts or getting my mind right."[13] But he also expresses doubt about ever making it outside prison.

> I just hope I can shake it [prison]. Because the more I try, the more I see how hard it is, the more I understand about it. The way you think, the way you perceive things . . . You have to change that. It's really hard to change your whole conception of things.

That conceptualization is, as he sees it, profoundly shaped by the institution. "Before you know it," he says, "it's part of you."

Janson and Tuttle both describe the extremity of prison in terms of "losing it" or "going crazy." They insist that strength and will power have to be repeated again and again in order to stay sane. As we will see in the next chapter, insanity is a possibility that exists in close proximity to these men, but I do not believe they mean it in any clinical sense. Rather, they are talking of the injunction to remain as self-sufficient and forceful as possible. Tuttle, for instance, says, "So the code is that you don't show what's going on, you've got to be strong. Whatever you are, you don't want to let them know that that's not really you, 'cause then you're weak." What is being said here is that the will is hard to find once and for all, but *willing*—as in Nietzsche's comment at the beginning of this section—is something complicated that must be repeated in order to be sustained. The complication for the prisoner is that the more his will is the target of enforcement, the more doubtful becomes the source of his actions.

STEERING

A perfected model it is, this prison life, with its apparent uniformity and dull passivity . . . Hidden behind the veil of discipline rages the struggle of fiercely contending wills, and intricate meshes are woven in the quagmire of darkness and suppression.

ALEXANDER BERKMAN, 1912, QUOTED IN
CHARLES STASTNY AND GABRIELLE TYRNAUER,
Who Rules the Joint? p. 1

Good order is the foundation of all good things.

EDMUND BURKE, QUOTED IN
JOHN DIIULIO, *Governing Prisons*, p. 9

I don't want them to leave [prison] without being corrected.

OFFICER, TALKING ABOUT THE DANGER FORMER
PRISONERS MAY POSE TO HER COMMUNITY

The central function of the prison—the work of keeping inmates inside and inmates and staff safe—is called "custody" or "security." The terms refer both to the task itself—"always maintain a security mindset"—and to the people who carry it out, as when a proposed alteration in routine is met with the objection that "custody won't like it." Custody is where the constraints of prison meet the inmate's will, but sheer force is not the primary method. Administrators sometimes say that the inmates are really in control of the institution. "We [just] steer them," said one. Prisons are orderly to the extent that prisoners' self-interest can be aligned with institutional rules, an alignment achieved primarily through the infraction system. The sanctions that back up the rules codified by this system depend on the assumption, in the words of an officer, that "behavior and thinking are a choice."

The infraction system shapes relationships both between inmates and staff and among staff members themselves.[14] As with the use of restraints, it raises the question of how discipline should be imposed in light of its close proximity to force. Are prison staff the impersonal vehicles of policy? Or are they personally involved in a struggle with the willfulness of the inmate? What does "personal" imply in this context? Before turning to this issue, we first need to consider how the system works.

Infractions are violations of prison rules for which inmates are punished; sanctions include not only time in segregation but also less drastic changes in housing and increased time in prison. Officers carry a laminated card listing offenses by number, and issue "tickets" to inmates caught in them. Some rule breaking is discovered through classic surveillance methods—cameras, glass walls, listening devices. Some is simply committed in front of officers—fighting, sneaking fruit out of the cafeteria (used for making an alcoholic beverage called pruno), threatening staff. Major infractions include homicide, assault, threatening an officer, interfering with officers, fighting, and possession of contraband. Most officers feel that punishment for these offenses should be swift and predictable: "If they cross the line and break the rules, they pay the price." Punishment for minor infractions, such as horseplay or lying, is discretionary. The "boundaries in inmates' minds" referred to in training officers are established and maintained primarily by this systematization of misbehavior. Thus, for example, signs next to painted lines on floors display infraction numbers referring to the consequence for crossing these boundaries.[15]

Violations of the system are adjudicated in disciplinary hearings, which are set up to resemble the criminal justice system—the "law"—as it operates outside of prison. Hearings include witnesses (usually officers) but no equivalent of a defense attorney for the inmate. Peter Owen was a prisoner with a long history of disciplinary problems both before and after his transfer to a control unit; his hearing notes, which include quotations written by officers at the time, convey how behavior, infractions, and hearings are related. At the age of twenty, Owen was living in a medium custody facility where he was "programming" and had a job. He had no infractions up to that point, which was about two years into his prison term. He was placed into a higher custody level for serious infractions 123 ("interfering with staff") and 456 ("general infraction likely to result in danger to life or limb"), when he "refused to stop interfering with a sergeant who was addressing another inmate." The next month, he received another infraction for resisting being uncuffed through the cuff port. An officer wrote: "I told him if he would not let me take the cuffs off he could wear them until he would. The inmate then spit at me through the door vent." During the same month, Owen was denied his shower because of "disruptive activity" that included his yelling at an officer, "Open this door, punk, and come in here like a man." A year later he was in segregation and receiving more infractions there. To an officer who asked him to calm down because he was shouting at another inmate, he said: "I don't care, you can't threaten me with a 789 infraction. You all already threw everything at me, there is nothing more you can do to me that you haven't already done." The officer wrote, "This type of behavior seems to be an ongoing problem with him."

Owen thus became increasingly entangled in a cycle of anger, infractions, punishment and more anger, the downward spiral often described as being "at war with the system." For several years he was enmeshed in this atmosphere of mutual provocation and refused to attend his hearings; the reports presented above were written without his participation. Later he explained to me that there was no point in going since he knew he would be charged. An officer described how staff at the time viewed this particular "war." "We played by the rules. If they wanted to be verbally abusive they didn't get fed, they didn't get yard, they didn't get shower. We didn't deviate from that."

The logic of the infraction system is intended to engage the rationality of the inmate. It posits that eventually—if staff hold their ground and refuse to deviate from supplying consequences—the prisoner will make a connection between what he does and what happens to him. And in fact, by acknowledging what he had done and avoiding the hearings Owen indicated, in his own view and that of the staff, that he did make the connection. When, in contrast, a prisoner seems unable to relate his actions to their consequences, his rationality may be suspect. An officer described an inmate who had signed his name to a threatening kite (a note from a prisoner to a staff member): since "threatening someone means a sure trip to seg, he is not thinking things out the way a rational person would." One administrator expressed his confidence that most prisoners could make sense of punishment as a consequence of their actions: "We put [misbehaving inmates] in strip cells where they have to earn *everything* back— [to get them] to where they can reflect in their mind: If I do this, this is what happens."

This administrator assumes (or hopes) that what is being reflected on is a straightforward cause and effect relationship between an act and its sanction. For many prisoners, however, the issue is more complex; they describe making choices in which an infraction is simply the lesser of two evils. Thus, as Hollister explained, going to a control unit can be seen as a way to bolster a man's reputation and protect him from assault later. A very young inmate said of his control unit sentence:

> I'm gonna come here anyways [no matter how serious the infraction required] if someone tries to mess with me . . . I mean, you look at me, I'm young, you know, I look like a fish [a new prisoner] . . . But I'm not gonna put up with that, I'm probably gonna end up getting in a lot more fights . . . It's kind of like a catch 22 because I ain't going to just let nobody take advantage of me, because if I [do] I'm going to come out on the streets a totally different person.[16]

Similarly, an African American prisoner, David Mattingly, had been held in segregation for months. He described later how he had been the target of a racial insult.

> There wasn't no peer pressure involved [in the fight that brought him into segregation]. I just went in and did what I felt I needed to do. As a man. My manhood, my integrity was challenged by somebody saying something that was totally out of line. I made a decision . . . I knew the consequences of it.

In the eyes of these men, these are rational decisions based on their understanding of the intersecting and contradictory rules that constrain their lives. For Mattingly, who said that inmates start "50 percent of trouble," his considered decision to respond to a racial attack is in contrast to senseless and self-defeating rebellion. This is how he described a cell extraction:

> For them to put on their outfits and come in to get you you've already done a whole lot at that point. If you refuse to cuff up they're gonna ask you a whole lot of times, they're gonna wait a while, they're gonna ask the sergeant and the lieutenant to talk to you, and then they're gonna put on their gear and ask you one more time. By then you gotta deal with whatever you've got coming.

Mattingly sees the prisoner, here, as retaining control over what happens to him; at each step, his refusal sets in motion an escalation by the staff. This is the view of those asking the questions as well: on the videos that record these situations each moment of questioning, each point of choice, is supposed to be clearly on camera.[17] The pepper spray, shields, mattresses, and restraints that overtake the resistant inmate are "what he has coming."

How such sanctions should be delivered is a primary source of tension in relations between officers and inmates. On the one hand, an officer who is a "hard-ass" and who (as one officer described it to me) "wants to kill 'em all" brings his attitude—inmates often describe it as his "bad day"—to all his interactions with inmates. As one officer put it:

> You become superman. Those are the scary officers, bulletproof and they show it to everyone, the power that badge gives you. You can run [an inmate] down and corner him and he'll "start it." And you've got a witness but they don't say that this bulletproof John Wayne should have kept his mouth shut. It's power.[18]

Power exercised in this way is called "personal." Janson's anger about the body cavity search centers on this personal quality of the attack on his manhood. He expresses no objection to being searched, which he regards as simply the job of the staff. What troubles him is that the search seemed intended to hurt him by exerting an obscenely close form of power—a kind of rape. Staff who can deal out the rules without becoming personal are compared favorably to those who say angrily, "You ain't got nothin' comin'," especially if the news is delivered respectfully. David Mattingly said of a request:

They rejected some magazines I ordered. So, [an administrator] came around, and I asked him . . . and he told me the reasons why they were rejected and he was real respectful about it. This is nothing personal, this politely is just rejected and you can't have them. And that was . . . a real positive experience.

Supervisors are motivated to prevent the "personal" from featuring in relations between staff and inmates, seeing it as a threat to the orderly operation of the prison. One administrator said that he felt it was his job to try to prevent staff from "becoming emotionally driven and out of control. It is creepy to have both staff and inmates yelling."

But on the other hand, impersonal and automatic imposition of the rules also troubles some inmates and staff. Taught that "enforcement is not personal but the law," officers may maintain a consistently cool distance from inmates. One described a fellow officer: "[She] writes 'em up for anything. Would you write someone up for giving his neighbor a cigarette? I won't give a ticket for that because I know what it feels like to need a smoke!" Prisoners complain about officers who seem like inflexible "robots," and some point out that impersonal application of the rules reminds them that they are subject to a larger agenda. One put it as follows:

I'm a pretty rational human being, when I think, you know. And I've sat and analyzed all this [how the prison system treats him] . . . I don't think it's anything geared specifically toward how to screw me over. It's just a problem that affects all people in prison and it's the system. It's the way it's set up. Basically what they're gonna do to us [is] try to rearrange our minds and try to make [us] become what society's so-called image of a model person is.

This man sees his own rationality emerging "when he thinks," enabling him to see how the "system" has his mind as its ultimate object.[19]

The mutually understood logic of the infraction system is seen by both prisoners and prison workers to be right at the edge of the use of force, which threatens on two sides. On one hand, the officers may take their power personally while, by implication, seeing the "person" behind the inmate's rebellion as an opponent or enemy. As Janson put it, "This is *their* prison. They're running it, and regardless of how much you resist . . . in the end you're gonna do what they wanted you to do . . . They are clearly in control, you know, there's no question of that." On the other hand, the effort to avoid violence may slip toward a mechanistic approach that accords no autonomy or will to the prisoner, making him seem more like an animal or a slave. It is only by harnessing discipline to its action on the person that prison can be a place in which Tuttle, for example, can discover his "bestself" through his choices and prison staff can "correct."

THE OWNERSHIP OF DEEDS

The criminal justice system focuses moral condemnation
on individuals and deflects it away from the social order.

JEFFREY REIMAN, *The Rich Get Richer
and the Poor Get Prison*, p. 158

Some inmates see themselves as victims and do crimes to
make themselves become victims of prosecution.

PRISON WORKER

You can say to an inmate [who is acting up] "You don't
have to do this." And he says, "You're right, but that
would negate everything I've ever done."

ADMINISTRATOR

The point of prison discipline, in the eyes of many workers, is to get inmates to move from positive small choices to revising their life as a whole. It is not clear to many exactly how to do that—the leap from small to large-scale change is often unexamined or mysterious. But the reason for this emphasis is not just a well-run prison, but the notion that the inmate is— and must come to see himself as—both owner and author of his own deeds. The two quotes at the beginning of the section from prison workers both make the point that people ultimately form their own lives—even seeking out prosecution in order to be a "victim," or refusing to change negative behavior because they have taken a lifelong stance as an outlaw. From this perspective arguments about environmental effects on behavior are either partial—perhaps the environment has some effect—or downright threatening.[20] The belief that the inmate moves in a charmed circle of his own reason and autonomy—or that he can be made to do so through discipline—is what ultimately justifies the practices of order within the prison.

Sometimes both inmates and staff talk in specific terms about how a prisoner is able to move in the direction of greater self-possession and control. An officer remarked on how much a particularly difficult inmate had changed.

> He would do anything to get in trouble. You name it . . . I mean, it was infraction after infraction. . . . [Sometime later] he was a totally different person. He had changed his behavior and his attitude . . . it was like talking to a brand new inmate. He changed his life because of the Lord. He found something he can take within and become a different person.

What gets "taken within" to make a different person may be, as here, religious, or it may be simply the prison rules themselves (the "boundaries in their minds"); as this officer added, "There are other ways [also] that have come into these inmates' lives." For Pete Owen—who was engaged in the years-long "war" described earlier—it was the books he learned to read in the control unit. "Look at me," he said, "I didn't read at all before, I have an eighth grade education. But in there I learned to discipline myself. I want to read. I want to be an individual."

Owen thus agrees—at least on this point—with those prison workers who believe that it is possible to move directly from discipline to "being an individual." The course materials quoted earlier in which the inmate is exhorted to find his true self are provided in a clear context of discipline, in which the inmate is expected to ready himself—fully dressed, not simply wearing underwear—for the teacher's weekly visit to his cell. A custody supervisor, Rick Trumble, explained his view that such small choices can lead to positive consequences.

> A choice is a series of events. The initial choice sets up other choices. You come to a fork in the road. One [way] leads to something bad—drugs, crime. One is the way you should choose. There's always another fork in the bad road; you can always get back to the good road if you are willing to make a good choice.

This process of choice making forms a life by producing a trajectory that must be answered for. I asked Rick whether he felt that to believe that someone has no choice is to diminish him, making him in some fundamental way less than a full person. Yes, he said, that is exactly what I think. We had both read Fox Butterfield's *All God's Children*, a book that describes a family in which several generations of violent men become increasingly numb to the sanctions of the law. Rick called the book "sad." But he also felt that Butterfield was too ready to blame history and social environment, especially in the case of Willie, the youngest in the family, who is held in a control unit as one of the "worst" prisoners in New York State.

> I didn't agree that it's all environmental conditioning. I agree that people are conditioned. But at some point they make a choice. When Willie said, "I'm gonna be the baddest," he *decided* to be that. [His father too] knew right from wrong. He wasn't "disturbed." He *knew* what would happen.

In this view Rick is in complete agreement with one stream of contemporary thinking about corrections that considers the attribution of responsibility a prerequisite for full humanity. "Talk of justice," writes Igor Primoratz, ". . . makes sense when we relate to a being who decides and acts freely, and therefore carries responsibility for its decisions and actions . . . [This is] a conception of humans as free, mature, responsible, self-determining beings. It sees and respects the offender as such a being, and relates to his act as to an act of such a being."[21]

Many prison workers readily acknowledge the effect of the prison environment. In a typical comment one officer remarked, "The environment has a big influence on people. It's intangible, but I'm sure there's an effect. People will react how you expect them to react." But workers nevertheless align themselves with these notions of responsible action and feel that too great an emphasis on influence robs the inmates of something—and for that matter robs them as well. One officer said:

> People defend [inmates] for reasons happening in their family. Well, the same thing happened to my family. So don't give me that as an excuse. I had a lot of decisions in my life. I could have [done] drugs. I have friends that have come through here [prison]. I chose to walk away. I *choose* to walk away.

Once bad decisions bring inmates to prison, many workers believe they must deprive them of excuses and offer small, repeated opportunities for the exercise of better ones. One officer said, "I want to correct them, that's why I came into corrections. I want to help them understand that there are consequences to choices."[22]

Yet the accountability so clearly articulated in these statements often becomes, in practice, a thoroughly murky business. An inmate describing the events that led him to a control unit expresses the kind of slippage about causation that workers find disturbing.

> Each and every person is an individual and they have their own set of circumstances. But from their [the staff's] point of view, they can't think any different than that I choose to be here. The little chain of events that came [happened] because I didn't—I wouldn't—snitch on somebody . . . So in essence, I did choose to come here. I chose not to tell on somebody. So I guess, yeah, I choose to be here—indirectly.

A little chain of events, a sense of indirect responsibility—how are these to be addressed? An officer described her interaction with one inmate who was in isolation for misbehavior: "He gets into this circle [with me]. I say, *you* chose to do this, you need to take responsibility. He says, no, you put me here. It's you guys' rules!" Staff and prisoners struggle over choice—whether there is one and whose it is—in a context where daily life is in fact tightly managed and events often reflect the conflicting sanctions of their respective "codes."[23]

This conversation within prisons reflects a larger national discussion of crime in which the notion of volitional wrongful action has become increasingly central.[24] Volitional criminology—or, alternatively, punitive individualism—includes an emphasis on the individual, insistence on accountability for "actions of choice," and a belief that rehabilitation is wasteful and useless. This perspective supports the public imagery surrounding the "worst of the worst" and carries the additional assumption that acts can be explained by their qualities. In other words, "acts are fun . . . or they are painful . . . and difficult."[25] Because these qualities, rather than social context, are the reason for crime, one need only look at immediate behavior (for instance, stealing cars) to understand its source in shortsighted pleasure-seeking (it is more fun to steal a car than work for the money to buy it). In this view the criminal is the only appropriate target of intervention while at the same time his individuality is collapsed or narrowed to the rather abstract status of "willful actor."

The cultural logic of volitional criminology supports the development of control units and makes sense of their relationship to prisons as whole.

It also articulates with and is reinforced by the increasing emphasis on rationality and governmental efficiency in prison administration. Nowhere is this clearer than in the way new technologies of control have come to participate in the notions of choice we have been exploring.[26]

TECHNOLOGY

To say that some technologies are inherently political is to say that certain . . . reasons of practical necessity . . . have tended to eclipse other sorts of moral and political reasoning.

LANGDON WINNER, *The Whale and the Reactor,* p. 36

If you relate, you have that moment when you put yourself in their place, and, man . . . !

OFFICER, OF INMATES

The Department of Corrections is bigger than me.

CONTROL UNIT PRISONER

One of the mock scenes set up to train prison workers opened on an "inmate" lying on the bottom bunk of his cell with an apparently self-inflicted injury created by the liberal application of ketchup. The injured man, in actuality a large and rather imposing custody supervisor, pretended to be too hurt and dizzy to get up, while his cellie "slept" soundly on the upper bunk. Concerned, the students rushed into the cell without noticing a shank on the floor. As they moved toward the "bleeding" man, his cellmate leaped from the upper bunk, brandished the shank, and yelled at the top of his voice: "You're all dead!" The moral of the lesson was that any situation can offer trouble no matter how benign or emergent it seems; in this case, "the appearance of injury doesn't mean he's down and out."

Intricate rules of operation and mountains of paperwork are common to many institutions; what differentiates prisons is a specific orientation to inmates as inherently *opportunistic*. "The bait was right there," scolded one of the instructors later as he debriefed the students on this session, "and you went for it." Malicious intent is the form of uncertainty specific to correctional work: "You don't know if it's a suicide, a stabbing, a self-mutilation . . . or a trap."

Thus the "worst nightmare" conjured up by an ad for video surveillance

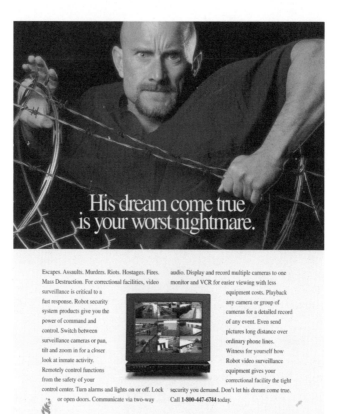

Figure 13. Correctional trade journal advertisement: "Your Worst Nightmare."

systems (Figure 13) is a cunning prisoner who has seized an opportunity. The text lists the disasters waiting to happen—"Escapes. Assaults. Murders. Mass Destruction."—and promises that remote control technology can prevent the convict's dream from coming true. Clearly the advertisers believe they are addressing the vulnerability and anxiety of those responsible for making sure that no one escapes on their watch, targeting prison administrators who see themselves employing ever-advancing technological expertise against ever-evolving inmate strength and skill. The technologies of control that preoccupy administrators and workers range from distant (perimeter fences, guns in the towers) to extremely close (cuffs,

Figure 14. Correctional trade journal advertisement: "When It Comes to Choices, They Should Be Yours Not Theirs."

body cavity search devices), and from the venerable (the towers) to the futuristic (electrical stun devices).[27] Like cuffs, most of these involve elements of judgment for the operator and a strong imputation of willfulness to the inmate, enmeshing both workers and prisoners in a calculus of risk and opportunity. Often the point at which opportunism meets industrial technology is explicitly framed in terms of its capacity to call forth rational— or at least very clever—choices. Another ad, this one for shatterproof glass (Figure 14), reads in part: "The opportunities, and weapons, for threat are tremendous . . . When you make security glazing decisions, the choices that leave no risk should be yours." Such highlighting of choice is repeated in many similar correctional advertisements offering technical support for what is framed as a battleground of wills.

At a meeting to discuss "behavior problems" in control units, administrators and prison officials framed disturbing experiences of danger and chaos in terms of the capacity of inmates to take advantage of vulnerabilities found even in these "secure" environments.

CONTROL UNIT
ADMINISTRATOR 1: We've had a serious use of force on our unit—a staff assault by an inmate. He ran from officers on his way back to his cell [from his yard]. They got hold of him, put him in leg irons and carried him to his cell. [He could] have done some damage and we could have hurt him, too. And we [also] found pruno and a shank in a supply closet, hidden by the pod porters . . . the best shank I've ever seen. That shank, it could have been [used in] a hostage situation.

OFFICIAL: There's a whole we/they fortress mentality among the [control unit] workers.

CONTROL UNIT
ADMINISTRATOR 2: A guy in my unit on the way to the shower cut an officer in the eye with broken TV glass. A guy broke the Plexiglas with his hand, another one of our guys had to be put in a restraint chair.

OFFICIAL: I'm concerned with the security practices at [X]. Prior to cuffing up the [inmates are supposed to] strip their coveralls off and pass them through the port. Where we get beat is some of that detail stuff: some of these folks [inmates] are opportunists.

CONTROL UNIT
ADMINISTRATOR 1: Yeah, some of these guys just go on and on.

There is a hint here of the context in which control unit administrators often experience violence on their units ("there's a whole we/they mentality"). But as in conversations about throwing, the major emphasis is on how the ingenuity and strength of the inmates constantly threatens to break the fragile structures of containment. Sometimes one can sense the feelings of exposure and physical vulnerability in the compul-

Figure 15. Correctional trade journal advertisement: "They Won't Get Past Your S.T.A.R."

siveness that surrounds this topic. To line staff, loose fixtures, aging buildings, inadequate fencing, and old equipment seem a direct statement about their worth—or their expendability. One said that during a period when the people working on his unit felt a "lack of confidence in the physical plant, everyone in there wanted to kill everyone [else]." Prison workers who do not feel supported may become preoccupied with violence—fearing, as an ad for body armor puts it (Figure 15), inmates' capacity to "stab, slash, pound, punch and burn you." As the ad implies, workers can "get stuck" with something "less"—and some, indeed, feel that they are considered expendable. Workers who do feel supported speak with approval and gratitude of the protection afforded by state-of-the-art gear and on-call emergency response teams. "I would say they are our heroes," said one officer of her prison's team.[28]

The conversation among control unit workers is characteristic, too, in its exhortation and worry about the "detail stuff" that requires an unrelenting focus on the material facts of institutional containment. Attention to the architecture, fixtures, and procedures intended to thwart opportunity is an open-ended practice, never settled, for the methods that contain prisoners quickly become obsolete. After an incident that engulfed a control unit in the kind of violence described in chapter 1, I stood on a tier with several staff members discussing fixtures, particularly some faucets that had been ripped out of the walls with apparent ease. The maintenance man explained, "The first thing they're going for is those handles. We have heavy-duty paranoid guys who are very, very strong." We went into a room where a large hole in the wall had just been repaired, the plaster still wet. "They're young" the maintenance man sighed. "Time is gonna wear them out." An administrator added, "But there are more guys behind them." The conversation turned to the merits and problems of different window materials. "Glass, if it breaks, they eat it. But plastic, they write on it, make swastikas and gang slogans."

Despite the fact that this conversation happened in a control unit, these workers assume that total control can never be achieved. Prisoners who attend closely to vulnerabilities of architecture and operation are sure to imagine, and occasionally achieve, a temporary reversal. Fishing out of cells, for example—using threads taken from clothing to pass notes and other items under cell doors—is thwarted by installing metal barriers to block the space between the door and the floor. One inmate, describing this change, said cheerfully, "It's just a matter of time, we'll figure something else out."[29]

The multitude of industries that supply prisons with "security" tend to push toward ever-greater efficacy. The most recent innovation is the development of devices, such as the stun gun described by Janson, that deliver an electric shock.[30] Electrical "demobilization devices," including stun shields, belts, and taser guns, are marketed by traveling sales people who make the rounds of prisons much as drug company representatives visit doctors. These devices are painful when touched to the skin; simply turned on, the shield and gun emit vivid blue sparks and a threatening crackle. In addition to the pain of the shock itself, they incapacitate by temporarily draining energy from muscles. The leading manufacturer, Stun Tech, describes the belt as inflicting a 50,000 volt shock and emphasizes its capacity to cause pain and immediate incapacitation. The company warns it should not be used to "unlawfully threaten, coerce, harass, taunt, belittle or harass any person."[31] As this statement suggests, the belt is "threatening" whether it is activated or not; the psychological aspect of control though fear is—from the perspective of manufacturers—one of its selling points. The use of these devices is described by Amnesty International and other human rights organizations as a form of torture, and there is evidence in some prison systems of extremely abusive—"unlawful," as the company sees it—use. Inside prisons, however, electrical technology is lauded for its intimidating effect; it strikes workers as a "clean" form of coercion. One officer explained to fellow officers who had never used one that "the electric shield makes sparks that often make an inmate real quiet. Just the visual display, and he'll say, 'I've had enough.'" Another asked me, "If you knew the belt you had on could make you mess your pants, wouldn't you decide to behave?"[32]

Prisoners describe the use of electricity as an attempt to reduce them to the status of animals. David Mattingly said:

A guy on my tier got shocked with [a taser gun]. The whole side of his face was black and blue, he looked like a vampire bit him . . . So he cuffs up [after an apparent suicide threat] and they get him in one of the holding cells and put the other thing [electric belt] on him to take him to the hospital . . . They do it to people who they feel could be a real risk. They've never done that to me. They never did that. I think you do that to dogs to stop them from barking, you keep your dog in the yard by an electric fence. Not to say that if a guy is hurting himself in the room, you gotta go in there and get him some way. There's different measures to take. I don't really see any problem with the spray and stuff. But as far as electric . . . there's no room for electric anywhere.

Mattingly is willing to put himself in the shoes of prison workers faced with an emergency. But he draws a sharp distinction between the use of pepper spray, which he considers legitimate, and the use of stun technology. His comments suggest that the taser gun exerts a specific and perverse kind of supremacy, one that damages because it dehumanizes the prisoner's will.

The concern about excessive force that emerged in the class on restraints focused on the possibility that officers might abuse the power vested in them. As the human rights and the trade literatures show, central to the debate over electrical technology is the question of what constitutes abuse in the first place. Is the problem that the technology has a legitimate use but can be abused? Or is it inherently abusive? Writers on state torture point out that it is not primarily about extracting something from the victim. Torture places the person in the clutches of a power that moves in too close—as Janson felt about the anal search—and threatens to make him nothing but a body. The abject state that results serves as evidence of the power to enforce, an invasive power that has escaped the law yet lends substance to its underside. It is little wonder, then, that one way the treatment of prisoners is contested is through arguments about what constitutes torture. For the Stun Tech Company, the law serves as the bottom line that legitimizes their products and makes their proper use a matter of training and individual choice. The difference between the position of the company and that of human rights advocates rests on the notion of deterrence and its ultimate referent in the will, not just the body, of the prisoner.[33]

Stun belts are used for the transport of prisoners to court or between prisons. The belt is attached to a leash held by the escorting officer, who can press a button to set it off. The belt also has a warning buzzer that sounds a few seconds before it is deployed. If the misbehaving prisoner ignores the warning, the electrical current runs for the prescribed number of seconds, making it futile for him to attack the officer in an attempt to reach the button. In preparation for the use of electric control devices, prison workers take a class offered by the manufacturer in which each class member must submit to the belt. At graduation they receive bright yellow-on-black T-shirts that display a leaping electrified figure and read, "*Yeeeow,* what a feeling!" (Figure 16).

A prison-made video of one class showed officers taking turns strapping on the belt and crossing a gym mat with the current turned on. Their class-

Figure 16. Stun belt T-shirt. Photo by Lorna A. Rhodes.

mates lined the mat, forming a supportive gauntlet to help them hold on, stay standing, and make it to the other side. One participant said, "For that eight seconds you're so intense on fighting that pain off and then once it's done, you're just wiped out." However, in contrast to the promotional video put out by the manufacturer that shows demonstrators rolling on the floor in a dramatic depiction of agony, the participants in the class appear to take a deep breath, grab their classmates' hands, and walk—quickly, certainly—across the mat. This is done, according to one participant, by *deciding* that you can make it, and by having support. "It's a macho thing," he says.

What is this "macho thing" that the students learn to do?[34] In his ethnography of workers at a nuclear weapons laboratory, Hugh Gusterson notes that in the face of the overwhelming physical vulnerability that would be exposed by the actual use of the weapons they make, nuclear scientists learn not to identify with their own "bodily subjectivity." The manufacturers of stun technology seem to understand that in order to use it, prison workers must dissociate from their fear and reactivity. Holding tight, squinching up their faces, they act out a moment of transcendence over pain and restraint. Like the nuclear scientists who joke about the vulnerability of the body to radiation, workers who have been through this training tease each other about "riding the belt" and joke about the bruises left by the shock. In this context dissociation from the body serves to maintain, as it seems to for nuclear workers, the "felt legitimacy" of the work itself.[35]

A second thing that enables the "ride" on the belt is the help of language. While torture distorts and silences the victim's capacity for speech, the class acquaints students with the "ride of a lifetime" in a social context that insists on the preservation of language.[36] "It's a team-building thing—we were just sweating beforehand and afterwards everybody's saying, 'You did it! You survived it!'" Riding the support of their peers, joshing one another about it later, students withstand the belt and preserve a sense of power in the face of it. They refuse to allow themselves to be harmed psychologically by dissociating from the over-closeness of the belt itself and focusing instead on the persuasive powers they are acquiring. One officer explained, "I know what it can do. I let [inmates] know, it ain't gonna be fun. They know that in the long run they are gonna lose . . . It is that basic dog psychology right there." By experiencing the effects of the technology—but having learned it through the mediation of group support—he enters into and wins the "dog psychology" of control.

Paradoxically, the moment at which force bottoms out in the belt is also the point at which—from the perspective of prison workers prepared by their own experience—the inmate's capacity to choose is at its most visible. Hearing the buzzer, getting "real quiet," he is at a fork in the road; as the officer said, "wouldn't *you* decide to behave?" All "opportunism" is blocked as the reason of the potentially troublesome inmate is enlisted on the side of obedience. Those who have gained the authority to use the belt know what the choice is, and they feel that it places legitimate force in such an acute, proximate, and yet at the same time merely potential form, that the inmate cannot help but choose to avoid pain and seek his own best interest.[37] The gulf between the position of Amnesty and that of many prison workers rests on this difference in the definition of the inmate's situation. For Amnesty, whether or not the belt is activated, it is still being used to exert a total domination over the prisoner. For workers, he is someone who has been placed in a situation so clear that merely by choosing to behave he can avoid coercion altogether.

What if Derek Janson doesn't get to leave the control unit, through no fault of the officers and other workers directly responsible for keeping him? They know of his desperate desire to be outdoors and want to find a way for him to work on the prison grounds. Stymied by the constraints imposed by his public image, they have proposed to "let him out on the belt." Janson agrees with the plan. "It would be a good first step, a good deal all around. I'm gonna have to build some trust. And after ten years it would be hard to adjust to being around people and [this way] I can work outdoors and get away from the walls." The unit staff are lobbying for the plan, hoping to shift the burden of trust to where they feel it belongs: the official decision-making that keeps him in the unit. But the idea worries John Larson, the administrator in charge. "I don't know," he says. "I don't want to end up zapping him."

Choice and obedience, will and enforcement overlap one another throughout the practices described in this chapter. The slow turning of administrative wheels will likely thwart the plan to give Janson a few hours in the open air. But the very existence of such a plan suggests that electronic control collapses these opposites altogether and allows both the obligatory nature of choice and its power as a sign of autonomy to come full circle. Janson has aligned with his keepers in a shared determination to place his will at the center of his situation, despite the fact that his body serves as its ultimate collateral.

PART TWO NEGOTIATING TREATMENT, MANAGING CUSTODY

Chapter 3 | THE ASYLUM OF LAST RESORT

> The mouth is indeed a strait place, the prototype of all prisons. Whatever goes in there is lost, and much goes in whilst still alive.
>
> ELIAS CANETTI, Crowds and Power, p. 20

> I'm like Cerberus at the gates of hell.
>
> PSYCHOLOGIST DESCRIBING THE WORK
OF SCREENING INMATES AS THEY ENTER PRISON

New prisoners arrive at the receiving unit on the chain bus or, in prison terms, "on the chain." They are shackled two by two in leg irons, their hands cuffed to chains around their waists. It takes each pair a long minute to climb awkwardly out of the bus and walk, steps shortened by the chain, to the low building where they will be processed into the prison system. Inside the locked double doors, each new inmate is moved through a series of steps; he will take off the orange jumpsuit in which he arrived, answer medical questions from a nurse, and stand for fingerprinting and photo identification. Between the fingerprint and the photo, he will be screened by "mental health" in the form of a psychologist, social worker, or mental health counselor. Stationed in small booths, these workers ask one inmate after another a series of simple but telling questions: Ever been hospitalized for mental problems? Ever attempted suicide? Have you seen things that weren't there? Felt despondent for weeks at a time?

Receiving is the moment when prisoners are inducted into the logic of systematic steering under the threat of force.[1] As we have just seen, these fundamentals of custodial containment depend on a capacity for rational response and some degree of self-regulation. Those arrivals who lack this capacity, however, have nowhere else to go. These prisoners—perhaps discovered in screening, perhaps emerging later as they encounter the prison's constraints and categories—become an internal other whose treatment both supports and contradicts the larger custodial project. In this and the next chapter, I turn to the dynamic relationship between treatment and custody. This relationship is pervaded by the residues of past historical struggles and the tensions of conflicting practices. Entering into this territory, prisoners are the target of a basic—but often difficult-to-answer—question: rational choice-maker or damaged patient?

I follow one of the mental health workers as he enters the receiving building for his morning's work. Directly inside the double doors several men, still in orange, are standing at a urinal with their backs to the door; one is washing his hands at the adjacent sink. A watchful officer takes a minute to explain that some have been on the bus for five or six hours. The barn-like building is sectioned on one side into several pens or tanks in which groups of men sit in varying stages of undress. In the second tank a heavy-set man, his belly spilling over his briefs and long black hair standing out around his shoulders, gives out a whoop and begins jumping up and down and beating his chest. The man standing next to him takes up the rhythm for a minute, and the group in the tank stirs and murmurs. An officer suggests that I duck out of sight before they all "go off" in the unaccustomed beam of my attention.[2] I turn away from a smaller group of men who are about to "get naked" and into a staff room where several uniformed workers are filling out paperwork or watching the inmates from the doorway. A familiar, lively conversation quickly develops about the difficulty officers have in "leaving it behind" when they go home from work. One man remarks that he has become much "stricter" with people on the outside. Says another, "Everybody's always studying the inmates. Nobody wants to make *our* lives better—and we ain't done nothing!"[3]

When I catch up with the mental health worker, he has just interviewed a "pretty sad little guy" whose brother recently committed suicide. Depressed, suffering from post-traumatic stress, and on Prozac, he is not sick enough for a psychiatric unit, but the mental health worker has made a note to check up on him the next day.[4] The next man allows me join in his interview. He is slight and pale, with longish gray hair and a nervous twinkle in his eyes. He answers no to all the questions, although to the one about whether he ever feels he has "special powers" he smiles and says, "Well, on certain drugs!" He agrees to speak with me privately for a minute, and we find a quiet spot away from the other men. I ask him what it is like to come through here. "It's very humiliating. I feel like a lab rat. I've been to prison before, and I try to shrug it off. But the older you get, the harder it gets, because every time you get out you gotta start over. Maybe I'll get myself right this time and I won't go out and get stupid again."[5] Later I speak with another man whose alert, expressive face is in contrast to the stolidity of some of those around him. In and out of prison several times in the past twenty years, he expresses confidence that he will weather this incarceration; "I did this to myself," he says, "but I'm not institutionalized. I'll do the program." In the course of describing his several returns, he explains that the receiving area used to be one big room with none of the booths and stations now set up in it.

And indeed, the design of this room perfectly reflects the shifting historical elements that lie behind these standard procedures for the management of prison populations. On the side with the tanks the men are organized and moved in groups, controlled primarily by the architecture and direct surveillance that are the most archaic and still the most fundamental layer governing the prison. Huge waves of incoming prisoners roll through these tanks, threatening to overwhelm the system trying to metabolize them. Just as they are here kept moving in a tight, calibrated mass, they will from now on be governed in groups. The turning away of the officers from the man who was beating on his chest is a first defense against one threat to this mandate: ignoring deviation in an attempt to keep it from infecting the group. As one of the officers told me, "We are just like the guys who work loading docks—we're trying to *move* stuff." One administrator explained that receiving is designed to "deal with a criminal who's here to be processed and moved on." What the officer called being strict is this suppressive, group-oriented stance toward individuals.[6]

On the side of the room opposite the tanks, the men are pulled out one by one to stand for momentary attention at fingerprinting and questioning, and data about them is fed into computers or marked on questionnaires. Here, both in support for and in contrast to the movement of the group, the prisoners' individuality is recorded and preserved. They will emerge from this building officially marked for tracking, but the mark is not, as they would say, "personal." As if to make this point, next to the photo ID station I find a big box full of discarded identification badges. Dozens of pictures of prisoners fill this box, men staring warily out of the laminated plastic. Some have closed, defiant faces, others are studiedly neutral; some are sad and exhausted, their eyes full of fear, and I see in one man the over-wide eyes of the fetal alcohol affected. Though the men who walk out of this building wear new ID photos along with their fresh prison-issue denims, they have been remade—symbolically at least—in one another's likeness. The hope of the system is that they will "maintain" by behaving more or less similarly in the large, minimally staffed housing units that are their destination.

The mental health workers process the majority of inmates as impersonally as the fingerprint machine. But they stop short and shift direction when they encounter a series of yeses to their questions.[7] One soft-voiced man answers immediately that he has been hospitalized and medicated for bipolar illness. Making an appointment for him to be seen the next day, the mental health worker asks him gently how he is feeling and whether he is nervous about prison. The task here is to snag out of the flow of passing prisoners those few who stand out as unable to manage in a group. The question behind the questionnaire, according to prison workers, is how much a prisoner may become "a nuisance to his neighbors." Given the limited capacity of the prison to provide help, those who work in receiving have no choice but to look, in the words of one administrator, for the "seriously crazy . . . If they can talk, even if they are squirrely, they are moved on."[8]

The passage of those with diagnosed psychiatric conditions into prisons is connected to events that have occurred in the larger society over the past thirty years. Most important is the deinstitutionalization of public psychiatric hospitals in the 1970s and early '80s, which shifted many who would have been hospitalized into prison as the asylum of last resort.[9] Ironically, the institutionalization of patients, which the closure of the hospitals and the laws against involuntary hospitalization were intended to avoid, returns in full force in prisons. A prison administrator expressed the feelings of many who find themselves on the receiving end of this change, "These decisions [by the courts] are so irresponsible. I don't think mentally ill inmates should ever get to a prison situation." Despite these objections, prison officials and administrators find themselves legally and practically required to provide an approximation of the treatment that used to be the province of state hospitals.[10]

The net slung across the receiving unit to catch those with serious mental illness is the first step in a process that resembles the intake procedures of a psychiatric facility. But it would be a mistake to make too much of this resemblance. In fact, almost all the men who pour into the wide mouth of the prison are tumbled together as they disperse through the system. The vast majority go on into living units at this and other prisons, sorted roughly according to their prior history of violence. Most of these men never or rarely receive infractions and live in general population units with a degree of autonomy. But over time, some will have difficulty accommodating to crowded and regimented conditions and will precipitate out of these units on the basis of their behavior. These are the inmates who accumulate infractions and—as though falling through a sieve—are sorted into control units and into special units for the mentally ill.

In this chapter I consider mental health units as enclosures: special environments in which those who precipitate out of general population are given a partial exemption from custodial expectations. This exemption is limited, temporary, and subject to ongoing negotiation. It creates space for the possibility that involuntary states of mind require specific forms of attention, while, at the same time, revealing the enmeshment of treatment in the project of control.

THE DING JACKET

[In prison] there's a very dangerous mentality that you have to treat everyone the same.

MENTAL HEALTH WORKER

You can't treat everybody the same no matter how much they ingrain it in you.

SUPERVISORY OFFICER

There is too many [mentally ill] people and not enough help.

OFFICER

Prison rules include an exception for incomprehension. The policies governing infractions are explicit that an inmate can be held accountable only for misbehavior that he understands and intends.[11] On one control unit a custody supervisor explained that he would not infract one inmate who had broken the window of his cell. Though the man apologized later, the supervisor explained, "It doesn't occur to him when he does it [that it is wrong]. Later he knows he did it, but he can't tell when he is *going* to do it." This prisoner seems unable to choose how he acts, because he only "knows" the rules after the fact. An exasperated mental health worker expressed the seeming self-evidence of this interpretation: "How can you discipline someone who isn't cognizant? How can we even *talk* about disciplining someone who is not responsible for their actions?"

But many situations do not have this self-evident quality. One officer on a special unit described how a mentally ill inmate had wet his bed. He was embarrassed and afraid she would punish him. "Don't worry about it," she told him, "just get it cleaned up." To me, she said, "He couldn't help it and he was truly sorry." It would be different if he were not mentally ill. In that case, "How do you know he's not doing it just to make you mad?" In a typical comment about this kind of situation, an officer defended his belief that an inmate should have been infracted. "He's *not* mentally ill!" he insisted. "He *knows* what he does." Custody and mental health workers who need to make decisions on the basis of limited information look for signs of intentionality. One mental health worker in a control unit described an inmate she felt was trying to extricate himself from his situation.

> He was laying in bed with a towel over his head. He went to a pitiful look and told me that his brain was blurry and he couldn't think straight. I tried to evaluate how lucid his thoughts were. How much was it that he just didn't like [serving his control unit] time? He got very fluent about how pissed off he was. He talked about not wanting to lose his privileges. His "voices" never appeared plausible and realistic to me. He had good insight into his situation.

This mental health worker is building a case for her belief that this man could understand the consequences of his actions. The delusional symptoms he described did not seem plausible to her because he was able to express and justify his preferences.

What prison workers actually confront in these situations is not "mental illness" but what is called "behavior": the pitiful look, articulate complaints, or wet sheets. The term implies that behavior belongs to the one doing the behaving, but it also suggests that it is in interaction—behavior in a larger sense—that what is later attributed entirely to the individual becomes visible in the first place. There are strong traditions that push this process toward abstraction, making "mental illness," "schizophrenia," or "post-traumatic stress" as thing-like as possible. At its most elementary, however, the process by which someone comes to be seen as mentally ill begins when "intolerable" behavior is reframed as opaque enough to become the province of experts. This does not cause control to become less central, but it does open it up to question and—at times—offer potential reframings for abject forms of otherness.

The insertion of psychiatric expertise into matters of punishment has roots in theories of motivation that developed in the nineteenth century as psychiatry evolved into a separate profession. By tapping into both romantic and neurological preoccupations with the hidden dimensions of human experience, the new science of the mind articulated long-standing notions of an irrational substratum of human experience. Armed with this apparent ability to explain deviant behavior by unearthing abnormal motivation, psychiatry became enmeshed with the criminal justice system in ways that remain with us today. But the issues most central to this mutual engagement—intent and accountability—have turned out to be extraordinarily difficult to resolve. By shifting intention into the shadows of human awareness, psychiatric theories threaten to exculpate the criminal on terms that are not accessible to everyone. Even the most obvious cases of psychosis, which may be relatively easy to resolve on a pragmatic basis, represent a rupture in the foundation of lawfulness on which an offender can be brought to account.

The word "ding" is used by prison staff and inmates to mean "crazy." It is often used in ways that seem synonymous with "mentally ill" but, as with the term "crazy," its range is wider than any psychiatric diagnosis.[12] To be a ding, or to ding out or become dingy means to exhibit crazy behavior—behavior that doesn't make sense. Talking to oneself, refusing to wash, mania, general strangeness of demeanor—all are dingy. The extent to which the "ding jacket" (prison term for label) is felt to be disparaging varies, with both inmates and staff making casual references like "This is the ding wing." An officer with whom I discussed the disturbing symptoms of a friend asked in a completely matter-of-fact way, "Is she dingy?" At other times, however, "ding" is highly pejorative. Control unit inmates speak with disgust of "these crazy dings they've got in here." Prison workers do not use the word in formal contexts or when talking to outsiders.

One mock training scene offered a window onto the custodial perspective on the inmate considered "dingy." The purpose was to teach the cell search, an essential skill of the correctional officer. To do a search, officers must systematically go through everything in the cell looking for weapons, contraband, and signs of impending escape.[13] They tap on the walls, look for seams made out of toothpaste, and rifle the inmates' possessions. The mock scene not only tested these skills, but also showed the students that they could not begin a search until they figured out how to get the inmates out of the way. Entering the classroom, they found the training cell occupied by two "inmates" (played by officers) and a typical assortment of their belongings. The teachers sat at a table, handing out cell search forms and instructions. The students were told sharply, "You have fifteen minutes to extract the inmates and search the cell and five minutes to do the paper work. Get in there and hustle. *Make sure to do the paperwork!* Any questions? Start!"

In the cell, an older "inmate" knelt by the lower bunk, carefully wrapping his Koran in a towel, while a younger prisoner sat on the upper bunk clutching his pillow to his chest. It became clear from their interaction that the older one was playing a hardened convict with a protective attitude toward his cellie, who had recently been released from a mental health unit. The younger man began insisting in a sing-song whine that the pillow was his "baby." "Are you a *mean* man?" he asked a student who was gently trying to take it from him. "*Don't* take my baby!" Awkwardly, the students gained control of the pillow and talked the two men into leaving the cell. The older one was barely willing to stand for the obligatory pat search. Finally the younger inmate followed the older to the "day room," announcing childishly of the student who took his pillow, "He is *not* a nice man."

Later the trainers and the two officers who played the inmates discussed the scene with the trainees. They quizzed them rigorously about the paperwork: Where does the pink sheet go? How do you avoid breaking the chain of evidence when contraband is found?[14] The teachers also told several of the more hesitant students that their concern for the inmate with the pillow undermined safety and efficiency; they stressed that in real life dozens of such searches must be conducted quickly. One teacher warned against getting too involved. "Tell them what you want them to do and the consequences." Too much concern might make the older, more savvy inmate think, "OK, I've got something over on *you!*" In one variation of the scene, the older "inmate" drove home this lesson: when a student hesitated to do a thorough pat down, he triumphantly hauled a sock-weapon from his crotch.

This scene enacts the dilemmas of an economy of attention. As in receiving, prison workers are expected to control *groups*. They cannot linger on interaction or take inmates' individual concerns too seriously.[15] The training encourages them to be sharply attuned to certain kinds of detail—the objects in the cell, signs of impending aggression from the inmates—while minimizing the differences between the two inmates in favor of studied efficiency. What the officers must deal with is "behavior"—that is, the slowness and complexity of the men's responses to their commands—while lingering on the cusp of any specific interpretation of this behavior. Even when an inmate is diagnosable from a psychiatric perspective, this exercise makes clear that it is not necessary to see his behavior as symptomatic. An overly expansive definition of illness would threaten to shift many prisoners from the bad into the mad category, not only diluting punishment to an unacceptable extent but also underscoring the lack of facilities for treatment.

When I talked later with the officer who had played the inmate with the imaginary baby, he explained that they had set up their scene to teach "that you don't want someone so focused on a search that they overlook other things . . . Security has to be first," he said, but he noted that some officers had little sense of proportion about it. He had seen a co-worker try to force an inmate off the toilet to do a count; "All he knew was 'We have to count these inmates!'" In his view one purpose of the session was to impart common sense—"To maintain security but relax!" A disturbed inmate who is oblivious to the demands of institutional order ruptures the sense of inevitability fostered by routine. He becomes a reminder that order is inevitable only if the prisoner cooperates with it and that there might be a hint of fun in the distancing effect of this kind of behavior. The officer who played the inmate with the baby added, "We were playing with them a little bit. Inmates will do that with us, too. We do exaggerate . . . There's humor and irony here. I don't know if we meant to tell them that, but we were building on our own experience and if you don't have that attitude, this place'll eat you up."

Disturbed inmates appear to be at the opposite pole from the rational mind and sharply defined boundaries of a Derek Janson. A prisoner who is having difficulty may engage in the extreme actions I described in the first chapter, throwing body wastes or erupting in unpredictable displays of violence. He may seem "pitiful"—deranged in his speech, disheveled, slow, or shuffling. When wheedling, "management," coercion, and irony fail and the individual sticks out of the group as "truly" abnormal, it becomes possible to consider alternatives. Mental health units offer a potential respite where a different set of questions—about the prisoner's history, mental state, and responses to the prison environment—can be asked. These questions shift the focus away from individual choice and open up the potential for a slight softening of custodial power at the same time that they insert the prisoner into psychiatric forms of knowledge. The result is to highlight the effects of both power and knowledge while revealing that neither is able to fully encompass the other. Instead, custody and treatment enter into a shifting tension that begins when disruptions in the routine of containment reveal the presence of those sliding, suddenly or in imperceptible degrees, toward madness.

SOME PEOPLE, THEY'LL BREAK

Prisons offer tests of resilience that nonresilient persons,
who disproportionately inhabit prisons, cannot pass.

HANS TOCH, *Corrections: A Humanistic Approach*, p. 138

At the onset of a psychosis . . . one begins to lose one's
willful control over mind. One cannot change direction
or linger over a detail. One cannot follow through, or
"think" through anything. One cannot stop or start . . .
one cannot "operate" the machinery.

EDWARD M. PODVOLL, *The Seduction of Madness*, p. 145

There are faulty human beings. You're weird. You're
irreparable. Why not just make room for someone else?

MENTALLY ILL PRISONER

In the control unit, just to one side of the door, built-in concrete benches form a rough circle. I am here with other visitors, including a consulting psychiatrist and the social worker, nurse, and resident psychiatrist who work in the prison's mental health unit. The big space is noisy: doors clang and officers shout back and forth as they pass out lunch trays. The keys and cuffs on the officers' belts clank and jangle as they walk by, ignoring our little gathering.

One person in our circle is the prisoner we have come to see, a middle-aged man in an orange jumpsuit named William Kramer. His long hair and full beard are matted, hiding his face as he slumps slightly forward and gazes down at the floor through his grimy, tightly clasped hands. The visiting psychiatrist, much younger, sits close to him on the bench. He leans forward and clasps his own hands in front of him, mirroring the posture of the prisoner. Slowly, as though he could easily sit there for the rest of the day, he asks Kramer if it is all right to talk in front of so many people. The prisoner nods yes, never raising his eyes from the floor. Softly the psychiatrist asks, "How can we be helpful?"

Kramer's voice is so small in the big noisy space that we make out only part of his words as he begins talking, haltingly at first. He tells the psychiatrist that he comes from a large family; we catch something about spacecraft mixed into what he says. There is a long, generous pause. "I like to work with my hands," he adds. The doctor picks up on this, and asks him about his work as a carpenter. The prisoner begins to talk more easily, a little louder, about the jobs he used to do.

Then the psychiatrist reaches out and gently takes Kramer's hands in his. He turns them over, delicately stroking the palms and touching the long, curling nails. "What do you think people should know about [you]?" he asks. Kramer is silent, but it is a not a tense silence. "It's been tough for you," the psychiatrist continues. The prisoner nods. "This isolation has sort of set in," he offers. The doctor waits, adjusting his posture slightly to mirror the signs of a slight increase in animation. The prisoner continues, "It [isolation] makes a person upset, and it's like you're diseased because you're upset. It's kind of a circle." His eyes suddenly fill with tears. "You certainly do get depressed."

Kramer is quiet now. The doctor says gently, "You've been all by yourself way too much, for far too long. We'll keep checking in with you about how we are doing [with you]. We'll work with you about how fast you want to be with people." The resident psychiatrist, a silent observer until now, turns to the prisoner and adds, "I'll bring in some nail clippers tomorrow and cut your nails for you. Let's just hope they won't fire me for it!"

Later, the visiting psychiatrist ends his consultation with some advice for the staff. "He's lonely and terrified that he's lost his mind. Anchor everything in the real world, play cards with him. He's interesting; there's a brightness in there that's still alive. That's what makes it hard. He knows what he has lost."

William Kramer was sent to prison from a county jail where he had been confined in isolation for two years. Charged with gradually moving him from the control unit into their facility, these mental health workers had already begun the process by removing his handcuffs. "Yesterday," says one, "we were afraid that we'd never get him off maximum security. We just had to observe him and act on faith [that he would not become violent], because he was mute. But we did it, and he is like a new person. He was sad and grateful when the cuffs came off . . . He seems less afraid he's in a death camp now." Even after studying the huge stack of records that arrived with him, the staff are baffled by his case. "This sort of situation shouldn't be happening," one says angrily. "This demonstrates our system's clumsiness."[16]

The task of these workers is well symbolized by the circle they form as they listen to Kramer: to encircle him with a rough approximation of psychiatric and social service. They are charged with easing his symptoms of paranoia, depression, and delusion, while recognizing that, as he says, these are related in "kind of a circle" to the treatment—or lack thereof—that he has already received. They also try, though the extent to which this is their charge is unclear, to protect him from the prison itself. We can see that the situation is tenuous. Kramer may strike out in fear and confusion, bringing down again the full weight of custody. They have no control over how he came to them and little more over where he will go when he leaves. And conditions are not conducive to their professional and personal inclination toward listening and care taking. As they take in what has happened to Kramer, the visiting psychiatrist offers sympathy for them, too. The resident psychiatrist may suspect that he won't be fired for slipping nail clippers into his pocket, but his remark points to his position as an outsider who is not fully aligned with custodial concerns. These prison mental health workers are not focused on the issue of whether Kramer "intends" his behavior. Instead, they offer a dilution of punishment that takes into account aspects of the prisoner other than his will, allowing Kramer to find temporary refuge from the relentless insistence that he be able to account for himself.[17]

Prisoners describe the malign conjunction of prison and madness as the experience of "being locked in a small space with intractable mental discomfort." Hans Toch quotes a man he interviewed describing how, in the confines of his isolation cell, his mental state became increasingly intolerable.

Figure 17. "Prison Torture" by Todd (Hyung-Rae) Tarselli. Courtesy of artist.

> I laid down on the mattress on the floor again, and I'd get all these bad feelings again . . . So I really got a bugged feeling in here. I started stomping around the room. This is on the third day. I built into this thing . . . and I said to myself, "I'm going to kill myself." I had started walking around the cell, you know? And then I had started going wall to wall banging myself, you know, my body into the walls . . . I was mad, you know? But I wanted out.[18]

A psychiatrist who proposes alternative approaches to mental illness suggests that we think of these conditions less as discrete entities and more as mind-states. What Edward Podvoll calls "wild mind" seems to begin with difficulties in changing the direction of thoughts.[19] In isolation or semi-isolation, there is nothing to nudge the mind outside of its self-preoccupation and discomfort; the ambiguity in the remark quoted above about being "mad" makes the point that for the prisoner anger and madness have merged and become a relentless pressure (Figure 17). One inmate described the feeling of speeding thoughts turning into paranoia:

> Thoughts just start racing through my head . . . I can't stop them. It's like a movie in fast-forward . . . I wasn't like that when I came in here [to the

control unit]. I mean, the paranoia is getting to the point where, you know, I actually see people [that aren't there].

One African American inmate, Stephen Tillich, had been in and out of control units for several years and described himself as mired in legal troubles, grievances against the corrections department, and multiple symptoms. He was in a control unit when he talked of his increasingly disturbed perception of his environment:

> I have a lot of fatigue and abnormal sleep patterns . . . The lighting [here] can be either poor or extremely light—the rays . . . just come in and hit you. I have hallucinations. I see things that is on the wall . . . that there is no explanation for. I know it might be a figment of my imagination, I don't know. Sometimes I see faces coming past my window when I am lying on my bed. Sometimes I see things on the walls . . . Sometimes I hear voices . . . My speech, my talk, my voice, it has all been changed, you know? This [prison] affects every aspect of my life . . . There is no hope for my future, no matter how hard I try to just be patient, be humble . . . There is nobody to talk to . . . and vent my frustration and as a result, sometimes I am violent. Pound on the walls. Yell and scream.[20]

The perceptual world of a control unit—and to some extent of any prison unit—includes flat, steady, artificial light, a built environment of harsh angles and flat planes, sudden noise and echoing voices that can't quite be made out, constant surveillance, and utter dependence on others for basic physical needs. This world is similar to that described by people experiencing certain extreme states of mind.[21] Paranoia about the cameras and being watched is common, as is the "peopling" of the isolating spaces with animals, people, and spirits (Figure 18). Other routine aspects of the physical environment—such as building maintenance or nighttime deliveries of medication—may also be disturbing. Tillich is in poor physical health, and the airlessness, smell, and mysterious activities of the unit create in him a sense of ominous strangeness whose meaning hovers just out of reach.

> There is no fresh air coming in—it seems like there is some type of chemical in the air like a gas . . . You can smell it. I have a feeling in my chest . . . I don't know what it is, but they have these yellow, these bluish tanks . . . and I don't know whether they are putting chemicals in the air or not. I know

Figure 18. "Sleep: The Convict's Only Freedom" by Ronnie White. Courtesy of artist. Previously published as "Dreamtime" in *Cellblock Visions: Prison Art in America* by Phyllis Kornfeld (Princeton University Press, 1997).

that they got this experimental thing with some of the inmates that take medication and stuff. Actually, they don't have this. If you requested medication in the past, then that gives them the OK to experiment with you without your knowledge and consent . . . It makes me paranoid. It's like being in a tomb.

Being in prison also involves constant exposure to threatening or difficult interpersonal situations—extreme expressions of anger, the use of force, threats and bullying, and constant talking and shouting. An inmate with an active delusional system may come to believe that the ever-watchful cameras belong to the CIA, that black inmates are robots who run the computer implanted in his brain, or that laser fire is being beamed at him from the towers. Prisoners who are not experiencing these symptoms are locked into close proximity to those who are.[22] Some feel sorry for deteriorating neighbors, but sympathy is rare in an environment where the extreme behavior of others is inescapable and potentially contagious.

> Some people, they'll break. You get the bangers on the wall and people that are going crazy and rubbing feces all over their cells and, you know, nut stuff, that's what I think it is . . . There's no way you can get away from it.

> There's people in the hole—dings, mental cases—they freak out. They're screaming and yelling, and [some] people, if they see that weakness, boom, they jump on it, like an animal thing . . . The guy's looking for some sympathy, and he's not going to get it. The idiot, he's screaming and yelling. Next thing you know he's trying to kill himself.

Kramer and Tillich both show signs of physical deterioration and neglect. Tillich speaks at length of the difficulty of keeping up his hygiene and the negative effects of confinement on his skin and hair. Kramer's long nails and matted hair are vivid evidence of his entombment. Their fragile bodies are not just evidence of poor hygiene; they also represent a descent into a radical otherness. As with throwing, the connection between failure to maintain the body and abject social status sets up a downward spiral of which Tillich, at least, seems well aware. In screening we saw men who, even as they emerged from shackles and were tumbled together into prison, washed their hands, changed their clothes, and emerged looking, in the main, neat and self-possessed. Kramer and Tillich, unable to "maintain," have precipitated out of this process. Their long months in isolation suggest that when both the mind and body of the prisoner become disheveled—no longer giving evidence of the self-regulation that stands in for social order—it is increasingly difficult for him to be imagined in anything less than permanent quarantine.[23]

The staff who reach out to Kramer challenge his isolation and in doing so they make the dual gesture that creates the foundation for mental health units. On one hand, they draw him toward them, encircling him and offering attention, touch, and the understanding that his situation is a human one, a mistake, and not merely his just deserts as a criminal. On the other, they begin a process of sense making that will enfold him in a new—or at least a modified—identity. This reentry into language simultaneously distances as it draws him in. With it he becomes someone who "has" a condition, someone whose depression, bipolar disease, or schizophrenia places him in relation to the norm—however remote normal may seem in an environment where everyone is defined as deviant—and explains his behavior.[24]

Some prisoners suspect that the same gesture that offers the respite of treatment will also give them an identity they will not be able to shed.

> With [mental health] people anything I say in confidence is going to be used, and biased against me, you know. They're employed by [the department] . . . [If] I have to go to court, my file's gonna be dragged up and here it is, my psychological mental health evaluation.

> The inmates call it dummy dope. Makes you stupid. They [prison mental health workers] wish it on you . . . they want you to take it. Mellaril, Thorazine, shit like that. You're considered to be a weak individual if you start resorting to that. I'm not weak. I won't resort to that. That's giving them a one up.

These prisoners recognize the stickiness of the ding jacket and the danger that it might harm them with their peers or in their ongoing struggle with the criminal justice system. Yet it can be equally hazardous for some inmates to persist in their struggle with the custodial order. One man who had refused treatment described his predicament:

> I've had one suicide attempt and one threat. I had a razor blade to my wrist and I threatened to cut myself. I was punished for that. This is what kills me about the system. They punish you when you need help. "We're punishing you for attempting to take your own life." Doesn't that sound ridiculous to you?

For this man psychiatry threatens, from one side, to turn both his despair and his resistance into symptoms while, from the other, custody punishes him for expressing them in the first place.

Stephen Tillich describes a suicide attempt that he felt even at the time was largely a call for help.

> I wanted to harm myself. I wanted to kill myself: dying would be better than what I'm going through here. I'm not getting any help. The staff's not helping . . . There's nobody [mental health workers] to come down and talk to you. And [talking to them] will be the only way that I can go to mental

health where I could speak to the doctor, where they could be concerned about me. [I tried to kill myself because] I wanted to die and I wanted some help, basically. They know that I have serious problems and I have that hope. I want the treatment if it's available for me.

Tillich believes that the "paper" identifying his problems (probably from his initial screening) is somewhere in the system and would hold the key to his situation if only someone would read it. For him, transfer to a mental health unit and the opportunity to talk to people who would recognize him as mentally ill cannot happen fast enough.

JUST ONE LITTLE THING THEY ARE SAYING

Autonomy and rationality always stand in tension with opposing tendencies and longings.

SUZANNE R. KIRSCHNER, *The Religious and Romantic Origins of Psychoanalysis*, p. 108

Their expectations of us are parental and they hold us to that standard every day.

MENTAL HEALTH WORKER,
OF INMATES ON HIS UNIT

I have a really sofe side and a very dark side of myself, so I ony showe the dark side or the tuff side.

FRAGMENT OF A NOTE FROM A YOUNG PRISONER
TO HIS COUNSELOR

Prisoners in mental health facilities are counted, searched, and surveilled just as they are in any maximum security prison, and the infraction system prevails as it does elsewhere. Daily life for staff is organized around standard security and lockdown procedures. Yet visiting these units, one immediately senses that the texture of institutional space has undergone a subtle shift. The self-evidence of this difference to prison staff is suggested by the way the term "mental health"—often said as though it were one word, "mentalhealth"—is used to describe these units, the people who work in them, and the inmate-patients who live in them.

Mental health facilities are often located in older buildings or sections of prisons and softened with inmate-painted murals of trees and flowers.

Prisoners are examined in glass-walled offices by therapists and psychiatrists; diagnosis, medication regimen, and family history are added to the classification information already available. An inmate's level of restriction may be adjusted according to his behavior. On these units some men watch television in sparsely furnished day rooms, while others are locked down in single cells. Some cells have a thoroughly lived-in look, inhabited by inmates with chronic conditions that make them poor candidates for transfer to regular prison units. Other cells are almost bare, testimony to the rapid passage of those who either get better quickly or so frighten staff and other inmates that they are promptly transferred out.

On a visit to one unit I sat with the supervisor in an office full of charts and posters, a large table with half-empty mugs giving evidence of a recent staff meeting.[25] Only the glass wall facing out to an officer's booth and the off-limits lines painted on the floor indicated that we were in a prison. A large whiteboard on the wall listed the names of all the unit's inmates along with color-coded information about their condition and treatment. The supervisor ran down the list, giving brief portraits of her charges.

Richards—His Axis I [major mental illness] has cleared and now his behavior disorder has surfaced more.

Monroe—Every time we send him out [to the general prison population] he comes back more decompensated.[26] He's at his highest function at the moment. He wants to come out [of his cell] so he can smoke, but he's too dangerous.

Harman is doing well. You can't believe how decompensated he was. He has decided not to be a skinhead anymore. He was afraid to come out of his cell because he was worried about his [Nazi] tattoos.

Mulroney—He's in the infirmary on suicide watch. He was banging his head so bad he had to have medical treatment. Almost every relative of his is mentally ill.

Korn—He's developmentally disabled, has epilepsy, he's assaultive. He loses ground every time, with every seizure he takes longer to come back.

And so she goes, through the borderline[27] who cuts himself, the young man with fetal alcohol effects who assaults people and doesn't remember it, the paranoid who won't come out of his cell. Even in this brief listing, the complexity of both the unit's task and of its overlapping conceptual frameworks is apparent. These inmates are described as individuals with specific constellations of symptoms (fear, worry, aggression), diseases (epilepsy), genetic tendencies (every relative is mentally ill), diagnoses (variations on those in the *Diagnostic and Statistical Manual of Mental Disorders*), behaviors (suicide, head banging), and responses to the prison environment (deciding not to be a skinhead, deterioration in general population). The supervisor accepts this complexity—many of the inmates, she notes, have "multiple diagnoses"—by trying to fit her charges into a multitude of available conceptions of the abnormal and problematic.

For some inmates—such as Harman—medication, attention from staff, programmatic interventions, and protection from other inmates result in marked improvement in their condition. Some of these men carve out a long-term niche in "mental health" that includes positive relationships with staff and routine accommodation to prison rules. The behavior of many inmates on this unit, however, is extremely problematic. Some throw feces and urine or smear it on themselves. Others mutilate themselves, refuse to wash, masturbate publicly, or fly into sudden and overwhelming rages. Some are developmentally disabled and have great difficulty learning simple cause and effect connections. The sometimes indistinguishable effects of illness and side effects of medication cause some inmates to mutter, shake, shuffle, and grimace.[28] Many embody an otherness that can be read as primitive or vaguely nonhuman. One officer said of a disheveled inmate, "He never stood a chance, he's like someone from the back woods. You should see him eat." She added of her charges in general, "It's hard for me to think of them as *men*." On another unit, a bald inmate who bites people reminded a counselor of "a billiard ball with teeth."

Both mental health and custody workers talk of the mix of fascination and revulsion occasioned by daily contact with people who are in raw states of disregulation and loss of control. A young officer described how she had become fairly comfortable with her job, at the same time reminding me (and herself) that she tries to hold in mind the prisoners' humanity.

> The mentally ill are unpredictable and entertaining, there's never a dull moment. I had never seen a man masturbate; a man hanged himself in here.

I saw I had to harden myself. I've been through five deaths now. [But] they *are* human.

The process of hardening can result in less gentle assessments. One older mental health worker offered a grim view of the prospects of his charges:

This is such a cesspool. In this environment, we're not gonna get healing. You need a change in the environment to heal—a sanitarium, a garden . . . I'm not gonna ever heal them if they are truly mentally ill. Mental illness is degenerative. These guys are gonna fixate, they'll lock in these behaviors. At best you can maintain them. They [the behaviors] aren't "episodes." Even if [an inmate] is a malingerer, he'll *become* mentally ill. The jacket sticks, the meds will make him sick. [Even] if you were superhuman, innocent, and had a support group you would be scarred for life.

From this perspective it hardly matters what the diagnosis is or whether the inmate is or is not "truly" mentally ill. Being in prison itself is bound to cause harm through either neglect or attention, the degeneration of the inmates evoking a contrast with better days—national and institutional as well as personal—in the past.

In large groups, the behavior of deranged, deteriorated inmates may make no sense except to signify the other, the disturbed, the less than human. Insisting, as do the two people just quoted, that either the humanity or the abjection of the prisoners entitles them to some sort of exemption is difficult in contexts where attention must be distributed evenly. But on mental health units the encirclement of "decompensated" inmates offers the prospect that their opacity can be deciphered. For staff the key to this process is to turn "behavior"—actions, in all their ambiguity and density—into words, with their potential for connecting the inmate to a version of himself that others can live with. One young prisoner had been sent to a mental health unit after spending six months in a control unit. He described how, teased by other inmates and distraught at news of deaths in his family, he threatened and attempted to urinate on an officer. I sat in on this conversation at which his unit supervisor and several others were present:

INMATE: I told the sergeant I was going to kill the next gang member I saw. I wasn't serious but they thought so.

SUPERVISOR: You threaten to kill people fairly regularly.

INMATE: (*laughing*) Yeah I do, I scare people. But I wouldn't do it. On [the control unit] I didn't have no space, but here I can cry in the shower.

SUPERVISOR: (*to the group of listeners*) But even here he's got a mouth. Some of it can be stabilized with meds. His communication is good, so you're not aware he's got mental problems.

This man's "mouth" is as problematic on the mental health unit as it was in the control unit. But here his words are less likely to be taken as signifiers of intended actions; instead they are simultaneously signs of his willingness to open up, of his illness itself, and of the difficulty of detecting that he is ill. Overcoming that difficulty is the task of the experts gathered around him, including the supervisor who brings into the circle his own authoritative description of the inmate.

Listening to inmates' words blends ordinary forms of social reciprocity with a larger purpose.[29] One officer remarked of the mental health unit in which he worked,

Here you can be more of an equal to [the inmates], and then really talk. If you wait about forty minutes with an inmate who is just venting and shouting he'll come out of that anger level. You can find just one little thing they are saying that's the key.

Finding that "one little thing" implies that unearthing what is wrong will act as a kind of window onto the irrational behavior and deranged mental life of these prisoners. An officer, putting this in the pragmatic terms most often invoked on these units, said, "When they start acting tweaky you can ask if they skipped their meds. If they say, 'That stuff is making me shake,' it's a place to start." The most important effect of this approach is to soften the prison environment by allowing what the prisoner says to become a clue to the meaning of his behavior. A mental health worker explained:

The biggest issue with the mentally ill patient [in general population] is that he doesn't get listened to or talked to by the line staff. What's important is if someone's psychotic you don't disagree. You try to get more information, you say, tell me more about it. [It's not a matter of] good or bad. Most guys want to cooperate but *can't*.

This attitude toward prisoners' intentions can significantly affect the degree of patience with which they are treated. On one unit, I saw an inmate suddenly stop on his way to yard and turn back toward the checkpoint he had just passed, necessitating the reopening of several gates just for him. The officer who tolerated this said easily, "He's in and out of la la land, he's a challenge."

Thus what distinguishes mental health from other units—before any consideration of "treatment"—is the interpretation placed on inmates' "need for attention." In the prison more generally the demand for attention is regarded as weakness or manipulation, simply another "want" expressing the inmate's desire to wriggle out of the equable distribution of control. In mental health units, on the other hand, the assumption that the inmate truly *needs* rather than merely *wants* attention creates the possibility of giving it to him. This allows for the questioning and observation necessary to prescribe and adjust medication, which is the main treatment available. One psychiatrist explained of his use of medication, "You have to develop a relationship to allow for a trial of these things. You have to pay attention and be flexible to see if the available drugs can help."[30] Attention also takes the form of a variety of interventions or "programming" such as cognitive behavioral therapy, behavior modification, and alcohol and drug counseling. The common denominator of these efforts is that prisoners are listened to, treated as impaired but social beings, and enlisted in their own redirection. "Isolation," continued the psychiatrist, "is always a mistake. You end up with wild critters with guards outside."[31]

The inmate who becomes the object of attention on a mental health unit, whose needs are attended to even if roughly, undergoes a shift in what kind of self he is perceived to be. Neither fully rational nor an incomprehensible "wild critter," he is understood to be influenced by his history and environment, subject to irrational impulses and feelings, and vulnerable to harm from others. Some prisoners embrace the mental health jacket when they see that its terms create the possibility for this change in how they are treated and, for some, in how they feel. One said:

This place surprised me. I thought they was trying to overdose me but I was so hyper they were trying to get me back to earth. I feel so good [now], my normal self, not so hyper or depressed. I was in bad shape on the streets.

Stephen Tillich, who eventually found his way to a mental health unit, explained what he hoped for from it and how he had shifted his energies from attacks on the "system" to a focus on his own problems.

I'm stressed. I would like the stress removed as much as possible. All I want is to do my time. And if I can do it in the mental health here, sure, I'd go for that, yes, definitely . . . I'm here to do my time, to be determined by what I need. I need to get educated, I need parenting class. I need to concentrate on staying out of prison . . . I'm depressed, but I know that there's hope, being that I've just got seen [for] my medication. Yes, just by that fact of starting to get my treatment, I feel very optimistic. I [didn't have] anybody to talk to [before].[32]

Another prisoner, Chris Halloway, described himself almost entirely in diagnostic terms. In jail before coming to prison he had requested psychiatric help; he was refused despite his insistence that he was "in touch with reality" and knew he needed it.

My behavior was pretty radical. I had psychological disorders . . . I was wild. I was violent. I said, put me on tranquilizers . . . Please put me on a tranquilizer, I know what's going to happen. And I was right, I just lost it. I'm much better [now] because I'm under control and I'm taking medication. The medication is extremely helpful. [Now] I don't go into the serious states of depression like I used to and my manic behavior is improving . . . It's like chemical handcuffs. It's difficult [now] for me to really lose my temper and go into a rage. I'm trying to maintain control over myself so that I don't revert back to what I was. And what I was was a stark, raving mad lunatic.

As he narrated his history of going back and forth into control units "like a ping pong ball," he added, "I feel intimidated by the prison population, to tell you the honest to God truth. I'd rather stay here as long as possible so I have access to the psychologists and the psychiatrists on a daily basis. I feel comfortable here."

Halloway suggested the process of adaptation to the terms of mental health treatment when he went on to say, "I'm kind of a case in a way." He saw himself as a "case" in both senses of the word: as someone who had made himself a case (a problem) by his actions—"many infractions in a short time"—and as someone who had allowed himself to become, for his own benefit, a psychiatric case. Halloway's description of himself and his symptoms resonates with the history of the psychiatric case itself. As psychiatry developed—originally as a hospital-based discipline with connections to social work as well as medicine—behavior, self-report, and personal history were woven into written accounts that organized and made sense of the patient as a problem.[33] Interaction with the person was reworked into knowledge of him as a case. As Tillich observed wryly, "These people [mental health staff] know more about myself than I do." In this process the stigmatized prison inmate moves away from being just a ding—a category arrived at through the seemingly simple measure of separating the insane from the sane. His individual experience becomes known in terms of symptoms, norms, and diagnoses that make sense of loss of personal control. Thus Halloway, who has joined wholeheartedly in this framing of his difficulties, refers to an earlier diagnosis of hyperactivity to explain his current problems with self-regulation.

Parenting.   Once a case is made it can support the diverse tasks that make up the management of mentally ill prisoners. But even before that happens, mental health units allow for a parenting orientation that makes both the dilution of punishment and the application of psychological theories possible. By seeing the inmates as in some ways like children, mental health workers can extricate themselves slightly from custodial imperatives. "Some [inmates]," said one mental health worker, "are just like little kids. They're *needy.*" This orientation is not necessarily "warm and fuzzy," though it can be. Rather it assumes that even limited and sometimes harsh parenting is better than nothing. One custody supervisor on a mental health unit said,

> I usually keep a professional distance but there's this kid, he could set the world on fire. With this kid I feel like a mother, he's an extremely honest kid. But for some, you need to just say cut the shit, that was the only way their parents ever communicated with them.

This parenting response gives shape and meaning to the exemption provided by irrational behavior. It allows recognition of differences among inmates, a certain ironic distance from prison procedures, and validation of the emotional reactions of both workers and prisoners. One mental health worker said tearfully of a young inmate who had died in custody, "He was a good kid, he never disrespected me. [When I showed up] he always looked like he was thinking 'Oh God, here's Dad.' He would *cling* onto anyone, cling like you wouldn't believe."[34]

Parenting as a central trope opens up a space in which compassion and the gathering up of the truth about inmates share a common ground. An officer who described reaching out to a deteriorating inmate said, "The guy was slipping . . . I don't have all the fancy mental health words . . . but I might have helped him. He's stabilized now." A mental health worker expressed what he felt was the definition of his job, "[To inmates] I say, 'I will try to be here to do the best thing for you.' [My job is] to help the human dilemma, even with the lowest, mentally ill, murdering rapist inmate." Within this general orientation toward helping, two main approaches are available for understanding prisoners. One looks to their histories for explanation, an approach that is psychotherapeutically based though not necessarily dependent on any particular psychological theory. The other looks to behavior. These approaches coexist despite contradictions between them, and in combination they make up the main alternatives available to workers attempting to intervene in the lives of their charges.[35]

The Past in the Present.   Many mental health workers take a developmental perspective on inmates' problems. Broadly understood, this perspective assumes that human growth, especially the development of children, is under ideal conditions "a movement towards greater rationality . . . greater individuation . . . and freedom from external constraint and internal conflict." The optimistic and teleological lines of this trajectory are often tempered by the additional assumption that—given the tragic dimension of human life—it can never be complete.[36] One mental health worker tapped into this narrative when he said of an intervention that had made him feel successful: "I asked one of my murderers how he could not make his a wasted life. Now he's a logical, coherent individual."

Because this is the ordinary language of self-development outside the prison, it does not take any particular specialization to see human motivation in terms of an "underneath" or "behind" rooted in the individual's past. This layer can be understood both as a cause (of the inmate's current experience) and an effect (of the inmate's early, negative environment). A mental health worker expressed the prevailing view, and went on to describe an example:

> The victimization [inmates have experienced] is tremendous. A lot of mental illness is due to early trauma. [That inmate] was jumping out of cars and buildings at three, he cried all the time as a baby. Was his mom drunk? Not paying attention? He was in and out of boys' homes.

For mental health staff with access to inmates' records it becomes transparently obvious that in most cases some relationship exists between past experience and current behavior. Histories of abusive and substance-abusing parents, head injuries, fetal alcohol exposure, abandonment, and multiple foster home and juvenile detention placements are common.[37] A man convicted of child sexual molestation, for example, was abused by his stepfathers and had fourteen foster home placements, in some of which he was raped. He has difficulty, according to a dry note in his chart, "learning appropriate social conduct from experience." But despite the culturally supported assumption of a transparent relationship between past and present, no single technique connects traumatic experiences and current motivations. Instead, staff feel they must attend to what emerges from "underneath" into daily speech and behavior. A mental health worker described her approach to the prisoners on her caseload:

> You have to be here with them—every little piece [of information] is important. Not just from the inmate, you go to every possible source . . . Do you get to the bottom of it? You have moments when things come together, but you never get the complete answer.

Getting to the bottom—penetrating the opacity of behavior and words—can involve a frustrating search for information about the inmates, which may or may not be something they can (or will) provide.

We never [get to] verify their self-reporting they did on intake. We build a history on this faulty thing [what the inmate says]. We *really* need to know who they are.

It takes time to find out what someone wants. You have to keep trying to get at the truth; only he knows it.

But even when, through listening and detective work, mental health workers begin to find out "who they are" and what they want, the knowledge is, in many ways, double-edged. There is no time to do therapy, as they would like; one counselor said wistfully, "I'd love to do some dream work. One guy who murdered his girlfriend, she comes to him [in dreams] and asks him why. He wakes up shaking, ashen faced." And what is unraveled may well turn out to be a horror story. One mental health worker said of colleagues sifting through the evidence of trauma, "Some of the counselors can't deal with it; their denial is tremendous." Unearthing what is "underneath" may increase the vulnerability of both staff member and inmate in an environment full of dangers for those encouraged to tell the truth about themselves.

The hope of the developmental perspective lies in depth, in the possibility that the damage haunting the present can somehow redeem it. The individual becomes the appropriate object of an attention that promises self-knowledge as the way out. For prison workers trained or willing to think in this way, there is no time or safety for a full exploration, only an almost utopian belief that—sometimes, somewhere—such explorations do succeed.

Behaviorism.   Behavioral psychology assumes that the individual is primarily influenced by a current structure of rewards—or motivators—and disincentives. Like development, behaviorism has a parallel in popular assumptions about motivation that are present in much ordinary child rearing. It is a theory relatively easy for mental health and custodial workers to agree on, but in practice the kind of consistency the theory calls for is quite difficult to sustain.

Behaviorism rests on the idea that attention—either in the form of interpersonal contact or as concrete rewards—is a method in itself. Behavioral approaches assume that the individual is capable of responding to a managed environment by deliberately choosing in his own best interest. "Self-defeating" behaviors (ideally considered that by both inmate and staff) are

the target of what one behavioral specialist called "an appropriate individualized plan . . . to address the issue at a point where the individual's
wants intersect institutional *needs*."[38] Intersection with institutional needs
can be created by tying these wants—say, being allowed to go outside to
smoke—to "appropriate" behavior. This approach does not depend on
changing the inmate's thoughts, only on finding where his desire articulates with his surroundings.[39] An officer described this approach with a
disturbed inmate. "You ask yourself, does this [really] need to be infracted?
[Instead] you walk him through [what he should do] over and over. When
he does it, you reinforce it and pat him on the back."

One common form of behavior management is the "step-up" or level
system common in prisons. An inmate considered a behavior problem is
initially placed in lockdown and gradually given increasing freedom or rewards as his behavior improves. I talked to one young man on a mental
health unit who had been transferred from a control unit. He was neatly
dressed and articulate, and it was hard to imagine that not long before, as
he described it, he had been smearing feces on himself. "I'm kind of a behavior problem," he said. He described the level program as "good" because by "staying cool" he could eat his meals out of his cell and hold a
small maintenance job. But he also described conflicts of interpretation
with staff, whose decisions he regarded as arbitrary. "When it goes wrong
I get a fuck 'em attitude and I don't care." Like control unit prisoners who
throw, he considered the mechanical imposition of obedience a challenge
to be met with whatever defiance he could muster.

Systematic behavior modification is coherent with the behavioral orientation of prison management more generally. Despite tension between
the notion of authentic choice and the manipulation of behavior to produce choice, in practice these ideas fit together on the grounds that quite
disturbed or antisocial individuals can understand elementary connections
between actions and their consequences. One inmate who was smearing
feces around his cell, for example, was placed on a "plan" in which he was
expected to clean it up immediately and, if he refused, to "stand still and
wait"—while the cell went uncleaned—until he understood that this was
the consequence of his behavior. Some behaviorally oriented staff believe
that this kind of management is less punitive and more useful to a prisoner than more psychologically intrusive approaches. They hope that environmental pressure can bypass self examintation and—if specifically and

neutrally applied—shift him toward an almost automatic response that will, despite the initial struggle, ultimately serve his interests.[40]

Prisoners whose intense mental distress shows in their bodies and behavior seem to have lost the ability to regulate themselves. Both developmental and behavioral approaches require inquiry into the "one little thing" that will give staff access to the mechanism of self-regulation, either through unconscious motives or desires in the present. Clearly some workers no longer have much faith that the special forms of active attention they bring to these approaches will result in adaptation to the prison environment, let alone the world outside. Nevertheless, they must approach their charges as potential self-regulators who might—someday—reap the benefits of stress management, anger management, and other forms of regulatory therapy. The practices and theories that allow them to do this also serve—as we will see—as strategies for the negotiation of relations with the larger custodial environment.

HE'S GONE IN THE STROKE OF A PEN

A woman stands by a street in a medieval city. A cart
is going by at breakneck speed; underneath, tied to
its wheels and barely on its feet, a small dog struggles.
Overwhelmed with compassion, she stops the driver
and buys the dog. But as you see her cradle the dog
in her arms, the camera pans out to show more streets,
the whole city. And the city is full of speeding carts, and
under each is a struggling dog. You realize there's no point
in rescuing just one.

STORY TOLD BY A FORMER
PRISON MENTAL HEALTH WORKER

Doesn't he just break your heart? I'd take him home in a
heartbeat, that poor kid.

OFFICER, OF A PARTICULARLY YOUNG
AND VULNERABLE INMATE

The state is criminally insane.

MENTAL HEALTH COUNSELOR, ABOUT THE TREATMENT
OF THE MENTALLY ILL IN GENERAL

One of the prisoners whose name is displayed on the whiteboard has been brought into the supervisor's office for his monthly interview with her.

Convicted of assault, in a few weeks he will return to the group home from which he entered prison. He is very young and has a strangely flat expression. As he sits before her in cuffs she asks him gently, "Are you trying to behave?" "Yeah," he says. "What is 'behave'?" she asks. There is a long pause before he says, tentatively, "Taking my shower?" He warms to the conversation slowly, but finally he brings up the topic that is clearly on his mind: When, exactly, will he get the "gate money" given by the state upon his release from prison? After she explains, he turns his large dark eyes to her and says, in the plaintive tone of a child, "When I get out, will they take the cuffs off?"

Abandoned to the clumsiness of a criminal justice system largely unequipped to care for him, this developmentally disabled and unpredictably assaultive young man was not allowed out of his cell. The supervisor, fully aware of how impaired he is, talks to him as gently as she can about the simple rules he is expected to follow. But she can offer only a partial dilution of the overarching project of control, and she is unable to do anything about his impending departure—perhaps to an even less nurturing environment.

Mental health units such as this one are frail bulwarks in a sea of need. For the former mental health worker who spoke of rescuing the little dog, the whole enterprise had come to seem futile, the questionable shoring up of a system he called a concentration camp.[41] Most mental health workers spoke of their work as meaningful, but subject to a nagging sense of incompletion. Following the departure from their unit of an inmate in whom they had invested themselves for months, a psychologist and a nurse discussed their uneasiness about what would happen to him.

PSYCHOLOGIST: I keep wondering if we could have done more. There was [still] something wrong with his mental status. I'm afraid he will get killed [in general population].

NURSE: I wonder if we'll see him [back here] again, sicker.

PSYCHOLOGIST: We poured so much emotional energy into him. I can't imagine there are a lot of people like him.

NURSE: Sometimes he'd have a big smile and his eyes would light up, he'd be so happy to see me. He really did think I was trying to help him.

PSYCHOLOGIST: We had heard that he's always been bad, but he wasn't.

NURSE: We did all this, and then in a stroke of a pen he's gone. There's no closure.

The incessant churning of prisoners through an overcrowded system means that a parsimonious care is directed primarily to the most immediate and pressing needs. We have seen in this chapter that one element enabling this attention to the most disturbed prisoners is a softening and redirecting of the issue of choice. Autonomy becomes less an inherent aspect of the person and more a—sometimes distant—goal. Individuals can be regarded—at least for a moment—as more important than groups. Thus the special needs of prisoners like the one whose face lights up when he sees the nurse create options not available to men whose needs are less acceptable or less in evidence. But these options occur in a larger context of custodial control in which treatment is more than an enclosure of specialized attention. To understand this context, we need to turn to the dynamic relationship at the border where "mentalhealth" enters into conflict and alliance with custodial power.

Chapter 4 | CUSTODY AND TREATMENT AT THE DIVIDE

> [The] analysis of violence should be limited to demystify-
> ing the contradiction between custody and rehabilitation,
> so basic to asylums and prisons.
>
> FRANCO BASAGLIA, *Psychiatry Inside Out,* p. 213

One day after going out to lunch with a prison mental health worker, I returned with him to the main gate of his institution. A buzz of movement and intensity signaled that something had happened: the prison was locked down in the immediate aftermath of an escape attempt. No one, not even someone making a delivery, was allowed to leave the grounds.

My companion tried to walk me into the interior of the prison but was stopped at a gate by the booth officer, who barked, "What the hell do you think you're doing, escorting someone through here right now?" I turned back, sat on a bench, and tried to make myself as inconspicuous as possible. After a while I realized that I was watching two parallel worlds. The uniformed staff—officers and their commanders—moved briskly through the gates, tense, talking tersely on their radios, checking with each other about the status of the lockdown. At the same time other workers in the administrative part of the prison near my bench—mostly women wearing civilian clothes—carried paper to copy machines and spoke casually to one another. Delivery people, maintenance staff, and religious volunteers walked in, looked around, and found places to sit and wait it out. These people could have been in the front office of an insurance company.

Finally I saw someone I knew from the mental health unit and went with her to my original destination. Along the way we heard that an officer had been injured and taken to the hospital—third- and forth-hand accounts in anxious, hurried fragments: "Who was it?" "I heard there was a lot of blood," "I heard that he's gonna be all right." When I got to the unit, an officer told me that the "mental health folks" were having a meeting. I knocked at a locked door and was admitted to a windowless conference room where half a dozen people in civilian clothes had just heard a presentation on schizophrenia. The speaker was packing up a large bound volume of diagnostic information. As soon as he left, the mental health workers began a tense debate among themselves.

One man argued that "treatment people" needed to maintain a stance of emotional detachment. "People [that is, mental health workers, ourselves] need help so that their feelings [about the inmates] don't get involved.[1] They need to be professional and *clean*, instead of getting angry and getting their feelings into it. Otherwise it creates an atmosphere of manipulation. We need to make the rules perfectly clear." "Heil Hitler!" said a co-worker sitting across the table. He added defiantly, "A few individuals are slugs. If we couldn't make [negative, angry] comments away from inmates we'd go nuts." The first mental health worker returned to his theme undeterred. "I'd like to see a clean environment where this [discipline] happens [to the inmate], boom, boom." "We might as well create a perfect computer to deal with it," retorted the second man. "The inmates have got us figured out. They *expect* a capricious system. It's OK to be natural with them."

Unable to resolve this obviously much-visited issue, the group moved on to why people are in prison in the first place. "We need to start at the juvenile level," one said. Someone else countered, "We need to get rid of the war on drugs." "No," said the first worker, "they're [just] gonna find something else [illegal to do]. These are youths with fathers and brothers in prison." "The taxpayers *want* all of them here," added another. The man who had just argued for being natural with the inmates complained, "But we just help people adapt to prison. Do we want them to be better prisoners? Or are they *citizens*? Can we help them learn how to live with integrity?"

The first thing that struck me about this incident was the disconnection between the mental health workers, encapsulated with their visiting expert, and the custody workers outside who were engaged in the defining moment of their work. The closeted treatment workers seemed to symbolize the position of mental health as an outpost within the prison. Prison workers take this view themselves when they maintain that custody and treatment entail inherently contradictory structural positions. But although descriptions of custody as hard-nosed and treatment as warm and fuzzy are important to workers' self-definition, this conversation suggests immediate complications. It appears that this small group of mental health workers has subdivided along custody/treatment lines. One man takes a position for a controlling, "boom, boom" approach to inmates, while the other argues for being natural and attending to social/psychological causation. The discussion does not lend itself to simple description as the "mental health perspective." Similar arguments and cross-alignments occurring within custody suggest a corresponding complexity on the other side of what is often called the "divide." One officer, speaking in a different context of how less experienced officers took the "tough" side of the job too literally, took a stance opposite that of the more "custodial" mental health worker: "I banter with these guys [inmates] a lot . . . Out here [on the control unit] there's just about nothing that isn't discussed. If you don't have any interaction with them you're not doing your job."

In the previous chapter I described the treatment context in terms of encircling attention to inmates' vulnerabilities. But that gesture is always in relationship to the complicated borderland formed at the conjunction of treatment and its custodial other. While the most obvious questions at this border concern the kind of attention impaired prisoners should receive, other, corresponding questions are asked by prison workers about themselves: Are treatment workers in possession of knowledge that reveals the true capacities of prisoners? Should—or must—custody workers punish those whose awareness of what they are doing seems limited, but not entirely absent? What about the dangers of responding empathically in the prison context?

For both custody and treatment workers it is axiomatic that friction between them results from their differential possession of power and knowledge. Custodial staff state as a brute fact of their capacity to inflict punishment: "It's about power." Treatment workers take their stand on psychiatric categories and approaches—specialized forms of knowledge—that sometimes skirt and sometimes support, but are always enmeshed in, custodial power. Sharing historical roots and a fundamentally similar method for locating individuals in institutional space, custody and treatment are united in mutual dependence. But this very interdependence also positions custody and treatment workers as one another's most vigorous critics. In this chapter I explore the "shifting and tentative alliance" through which custody and treatment—power and knowledge—thrash out their relationship. Individual workers are necessarily caught up in the available terms, but they are not docile subjects of their job descriptions. Rather, as in the moment that followed the escape attempt, staff work out their relations to one another's projects on the shifting ground of their interpretation of prisoners' behavior. They are constrained on all sides by the structures and logic that hold custodial power in place. But their most fundamental argument—taking as its object the will of the prisoner—remains unsettled, an ongoing contradiction between custody and rehabilitation, in Basaglia's apt phrase, that is indeed basic to prisons.[2]

CLASSIFICATION

When John Howard, [the inventor of the penitentiary, visited prisons and jails in the 1770s] what offended him was the evidence of disorder and inattention, the failure to post rules, the indiscriminate mixing of inhabitants, and the unregulated boundary between the prison and the community.

RANDALL MCGOWAN, "The Well-Ordered Prison: England, 1780-1865," *Oxford History of the Prison,* p. 78

Classification and segregation of prisoners have been preached for over a hundred years. Officialdom has turned a deaf ear to both projects. We have arrived at last at a classification stage.

WARDEN LEWIS LAWES, *Twenty Thousand Years in Sing Sing,* 1932, p. 176

Bureaucratic professional administrators now attempt to control prisoners through increasingly formal and rational systems.

JAMES AUSTIN AND JOHN IRWIN, *It's about Time,* 2001, p. 99

The centrality of classification to prisons has been repeatedly stressed by reform-minded wardens and officials. At many points historically it was probably little more than a dream of order.[3] Better, more scientific or more practical classification systems have been—and still are—the major offering of many efforts to change prisons. As Irwin notes, they have an attractive

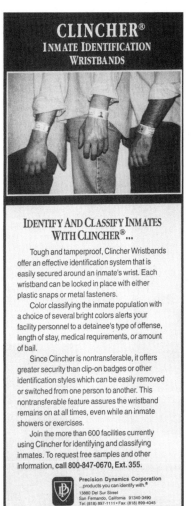

Figure 19. Correctional trade journal
advertisement: "Identify and Classify
Inmates."

formality and rationality; thus they can be misunderstood as descriptions
both of individuals, and of what takes place in the actual interaction of
individuals with "systems." But classification is in fact a set of practices,
one of the primary areas where the abstraction of management meets the
concrete facts of prisoners' lives. As an ad for wristbands suggests (Figure
19), the purpose is to fix a "nontransferable" identity to the inmate. Made
up of type of offense, length of sentence, and many other elements, this
identity should, as the ad promises, "remain on at all times," indissoluble

and "tamper-proof." Thus identified, the inmate can be "placed"—located and managed—within the security system of the prison.

During classification hearings the prisoner is brought before correctional counselors, unit managers, and mental health workers. Correctional counselors are responsible for determining where inmates are housed, calculating the effects of infractions, balancing available beds against inmate needs and wants, separating inmates from specific friends or enemies, and planning for release. They are also the inmates' link to the outside world, with the authority to arrange contacts with families and courts.[4] Sometimes the result of a hearing is curt dismissal at the hands of unsympathetic staff, with the prisoner, who must represent his own interests, having no real recourse. As one prisoner said, "[When you] bring me in for a five-minute interview . . . I know how you're looking at me . . . All you're doing is making a determination based on the paper in front of you."

But hearings can also allow for negotiation and offer a rare opportunity for self-advocacy.

At one hearing the hearing officer says to the prisoner: "We are recommending you remain in close [custody]. You also need to take substance abuse and anger management." The inmate counters, "But I already had medium custody for two years!" An officer points out to the counselor that the inmate was probably denied last time because of a major infraction that sent him to a control unit. Looking more carefully at his record, they note that he has had no infractions for over a year. They decide to recommend medium custody.

At a hearing in a different prison, an inmate describes in detail why he does not need to be kept away from one of his "separatees." When the hearing panel finally cuts him off with a promise to look into it, he breaks into a broad grin and says, "I've been working on this pitch for weeks!"

A prisoner in a control unit says, "Every time I go to a hearing they use my history. I'm in here for a violent crime and since I've been down, I've been caught with a shank, had seven assaults. . . . My last hearing, as soon as I came in they says, 'Well, what do you have to say for yourself?' And I said, 'Well, I'm really trying to get out of the hole.'"

Each of these individuals is placed according to his history—including his criminal and infraction history—in a way that reflects the logic and limitations of the larger system. There is not enough flexibility, for example, to send everyone to a prison near his family.[5] Nor, of course, do those in charge of placement decisions want to be considered responsible, later, for an assault. One counselor explained, "Inmates misperceive the role of the counselor. They think he's there for them, but he is looking out for the interests of the state. We have to document what we've done to provide services. *Something.*" The something is usually programming—the courses that are the current remnant of earlier rehabilitative exercises. In apparent recognition of this state sponsorship, prisoners use the word "program" even for unwanted or aversive placements (as in "I am doing this control unit program right now").

Classification hearings are routine for every inmate. Disciplinary hearings, on the other hand, occur in response to specific situations. A prisoner in trouble, most often for fighting, is brought before a disciplinary hearing in which he may be placed into segregation or a control unit—and his record amended to preserve the incident for future consideration. As with the second prisoner above, the specifics of such events may dog his placement for years or, in a few cases, decades.

One day in a control unit a series of disciplinary hearings follow on the arrival of several inmates admitted after a fight between rival groups at another institution. The first prisoner has a nasty black eye. He is escorted into the glass-walled room by two officers who, once he is seated and cuffed up, stand impassively on either side of him. The psychologist, unit manager, and classification counselor sit at the round table across from the prisoner. The unit manager introduces himself, his co-workers and me, and then asks the prisoner what happened. The man readily admits that he fought out of loyalty to his friends. The unit manager gives a short pep talk about the consequences of the path he is on: "You'll get a felony! You'll be in prison longer!" He asks rhetorically, including everyone in the room, "How many times have I given this lecture?" He questions the prisoner about whether he has any friends or enemies at another facility. When the answer is no, he agrees to send the inmate there, and the officers escort the man from the room. He will be returned to his cell to wait—for an unpredictable length of time—until the transport arrangements are actually made.

Classification separates and homogenizes inmates while at the same time attending to individual characteristics that allow them to be clumped into workable groups. Seen in terms of the management of large populations, it produces an orderly grid that can align the prisoners, in all their diversity, with the limited physical enclosures of the prison system.[6] But classification also opens up a space of unequal but not completely closed negotiation. For example, prisoners and staff in disciplinary hearings are adept at acknowledging the social situation behind an incident while evading the specifics. They speak, for instance, of how fighting is both necessary and punished.[7] Dan Garrity, a prisoner whose tattoos marked him as a member of a "security threat group" to prison intelligence officers, said of the fight for which he was segregated, "If you don't help your partner it is considered weak. You got to live on the main line . . . So I ain't no tender guy." An administrator acknowledged:

> You know it's a Catch 22 for inmates. You've got to fight at times. You've [either] got to have a huge reputation built on the fact that you fought before or you've got to fight now. And when they fight, of course, if we catch them, then they might end up [in the control unit]. And we tell them, "Don't do it again." But they've got to do it.

An African American convicted of a drug offense, Garrity went on to explain the complexity of his relationship to classification.

> [Staff] keep bringing up, You was affiliated with a gang, so you dangerous to the main line. [But other] people in here kill for cold-blooded murder! I am not holding it against them, but they are more dangerous than me . . . That is what I don't understand. Some [unit staff] is fair . . . They said, why would you get in this trouble [on main line]? And I said 'cause they was harassing me over there, treating me like bad, bad, and fabricating infractions on me . . . I write the superintendent, I tell him, look at my record . . . Back here [in the control unit] these [staff] people treat you with respect . . . They are changing me. I took the program. I am moving forward now. But if you keep on giving me this theory, telling me that I am dangerous, making me think that I am nobody . . .

Garrity vigorously takes up, argues, uses, and contests the issues and forces bearing down on him, protesting against the assumption that he is a gang member, comparing himself to "worse" inmates, describing how his own behavior has differed depending on context, making careful distinctions among correctional workers, and writing a letter of protest to the superintendent. He responds to the fact that classification is both a set of rules that governs the sorting of inmates *and* a space of negotiation in which a variety of assumptions about behavior and learning are in play. A custody worker noted that what happens to inmates depends on "the way that they carry themselves . . . their history, too. [We] err on the side of caution." Issues of self-defense, rules about gang affiliation, efforts to avoid damaging jackets, and punishment are all on the table. On the table also is psychiatry, for whatever its diagnostic categories may mean outside prison, inside they provide an additional way to make sense of how the prisoner "carries himself."

CLEAR AND DISCRETE DISORDERS

The current *DSM* process gives the image of precision and exactness. In fact, many have come to believe that we are dealing with clear and discrete disorders rather than arbitrary symptom clusters.

GARY TUCKER, "Putting *DSM*-IV in Perspective," p. 159

Prison is a botanical garden of the *DSM*.

MENTAL HEALTH WORKER

Schizophrenic, schizoid . . .

PRISONER, DESCRIBING HIMSELF

Control, rehabilitation, and psychiatry have been deeply enmeshed—in changing proportions—since the nineteenth century.[8] Sociologist John Irwin describes the effects of shifting political tides just since the 1950s when he was imprisoned at Soledad. At that time many prison departments took up an optimistic medical model of criminality and changed their names to "corrections." By the early 1960s "the treatment era was welcomed with general enthusiasm . . . Convicts . . . were led to believe that they would be able to raise their educational level . . . learn a trade . . . and receive help [to solve] their psychological problems." In the 1970s, however, prisoners began to suspect "a grand hypocrisy in which custodial concerns, administrative exigencies and punishment are all disguised as treatment."[9] The 1980s saw a renewed emphasis on incapacitation and punishment as the most rational responses to crime. Describing, in 1997, a control unit cell extraction, Irwin and James Austin note sadly, "Rehabilitation, the guiding principle of penology, has fallen into disrepute."[10]

The current reduction of treatment from a global project of corrections to its current identification with "mental health" is one consequence of this history.[11] Treatment in this narrower sense requires that mental health workers police entry to their limited beds, relying primarily on the standard psychiatric taxonomy. The *Diagnostic and Statistical Manual of Mental Disorders*, Fourth Edition (*DSM*-IV) can be found on the desks of psychiatrists and mental health workers everywhere. Viewed in light of the overwhelming numbers involved in contemporary incarceration, the key virtue of this bible of psychiatry is that it separates the mad from the bad in a seemingly definitive way. In their conference during the escape attempt, for example, the mental health workers were refining their knowledge of a category recognized by the *DSM* and the prison system as "serious mental illness." To diagnose schizophrenia, a mental health worker can use the decision tree in the manual to check whether certain sets of defining symptoms are present: "Schizophrenia . . . lasts for at least six months and includes . . . [two or more] of the following: delusions, hallucinations, disorganized speech."[12]

One day I followed an inmate, Eddie Mullen, as he was admitted into a mental health unit.[13] Recently sent to prison for a drunken attack on family members, he was a small, disheveled man with several tattoos and scars. The admitting mental health worker questioned him carefully about his crime and his symptoms. Mullen described himself as "hurting inside" and suffering from paranoia and anxiety. "Sometimes I hear things that aren't there, but I can't make them out . . . I black out from anxiety—anxiety attacks, that's what they're classified as. Last year I planned to blow my head off, but I lost my nerve and chicken-shitted out." He expressed remorse, crying and wondering if "I'm gonna be able to forgive myself for what I did."

The mental health worker listened attentively. He gently suggested that Mullen exercise in the yard, shower regularly, and begin programs to address his anger and substance abuse. The critical thing, he said, is "to get yourself under control." Mullen agreed, "That's why I came here, to get the fundamentals." After Mullen was taken out of handcuffs and escorted to his cell by an officer, the mental health worker turned to me:

My guess is personality disorder. The tattoos suggest an antisocial, maybe we will find a fair amount of anger. Also we need to rule out borderline, which is suggested by his hitting walls . . . There's a borderline feel to it. Sometimes he hears voices, but he's not schizophrenic. There's lots of emotion, maybe he has an anxiety disorder, but I'm guessing it's secondary. What does his remorse [really] mean?

This comment—and the whole conversation with Mullen—reflected the everyday use of the categories of the *DSM* and the assumptions that lie behind them. Mullen was interested in presenting himself as seriously mentally ill because he did not want to be sent to a more threatening environment.[14] He described himself as paranoid, anxious, delusional, and remorseful. The mental health worker expressed suspicions centered on different diagnostic categories: antisocial or borderline personality disorder. He looked for clues above and beyond what Mullen said about himself, such as his anger, tattoos, and scars. He did not trust Mullen's remorse.

The diagnostic definitions of the *DSM* do not refer to individual persons, their histories, or even their personalities in any specific sense; instead they provide a language for describing sets of features that should be clear to any trained observer.[15] Disorders are divided along axes, broad taxonomic categories that differentiate between diseases (or "states") and character (or "traits"). Axis I is for clinical syndromes and includes the major mental illnesses of schizophrenia, depression, and bipolar disorder. In the idiom common in psychiatry, this axis is for the "mad" whose symptoms are recognizable and often florid, but for whom, in general, some (almost always pharmacological) treatment exists. Axis II refers to personality disorders (and some developmental disorders). It encompasses the "anxious," "eccentric," and "erratic"—those whose traits emerge from and result in "conflict between the individual and society."[16]

Mullen's suggestions for diagnoses fall onto Axis I. A diagnosis of paranoid schizophrenia or anxiety disorder would allow his behavior to be viewed as symptomatic and would suggest medication. He would *have* a condition.[17] But if he is to be diagnosed, as the mental health worker suggests, on Axis II, the implication is "characterological." His antisocial behavior would be seen as a trait ingrained in his personality and not susceptible to change through medication or any kind of treatment. He would *be* "behavioral."

Psychiatric diagnosis is a primary mechanism through which mental health workers negotiate the acceptance or rejection of those referred to them. In their view the diagnosis of a major mental disorder indicates that the prisoner can be helped by what they have to offer, particularly medication. The control unit prisoner in the last chapter who said that mental health workers "wish [medication] on you" was close to the mark in one sense: the wish of treatment is that there should be a treatment. In the circular logic of biological psychiatry, when antipsychotics or antidepressants work it is because the prisoner is psychotic or depressed. Encirclement then makes sense because what the patient says about himself is taken to point either directly, or through various clues, to his condition. In clinical case notes, Axis I diagnoses include speculation about the effects of past trauma, consideration of delusions and paranoid ideas, and accounts of suicide attempts and self-care problems. One mental health worker said, "Our power is approaching the person with the assumption that you *can* change him." In other words, what he has is a state.

How is the difference between state and trait determined? Diagnostic features—such as the coherence of Mullen's speech and whether he expresses remorse—enter strongly into the equation. But when the mental health worker said, "There's a borderline feel to it," he also treated his own emotional reaction as a clue to diagnosis. Describing the training of young psychiatrists, Luhrmann writes of the Axis I/II distinction: "It is the general idea of the personality disorder, with shades of awkwardness and annoyance, rather than a specific diagnostic category, that is invoked [with the phrase] Axis II flavor." For many psychiatrists outside prisons, "Personality disorder patients are the patients you don't like, don't trust, don't want . . . One of the reasons you dislike them is an inexpungable sense that they are morally at fault because they could choose to be different."[18] The issue inside prisons is not whether psychiatrists themselves "believe in" the Axis I/II distinction—many have a highly nuanced view of its uses and limitations—but how the seeming clarity of the taxonomic system is used by mental health and other prison staff who carry out the everyday work of classifying and interacting with prisoners.

The interview with Mullen suggests how the diagnostic taxonomy can come to matter in the prison context. The *DSM*'s shorthand method for separating "illness" from "behavior" is in the background of the conversation for the mental health worker, and even for Mullen, in the sense that he too uses the vocabulary of psychiatry. They are sparring over the discovery and definition of the "truth" about him, a truth in which each has something at stake. The mental health worker does not want to miss the diagnosis of antisocial personality disorder, which is the most common Axis II diagnosis in prison and largely synonymous with male criminality. He fears that if he does, Mullen will harm the more vulnerable inmates in his care or, perhaps, his staff. From Mullen's perspective, if he is diagnosed antisocial he loses his best chance to be treated as someone who is damaged rather than bad. If he were a plant, he would hold still as he is sorted for entry into the botanical garden of the *DSM* that, in the eyes of the mental health worker quoted at the beginning of this section, makes the prison a fascinating place. As a human speaker, however, Mullen himself attempts to participate in his placement in the diagnostic taxonomy. But his words, by the very fact that they may not be the truth about him, may tell the further truth that he is manipulating. In that case, also, he has a place: it is not in the enclosure of treatment but out on the main line where the antisocial character belongs.

HE TEETERS ON THE STUPID SIDE

Sometimes I get sick of them being so stupid. I yelled at
[an inmate] the other day, it just came out.

> OFFICER ON A MENTAL HEALTH UNIT

To be rational means not questioning irrational
conditions, but to make the best of them from the
viewpoint of one's private interests.

> THEODOR ADORNO, *The Stars down to Earth*, p. 43

You make your own nest. If you want to live in feathers
and down, it's nice. If you put in river rock, it's going to
be a little lumpy . . . And that goes for . . . whether you're
staff or inmate.

> OFFICER

Classification and the *DSM* are brought to bear in situations that require explicit decisions about placement. But what of the average prisoner who gets into trouble? A vernacular logic that deals with everyday misbehavior forms the background of the relationship between custody and treatment. It privileges custodial forms of expertise that do not require a decision about what the inmate *is* (his diagnosis) but rather focus on what he does.

To "get stupid" means to behave badly or irrationally but in a way that does not require consignment to a category. The "stupid" inmate is considered capable of rational choice, but not up to exercising this capacity. The notion is pervasive in prison, and does not mean what it does in everyday talk outside. I first realized this in a conversation with a teenager in a mental health unit. Sweet-faced, light hair curling in a nimbus around his head, he had been brutally attacked in a four-man general population cell. "Being in prison is rough at my age," he said, "a lot people in here prey on the young. [Some of the] guards try to get you mad and get you in trouble. There are a lot of people to stay away from. But in here it's pretty safe." He described how the inmates he left behind in general population were trying to get him to carry out a hit job on another inmate in his present unit. Some of them, he said, "have no morals." An officer on the unit came into the office where we were talking and heard this last comment. To me she said, "He teeters on the stupid side." The boy enthusiastically agreed. "I get stupid sometimes. What helps me is [this officer, who takes a friendly interest in him], the guards who yell at me, and my friends [in here]. People tell me when I'm out of line. There are so many ways to get in trouble."

In a context of multiple pressures and temptations, this conversation speaks to ordinary difficulties of self-determination and the possibility of immediate, local intervention. Later, after I had heard about getting stupid in other contexts, I asked an officer to clarify.

OFFICER: Getting stupid means that they basically did something that they would not have done [normally]. They were being escorted and turned on an officer for no reason, just got stupid and got thrown down for it.

LAR: So, when the officers say that he got stupid, they mean going off for no reason?

OFFICER: Going off for no reason . . . [An inmate] tries to go across the table after the hearings officer. Or, he is being escorted and tries turning on an officer, stuff like that.

LAR: So, it is not stupid in the sense of . . .

OFFICER: It is not stupid in the sense of being dumb. No, not at all.

LAR: It means doing something without . . .

OFFICER: Without real justification.

LAR: If somebody did something like that, and then later he said, "Well, I did it because so and so disrespected me," would it still be stupid?

OFFICER: Depending on what it was. If he did it because an officer did something to him, but it wasn't the same officer, it is still pretty much [stupid]. But, if he did it because that officer did something to him while he was escorting him, it varies. The officer will still consider it getting stupid. For the inmate, it has justification.

This is a thoroughly social concept—not a description of a prisoner alone in his cell, but an account of seemingly senseless or poorly thought-out social behavior.[19] The inmate fights something he cannot win and does not think of the consequences. Further, whether any particular act is stupid depends on whether justification can be found for it, and that justification may depend on the person doing the describing.

Getting stupid can be applied to oneself or others, and to inmates or staff. One prisoner, Sam Delano, said contemptuously of his former cellmate,

He killed a guy for some dope. Eleven dollars worth of poison. That was stupid. If the guy rips you off or disrespects you, sure, kick his head in. Teach him a lesson. Don't kill him, or don't get caught at least anyways, you know. If you get caught, then the law says you will be here. Boo hoo, you know.

An officer in a control unit described feeling some frustration with young officers who seemed to have little awareness of the consequences of their behavior with inmates.

For every action there's a consequence. When I get stupid at the big yard gate, shakin' inmates down, or I get stupid in the chow hall and I put the guy on front street, he has to defend his honor among his peers. I have no business as another staff member dragging you in with me when I dig that hole. Don't create a situation that doesn't need to be created.

To create a situation that doesn't need to be created is the essence of getting stupid. Delano is enthusiastic about the use of violence, but considers murder—or at least getting caught—to be stupid. The officer's admonition to his younger peer points to the context of respect and performance within which such unnecessary actions produce their consequences. A prisoner said, "I knew they were going to take my radio so I smashed it up and threatened [officers]. I just acted stupid for a while."

Some staff and inmates place stupid behavior in a larger social context of alienation and lack of opportunity. One staff member said of the young inmates on his unit:

> Ordinary life is unattainable to most of these kids. [When they get out of prison] they get off the bus and they're lost. They can't read the street signs, a relative or parent doesn't arrive. They think they have the penitentiary stink. They're treated just like any other welfare inmate. [It's] just like a kid with his nose up against the toy store.[20]

Wondering about larger contexts of constraint, I asked whether he thought this was about class. "Yeah," he said. "But it's almost invisible [to them and to us]. They're *used* to being shoved to the back of the line. The only way they got attention was being destructive." One prisoner, less than twenty years old, provided much the same analysis of his own loss of hope in the future:

> I am pretty rebellious and antisocial, pretty violent . . . I am not very susceptible to rules . . . I will probably be coming back to prison . . . I talk a good game [but] I am not doing good. I get out [of prison] soon but I ain't got nowhere to go . . . I don't got a lot going for me . . . I am a convict, and nobody will give me a job. It is terrible, but I am a drug addict, an alcoholic. I like doing what I want to do. And I really don't have very good self-control. I had a rough life, and that could be my excuse to be a drunk loser, a punk the rest of my life. I want to change but what is the full benefit of it? Squares that got a job, they are struggling, they are bored . . . Is that the way I want to be? I don't have anybody that loves me, so what's the point?

Speaking of young prisoners like this one, and in further response to my question, the staff member added,

> [It's about] pleasure and pain . . . These guys don't make the connection between consequences. The word stupid has been used against them all the time. They never had anything, everything could be taken away at any moment. [You and I] know cause and effect. We look forward to our grandchildren. They see about six months ahead.

Like Bentham in the late eighteenth century, this man sees the problem with what he regards as the criminal classes to be their inability to reason, not because they can't, but because their environment has never made it clear why they should. The "stupid" prisoner—as the young man who considers himself one is quick to point out—is capable in the abstract, but too young and too warped by his environment to manifest the capacities he has. It became clear in the context of a long conversation with this prisoner that he did see the effects of his actions: addiction, an irresistible desire for power over others, and lack of incentive to do anything else are leading him inexorably to another prison term. He considers himself—just as the prison worker considers those like him—irreparably damaged. Later in our conversation he described his difficulty sleeping and the dissociative experiences that haunt him in isolation.

> I see myself slipping into somewhere I don't want to go . . . It is like my mind is trying to go somewhere else. Something real bad happened to me [as a kid] and I used to try to do things else when it was happening, block it off and go to a different place. [That is happening in here too].

The developmental orientation of mental health workers who might pick up on this admission seemed remote to the context of this conversation, conducted in the visiting booth of a control unit. But a rough and ready form of intervention does sometimes interrupt the mix of toughness and fragility conveyed by this prisoner. The practice associated with getting stupid was touched on by the prisoner who talked of how the guards helped him by "yelling at him." Both officers and inmates believe that exhortation—a kind of no-nonsense coaching—can pull the stupid prisoner back from the brink.[21] Talking to prisoners about just where their actions will lead—as many prison workers explain they would with their own children—does not require some sort of special expertise. They need only be willing to step in and directly apply the assumptions about rational choice that are central to the infraction system. Sam Delano, who criticized his cellmate in the quote above, was eventually released from the control unit into a transition program in which he was expected to learn to live in general population. Within a week, according to a worker from the control unit who took an interest in his success, he "did bad." He altered his name tag so that he could get into the weight lifting room, thus earning an infraction for "forgery." This is a good example of the "stupid" act performed by a rational individual who ignores obvious consequences in order to attain a short-term objective. The control unit worker went to see him and "chewed him out real good." Delano "got the message and ever since then he's done well." Eventually he was recommended, with the support of this prison worker, for a less restrictive unit.

A control unit supervisor gave an example of this approach with an inmate whose intractably strange and self-destructive behavior—and the assumption by staff that it was volitional—was the reason he was being kept in a strip cell.

> We don't personalize it. We say, hey, here's your choice. I talked to him. I says, listen, let's work together. Do you think we want this? Do you think we want to have you in this demeaning [situation] with only a blanket? I mean, come on. Get real. We don't want this to happen to you. You need to cooperate with us and let's go forward. It's as simple as that.

A mental health worker described a similar conversation, what he called a "father-son talk" in which he told a disturbed, tearful inmate who was being moved back and forth between a mental health unit and a control unit: "This is stupid. This [behavior] isn't getting you anywhere, this has got to stop. You can get through [your long control unit sentence] if you can just keep your chin up."

These efforts on behalf of inmates who have "gotten stupid" are the custodial version of the parenting and encircling gestures of mental health. To be stupid is to be neither mad nor bad, but "teetering." Through exhortation, prison workers attempt to call forth the prisoner's underutilized reason before he receives a lowered classification or is transferred to a control or mental health unit. This locally informed, seat-of-the-pants effort to change behavior assumes that the prisoner's susceptibility to reason is so obvious a human quality that the intervention of experts is not required. And because it is human susceptibility, not character, that is implied by stupidity, prisoners also rely on its explanatory power. Recognizing and addressing stupid behavior is thus the backdrop—for both staff and inmates—to the more formal knowledge systems of classification and psychiatric diagnosis.

I said, You treat mental patients like this? I have a psychiatric disorder. Why am I being treated like a subhuman? You put me in restraints and it's not necessary.
You come in with pepper spray. This is not how you deal
with an individual who has psychological disorders. And
the psychiatrists and the psychologist said, "Well, our
hands are tied, you know. You violated the rules and
regulations of this facility and they dealt with you ac-
cordingly." And so, it was a war.

CHRIS HALLOWAY, ON HIS EXPERIENCE
IN A MENTAL HEALTH UNIT

A guy had been hiding in his cell in the control unit, refusing to cooperate with any treatment. He was perched
like a bird on his sink. Stark naked all the time, perched,
wouldn't talk or get his food. The psychologist said,
"This is behavior, he's not psychotic." I said, "We have
a responsibility. That's not normal, that *ain't* normal!"
The psychologist said, "You can't tell me what's normal.
If he has no prior diagnosis and he doesn't want help,
we can't test him." That means that he's only a mental
patient when he [already] has that diagnosis. It makes no
sense! I grabbed a mental health worker who had recently
started at the prison [and insisted he visit the inmate].
He said, there's something wrong with this guy. He took
him to the [treatment unit]. The guy deteriorated so
badly there, he wiped feces all over himself. He was
kicking the door and acting out . . . The mental health
worker tried to get him to stop. Finally he said, I will
help you. He got a towel and took the guy's hand—it was
covered with feces and there was a couple of day's worth
of smell. He took his hand, and he said, I will come with
you, we'll talk. He led him to the shower and talked to
him and got him cleaned up and in a clean cell . . . He
walked him through it one step at a time. The guy's
hurting, is what he said.

A CONTROL UNIT ADMINISTRATOR DESCRIBING HIS
ADMIRATION FOR A MENTAL HEALTH WORKER

On the cusp of mental health, these two prisoners are caught in a confusion of categories, intentions, and missions. Halloway is relying on diagnostic norms to make the case for his psychological condition. He has been

disciplined for what was undoubtedly described as his "behavior," and in the course of it realizes that staff adherence to custodial rules is stronger than the psychiatric discourse into which he wants to insert himself. He insists that his war against the system started because the system was at war with itself. The story of the second prisoner expresses the inscrutability of psychiatric classification. The psychologist is represented playing the card of his expertise—"Trust me, I have a degree," as one person sarcastically described it. He defined the normal and insisted that no matter how bizarre the behavior, it did not qualify as mental illness. The second mental health worker is described reaching beyond himself to contact and transcend the abject body of the prisoner. He reframed psychiatric categories as suffering and, like the psychiatrist who took Kramer's hands, made himself available to the prisoner at the most concrete and—to the administrator telling the story—human level.

I have so far drawn a picture of mental health units as enclosures where there is substantial agreement on treatment. While this is a necessary starting place, it does not do justice to situations like these, in which complex alignments and disagreements occur between custody and mental health workers over specific issues of interpretation. At one hearing I attended, custody, mental health, and administrative staff were deciding whether a prisoner's claim of mental illness entitled him to transfer out of general population. As they gathered around a table with the inmate's records, one person explained, "We don't know if he's a legitimate mental health guy. He *wants* to be mental health, and he's trying to convince [his unit supervisor] that he's crazy." A custody supervisor from the inmate's general population unit said, "He's acting like a true mental health guy, he holes up in his room and acts loopy when you talk to him. But he has grabbed staff through his cuffport, he's throwing, threatening. It's hard to tell if he's mentally ill or faking it. Sometimes he *says* he's making up false symptoms." Various speakers questioned the validity of past diagnoses and speculated that the prisoner wanted out of general population. A treatment unit supervisor said, "I think he's just a manipulator. Does he have mental health concerns or is it all tied in with his antisocial stuff?" They studied his file: he was not on medication and had symptoms such as hearing voices, paranoia, and—less convincing to the group—seeing "blue lights switched to red." The supervisor read out loud, "He does not have a thought disorder but is more characterological." Someone else said uncertainly, "Well, he sounds convincing. There's lots of mental information here, *and* he's a manipulative thug with an antisocial personality."

The prisoner, a short, serious man named Andrew Gomez, was called in and sat at one end of the table, nervously swinging one leg as he talked. He had spent four years in a control unit.

GOMEZ:	I need to see a psychiatrist. I see voices; at times they are introverted and sometimes they are out. I've been thinking it's telepathic, from the officers.
SUPERVISOR:	They said you're just faking.
GOMEZ:	They gave me just a little pill.
SUPERVISOR:	Are you afraid to go out in general population, is that the bottom line? Because I'm not buying this.
GOMEZ:	I thought I was being attacked psychically.
MENTAL HEALTH UNIT CUSTODY WORKER:	I don't buy what you are saying. You can't come to a mental health unit and play games [when] your problem is behavior . . .
SUPERVISOR:	You've got lots of staff assaults. It bothers me, especially when you're antisocial.
GOMEZ:	I done a lot of bad things. I got hit on the head and voices are getting in.
SUPERVISOR:	We won't put up with it. The first behavioral problem [you have] you're out, you're antisocial. There are mental health counselors over there and you are going to have to deal with them. You want out of general population.
GOMEZ :	(*letting out a sudden sigh*) I was *told* I was gonna get shanked over there.

The staff reluctantly agreed among themselves to send Gomez to mental health, but not before warning him that by seeking the "mental health jacket" he was creating a new set of problems for himself.

The most immediate issue here is placement: where does this inmate belong? The staff of the unit to which he wants to go express their primary concern: Is he violent? What about his staff assaults? Gomez is also, at the very least, trying to solve a placement problem of his own. The Axis I/II distinction is implied in the effort to sort out whether he is mentally ill or antisocial. Though one staff member suggests that he is likely both, they must settle on one side or the other. Thus the terms of a minimal psychiatry—antisocial personality and, as Gomez clearly knows, hearing voices, hallucinating—are the terms in which this decision must be framed. Contained within them is the same issue suggested in the conversation with Mullen: are the inmate's words "truly" reflecting "real" mental illness or are they a manipulation intended to perform a version of mental illness that will get him where he wants to go?[22]

Aligning on Common Ground.   The decision about Gomez shows custody and treatment staff aligning in their use of the psychiatric vocabulary, which here supports their desire to keep separate the functions of treatment and general population units. The group as a whole considers the available categories, trying to make sense of how they have been applied in the past and strategizing to get them to work in the present. With only two options, they make a placement decision that goes against their preference for the Axis II interpretation. Andrew Gomez gets what he wants, but only after the terms on which he is trying to get it, as well as his truthfulness, are subjected to their shared, and suspicious, gaze.

In mental health units, control units, and hearings, the practices of the security staff and the mental health staff are acutely visible to one another. The glass-walled offices of counselors are only one sign of a myriad of situations that create this transparency; thus, for instance, at Gomez's hearing a supervisor insists that the inmate "deal with mental health." In terms of how custody and treatment staff come to see their interactions, no one result flows inevitably from this. One possibility is that they move closer to one another, acknowledging their mutual dependence and intertwined, often similar, skills. On one mental health unit a treatment worker and an officer were at pains to make clear to me the complementarity of their roles. The mental health worker explained that he was not such an "inmate-lover" that advantage could be taken of him. "The inmate knows I'm gonna dump [punish or infract] him just as quick as an officer." The officer said, appreciatively, "He'll talk 'em down with me." Each saw the other as providing a kind of backup and capable of performing the role usually attributed to the other. The mental health worker added quickly,

"But I'll advocate for the inmate, write letters for him, go to store." These are things the officer cannot do, but she nodded in understanding. Then she turned to me and said, "Now listen to this guy, this is reality. Sometimes I get frustrated by the little communication between us and psychiatry [the psychiatrists who work on a contract basis for the prison]. But we don't have one mental health worker that walks down the tier [that is, responds] when an inmate cries. They know a game."[23]

Officers and mental health workers are brought together in part by these shared experiences of their "reality"—situations that place them on the inside of a world comprehensible only to them. A mental health worker said:

> In here you have close relationships with people who've done things so outcasted. A hard-line custody guy was joking with an inmate who killed twelve people. You get letters from child-molesters. That relationship can only be inside here—it's a bond.

On special units where custody and treatment staff have close daily contact with inmates, they may develop substantial agreement. A nurse described how all the staff in her unit became invested in a charismatic and difficult prisoner:

> [The officers] got along with him. They talked to him through his door for a long time. A few swing shift officers would talk and talk. His counselor also saw something good in him and wanted to help him. People were pulling for him.

Similar agreement can develop about the effects of medication, which are often the most visible and dramatic evidence of the value treatment can have to custody—and also the one least subject to interpretation in terms of manipulation.[24] Custody staff often advocate for a "trip to mental health for a tune-up." An officer said approvingly about one inmate, "For a while he was on meds that seemed to just make him human." Whatever medication does or does not do for a prisoner's experience of his mental life, it may help him fit into the situation of group living.

In these examples, what the mental health workers know—diagnosis, medication, ways of classifying inmates, interpersonal skills—is seen as supporting custodial control. One mental health worker remarked that this relationship is at its best when it is informal—when the mental health workers refrain from "reminding custody that 'we have the degrees,'" and when a "common language" allows everyone to say both "whacko" and "decompensated." In these moments of alliance, respite from difficult inmates—regardless of diagnosis—is accepted by mental health workers as a reason to admit them to mental health units and by custody workers as a reason for a stay in a control unit. One disadvantage to prisoners of this kind of harmony was noted by this mental health worker when he said that mutual understanding can develop—"none of it said"—that sends an inmate into a control unit regardless of his mental state. An advantage is that custodial workers who trust "mental health" may provide some space in which treatment workers can approach and offer help to a disturbed, violent prisoner.

Conflict at the Divide.   Cooperation between custody and treatment is commonplace, but fragile. Custodial staff complain that mental health workers do not appreciate that they are working in a prison. An officer on a mental health unit made these bitter reflections on the increasing number and influence of mental health workers during his tenure there:

> Mental health thinks we're just brainless blue shirts beating them up. Anybody that comes here to work should be on line as an officer before they step up into their high and mighty job. Custody works with the inmates constantly; everything they want comes from us. Mental health talks for an hour and writes for three hours. You're dealing with all one hundred of them. You can't pick one out but mental health can show some favoritism.
>   They talked one guy down, did their school stuff and made a deal with him.[25] It's like one parent saying no, the other yes. The inmates play us off against each other. If [mental health workers] cross the line of security that's been battered into our heads . . . they lower blue shirt opinion of ourselves, and we start putting up a wall against them. It's like getting beaten down one pebble at a time.

This passage well represents the variety of issues that custody workers have with their position. On the most basic level are some practical and safety matters on which they feel that mental health workers "cross the line of security." Granting exceptions to rules is a problem that reveals fundamental disagreement about what kind of person the exemption is being given to. Custody workers tell cautionary tales of mental health workers who are too eager to see inmates in their offices and—glass wall or not—end up being attacked and injured, or who grant some privilege only to find later that they have been lied to. The custodial point is that prisoners—no matter what their symptoms—are more willful and their intentions more malignant than mental health workers want to believe.[26]

In this conflict, treatment can become equivalent to "care," which is then conflated with the amelioration of deserved suffering. At its sharpest, the custodial critique suggests that criminals simply do not deserve the privileges that are the province of mental health workers to dispense. This is a comment by an administrator:

> There's a contradiction in rehabilitation. Our first mission [as custody] is to protect citizens and staff but mental health professionals want to cure everybody. Inmates have to *want* to rehabilitate. It makes more sense to dispose of [execute] mentally ill killers.

An officer in a control unit said bluntly, "I am not a treatment person. I really don't care about the inmates. You did the crime and I don't care if you suffer." Referring to the either/or quality of this argument, officers say of one another, "He's a black and white sort of guy." One explained to me, "I have a hard time with gray. I like black and white."[27]

In order to keep this perspective in place, the inmate has to be seen as rational, and knowledge of his rationality—which is a form of knowledge that custody workers feel they have—given priority over diagnosis. A custody supervisor gave his opinion of a conflict on his unit about an inmate who had repeatedly cut himself.

SUPERVISOR: He knows what he's doing. He's manipulating, he's playing us. Now mental health has a different view. But I think that within his limited scope, [he's still able to make choices]. If [we set things up] so that there is no choice [that is, so that there is no escape into mental health] then we can show alternatives and show that they have consequences. My experience with this guy is that he has been trained that good things happen to him when he acts as he does [he is sent to the infirmary, gets attention]. How do we change that? We make sure bad things happen and steer him toward the results we want. How? We

> stop letting good things happen and start making him suffer consequences.
>
> LAR: Do you see him as rational?
>
> SUPERVISOR: I've been around him for years and he's very rational. His *reaction* is irrational but *he's* a rational person.

If the inmate is rational "himself" or "in himself"—as many people believe is the case for a misbehaving child—then it is the responsibility of those in charge of discipline to make sure that he experiences consequences that will speak to this aspect of himself. When this prisoner later "got stupid" and spat at an officer who was escorting him, one officer went to him afterward. "Is this how you want to live your life? Don't your parents care [what happens to you]?" The prisoner's only reply was "Fuck you!" "He's just so angry," she said to me later. She speculated that he might have been abused, but at some point—as a teenager, at least—"he has to take responsibility for his actions." Some officers feel that psychiatric medication interferes with this potential for responsibility; one objected that if prisoners are medicated "you can't get into any of the causes of their behavior. I mean they can't think, they're drooling." In this view inmates need to experience the pain that will connect them to their capacity for reason.

Mental health workers describe frustration with this perspective. A counselor for the inmate who cut himself sees him as depressed and suicidal. He finds it difficult to see inmates infracted for behavior that he feels is not volitional and suggests a more complex approach to motive; "You can get into the inmate's head and avoid these things." Another explained,

> It's a dichotomy of mission. The counseling mission isn't well defined. When the officers are faced with an inmate who is brain damaged and unable to learn, they insist that he's just playing, just manipulating us. We'll say, he's *unable* to conceptualize. Officers talk the same way about children, that the "threat of punishment" will change behavior. They say, "They *know* what they're supposed to be doing." Yet we see borderlines, schizophrenics, fetal alcohol syndrome, all from broken homes.

Discouraged mental health workers complain about specific ways in which custodial routines and regulations interfere with their efforts to provide treatment. "I give them something for sleep, and then the nurse wakes them up at 4 A.M. for meds!" Others simply protest, "No one gives a shit about the inmates."

In these conversations the divide between treatment and custody marks a string of oppositions: a division of labor, a disagreement about volition and responsibility, friction between security and care. Prison workers cross back and forth as they argue with or strategically enter into both the custodial and psychiatric perspectives. Some individuals, like the "boom-boom" mental health worker who spoke at the beginning of this chapter, stand firmly on one position—his, of course, being the opposite of what one might expect. Others mix and match interpretations, making strategic use of the alternatives available and fitting them, as best they can, into the difficult situations at hand.

SIGMUND FREUD COULDN'T DO ANYTHING ABOUT IT

Custody people say he's got to be crazy, but we know he knows exactly what he's doing. He's an antisocial guy who demonstrates he can give out more crap than we can handle. Sigmund Freud couldn't do anything about it.

MENTAL HEALTH WORKER

They stopped my medications and then they said, there's nothing wrong with you, you're just a behavioral problem. That's what people use to abuse you—oh, he's just a behavioral problem, look at his record. It's easy for people to say that, because they can just justify everything.

CONTROL UNIT PRISONER

Classification and diagnosis work to connect the behavior of an inmate to a stable identity—to "clinch" him into place as mentally ill or not. This work is at its most problematic—and the seams of the system most apparent—when it comes to what is simply called "behavior." Two mental health workers told me—only half joking—that the "evolution of a behavioral diagnosis" goes like this: "1) he's schizophrenic—crazy, really ill, 2) he does that on purpose, 3) have you noticed that every time he wants x he does y? 4) he's manipulating us, 5) I really wonder if those guys knew what they were doing with that diagnosis—and finally, 6) this guy's behavioral." The point is that the inmate who appears to connect his "y" with the "x" that he wants can't be crazy because to be crazy is, by definition, to be wholly unconscious of such cause-and-effect relationships. We have seen this calculus of inclusion and exclusion threading through conversations in which prisoners are confronted with evidence of their intentionality and staff argue among themselves about whether, in any given case, a prisoner "knew what he was doing." Room for interpretation is greatest when a prisoner's behavior is clearly aberrant yet seemingly useful to him.

The rejection by mental health units of inmates diagnosed on Axis II—particularly those whose aberrant behavior, like throwing, is extreme—makes no sense to custody workers. "There's behavior beyond the scope of custody," said one custody worker. "If you crap on the floor and play with it—it's nuts! What does it *take* to classify it as a mental health problem?" Mental health workers counter that they should not be expected to do the work of custodial containment. One said wryly, "Maybe they'll find a drug for antisocial personality. You can't make somebody do something they don't want to."

Yet of course the project of the prison as a whole is to make people do what they do not want to do. Custody and treatment offer ways to frame this project that differ just enough to provide alternative interpretations of misbehavior, yet not enough to allow either side to escape the other's terms. A control unit administrator explained why prisoners, whether mentally ill nor not, end up in control units:

> Their behavior is a disruptive element in our system . . . so you have the punitive measures because of the behavior. Same thing with the mentally ill. Maybe they weren't thinking right . . . but you still have to punish the behavior. So we're in a real quandary [if prisoners are simply given treatment] . . . where's their consequences? It's not a real pretty picture.

This comment acknowledges irrational thinking but not in a way that affects what happens to the inmate, which is nevertheless framed in terms of punishment. A mental health worker takes up the same logic but resists it as she argues for the impairment of one of her charges:

> Maybe he knew what he was doing with that assault. But I don't see him as that calculating. One day he refused to cuff up, and I said, "I know you

don't want them [custody] to come and hurt you." He was sitting on the toilet wringing his hands. I don't think he could calculate like that.

In other words, can this prisoner "think right" enough to get himself out of trouble? Should he be punished whether he can or not?

Classification and diagnosis are brought to bear on these recurring questions, but they do not simply fit down over the prisoners like a grid. Instead they have to be thrashed out, as we have seen, in the practices through which custody and treatment not only control and manage prisoners but constitute themselves as reasonable. The prisoners who are the object of these practices experience effects ranging from irreparable harm to compassionate attention—effects, as we have seen in this chapter, that are not the simple product of one side or the other of the "divide." Paradoxically, in fact, prisoners sometimes gain some space for maneuver from the moments of fragility and indecision that accompany the process of negotiation.

In some cases, however, there is a further possibility. A mental health worker argued for it when speaking of a proposed transfer to his unit. "You're not going to do anything with [that inmate]. He's a *control unit* inmate! Lots of them have life sentences, they are institutionalized. Why pour resources into them?" We have seen in this chapter that in the case of the prisoner who is considered "stupid" or "behavioral" the question of intention has a little space in it, some room for argument. The next chapter turns to what happens when the elements of custody/treatment alliance coalesce around the long-term control unit prisoner.

PART THREE   QUESTIONS OF EXCLUSION

Chapter 5 | THE GAMES RUN DEEP

> In the control unit you're creating your own monster.
>
> PRISON WORKER AFTER MANY YEARS
> WORKING A CONTROL UNIT

> It kind of builds you into a monster, because it hardens
> your feelings.
>
> DEREK JANSON, ABOUT HIS YEARS
> OF CONTROL UNIT CONFINEMENT

> I was certainly put on that assembly line for a manufac-
> tured human monster.
>
> SAMMY ANDREWS, LONG-TERM CONTROL UNIT PRISONER

The first time I met Pete Owen, all I could see through the door of his control unit cell was his shaved head and pale young face, somewhat indistinct
in the murky winter light filtering through the frosted window. When I interviewed him later in a visiting booth, the rituals of escorting and cuffing
surrounded him, as they do all control unit prisoners, with an aura of danger. At that point he had lived in a control unit for over five years—the better part of his twenties—following his participation in a violent incident.
Some time later, through efforts of staff I will turn to in the next chapter,
he was released to a less restrictive unit. There prisoners moved and spoke
with one another freely in an open day room. Free of restraints, wearing a
T-shirt and jeans and carrying the key to the cell he shared with another
inmate, Owen came without escort to a cluttered counselor's office. Asked
to reflect on his experience of intensive confinement, he said, "For someone in one of those cells every day is extreme. It's like a polar environment—
you're living at a pole. You develop a reactive armor."

Sooner or later most control unit prisoners negotiate passage out of
the polar environment in which they have been contained. Some do so

quickly; others, like Owen, only after years of intensive confinement. But a few prisoners remain for many years with little likelihood of release.[1] These longer-term inmates are known by name to many prison workers who have never met them or even, in some cases, seen the inside of the facilities in which they are held. They may be known to other inmates, too, making for complex placement difficulties. Once someone like Owen is linked, in the minds both of staff and of other prisoners, with the symbols and routines of total control, other custody levels seem inadequate to contain the danger he represents.

Up to this point we have seen that the work of negotiation between treatment and custody involves the difference between symptoms (the states mental health staff feel they can affect) and bad (antisocial) behavior. The contested issue is whether any particular behavior—such as throwing—is within the inmate's control. But for some long-term control unit inmates, months and years without infractions—without "behavior"—do not result in less restrictive placement. Whether good or bad, chosen or not, the actions of these prisoners become unmoored from systemic reward; punishment, no longer a "consequence," becomes the status quo. Paradoxically, however, this status quo continues to be seen—in fact, is seen even more intensely—as a matter of choice in the larger, institutional sense. Long-term prisoners come to represent not only the past behavior that brought them into the control unit, but also the *character* behind that behavior. And their character is constituted as a perfect fit with—and perfect reason for—the environment in which they are held.

Thus long-term control unit prisoners are the limit-case of the cultural logic of the prison. Just as those eventually regarded as mentally ill precipitate out of a sorting process as irrational and unable to manage themselves, so those consigned to long-term control precipitate out of this same process as quintessential rational actors. Although in the prisons I describe here they are relatively few in number, they are important to an understanding of the compelling yet paradoxical "systemic compulsions" that make up the maximum security environment and its inhabitants.[2]

In chapter 6 I consider an effort to interrupt the process that keeps this kind of confinement going. Here, I turn first to several elements that maintain long-term confinement—that "defer, defer, defer" the difficult issue of less restrictive placement—despite the contradictions posed to the system's behavioral logic. My aim is to open some space in which to ask not who is the "worst" prisoner and what is his nature but rather, what aspects of this context cause a particular reading of his nature to make the most sense? Prisoners held indefinitely in control units are at the center of several intersecting influences: the socialization of prison workers to expect manipulation by inmates, the mechanical and intrusive forms of control that enter into prisoners' responses to confinement, psychiatric theories of pathological disconnection from the human, and historical assumptions about individual pathology and motive. We have seen that a surplus of power accumulates around the bodies of prisoners, particularly in control units. Paradoxically, however, the more tightly the prisoner's body is controlled, the more his production of language comes to seem autonomous, seductive, and threatening. In a mutually reinforcing cycle, reactive armor is characteristic not only of the prisoner but also of the staff and, of course, of the prison itself. In this process certain prisoners come to represent a shadow side of human nature that crystallizes danger and extends the logic of consequences into the finality of the warehouse prison.

MANIPULATION

Manipulation means to control . . . by artful, unfair or insidious means, especially to one's own advantage.

SGT. JAMES TOPHAM, "The Sting," p. 21

[That inmate] is a manipulator. He's bright, always trying to schmooze and talk to you. He's always trying to get your attention.

OFFICER, OF A CONTROL UNIT PRISONER

I am sure they are trying to make you see [this prison as] good . . . what they tell you [me, LAR] and what they do to us is two different things . . . what they say is supposed to be better than what we say [but] it is a whole bunch of hogwash.

PRISONER, OF STAFF

They don't trust me. I can't say I blame them.

CONTROL UNIT PRISONER, OF STAFF

One day a small group of treatment workers debated whether a certain control unit prisoner could ever be an appropriate transfer to their facility. One person who had treated him during a previous placement said carefully that the inmate had not "fooled" him: "I saw what was in front of me." He then went on to suggest, rather hesitantly, that he was sympathetic to the prisoner's plight. After so many years, he said, "The control unit's driving him crazy." This mental health worker was clearly aware that before he could indicate his willingness to imagine the prisoner's suffering, he had to defend his competence in an environment where manipulation and deceit are pervasive themes. To see what is in front of one is sometimes a very concrete matter in a prison, as literal as detecting the toothpaste seam between concrete blocks that signals an escape attempt. The mental health worker wanted to insist that he could carry out a parallel kind of seeing—seeing the inmate's true character—and still sustain the possibility of empathy. His colleagues soon pulled him back from this idea—which, as we will see, contradicts the logic of long-term placement—by insisting that the prisoner was "glib, charming, and dangerous." They reminded their colleague that the problem of long-term confinement for this type of prisoner was not theirs to solve.

Officers are taught about manipulation during their training in what is called "verbal tactics"—that is, methods for substituting words for the use of force.[3] A class on "inmate manipulation" included an exercise in which a student was paired with an experienced officer who played an inmate. The student picked a card that described an inmate "setting up an officer to get into his work crew" by telling him where to find a shank. Though no shank was found, "the officer feels good he was trusted." Student and "inmate" improvised an enactment of this scene under the watchful eye of a teacher.

STUDENT OFFICER: I'm gonna keep documenting this [the tip] and pass it on to my supervisor. It's good you told us.

"INMATE": You live local here?

OFFICER: I live in my office. I'm dedicated to my job.

INMATE: All the information [I gave you], keep it confidential, OK? . . . Could you get me a coffee?

OFFICER : Nah, I can't do that, it's against the rules. It wouldn't be fair to others.

INMATE: (*persisting, whiny*) Auwww, do me a favor. I did you one.

OFFICER: (*hesitating*) I'm busy. Now I'm gonna infract you if you don't leave.

The teacher interrupted at this point and criticized the new officer for allowing the inmate to edge toward him and attempt to bargain. "You need to maintain that distance. If you gave an order and he refused to leave, you are *required* to write a major infraction!" The teacher suggested that the student get more practice dealing with prisoners.

The inmate who shows signs of psychological disturbance may be approached, as we have seen, in terms of whether he knows what he is doing. In this exchange, on the other hand, the prisoner is believed to know all too well; the question is whether he means what he is saying. The issue of manipulation has been in the background of a number of situations I have described thus far. For example, the staff defense of Derek Janson's truthfulness—and his defense of himself—occur in a social world often framed as a game in which, as one officer said, "Any sign of weakness and you get eaten—you gotta be rigid, tough, and guarded." An advertisement for protective clothing (Figure 20) suggests that it is "tough on the inside" precisely because "what's behind the bars"—represented by dark-skinned hands—cannot be trusted.[4] The proposed remedy for the "daily threat" of "vicious attack" is a material form of reactive armor. "Knowing a game" is the social equivalent of this protective clothing, a valued form of expertise that buffers the correctional worker by allowing him to anticipate and not merely contain the threat represented by the inmates.[5]

The teacher of verbal tactics thus promotes an instrumental view of language and a focus on strategy. To reinforce the lesson, the class is given a trade journal piece entitled "The Sting: Anatomy of a Set-up." The author, a correctional sergeant, contrasts the premise of everyday social life, in which "we . . . give people the benefit of the doubt," with the verbal and bodily habits needed in the prison environment.[6] One of the teachers explained, "We teach [the students] that their safety is more important than inmates' distress and that the inmates may be *faking* it." An administrator elaborated the point:

> The inmates know the game. They know what to say . . . you have to be really guarded on that. You'd like to think that they're not animals, that these are human beings: (*imitating "innocence"*) "Oh, my gosh, [he] won't do that. And he even promised me." But that is not the reality . . . there's always the risk that the person is just playing the game.

Figure 20. Correctional trade journal advertisement: "When You Can't Trust What's behind the Bars."

For staff, the lesson here is that to guard prisoners is also to guard oneself. "You live local?" is a reminder that the officer must "stay clean" and vigilantly patrol the boundary around person, family, and home no matter how amiable, reasonable, or unhappy the inmate may seem.[7]

One custody supervisor described how, as a new officer in a medium custody general population unit, he learned not to be "natural" in his responses.

SUPERVISOR: I've been manipulated [more than once], I'm sure. The games run deep. I'll never forget one of the first times I got it. I was bringing a plate of chicken nuggets back to the kitchen and this inmate says, well, gee, you know, I'm hungry. I didn't get enough. And I held out my plate for him to take some because it was not a big deal for me.

LAR: Why not [give it]? It doesn't seem like that big of a deal.

SUPERVISOR: Of course, the lieutenant came out of his office [and] I got to sit right there and watch a video on inmate manipulation. Because it never struck me there was anything wrong with that.

What makes a game deep is not its content, which can be as trivial as chicken nuggets. It is the fact that a person's automatic social habits—normal good intentions or just politeness—can be enlisted against him by engaging his use of everyday language. "There is such a fine line," a prison worker explained, "between that pathos for someone and saying, 'Hey, I gotta be careful here.'"

In an environment already labyrinthine in its potential for conflict, this wary stance requires several reversals. The first is a reversal of the structure of power. Here it is the inmate who is powerful, and his power consists in getting what he wants. In both examples the prisoner is trying to gain something that is a matter of intense competition over access and that—through a circular logic—cannot be considered a need. As a consequence of this perspective, unless he is floridly psychotic he has the near impossible task of proving that he is not manipulating. Second, the contention in these examples is that "inmates use the traits of the potential victim that most would see as good." Empathy, kindness, and trust are virtues on the outside, but hazards here; the hard heart and closed face are signs that one has learned correctly how to be in prison. Finally, normal assumptions about docility are reversed: the most obedient prisoner may be the one most adept at hiding his true desires in order to "manipulate the will of another person [for] coercion." Here the link between behavior and the steering mechanisms of the prison breaks down, as a positive response to pressure for good behavior comes to be seen as nothing more than a waiting game.[8]

Many prison workers and inmates describe a play of faces or fronts that takes the game beyond the issue of managing these reversals. The story of the chicken nuggets presents the naïve officer as innocent of "face"—that is, at the beginning of the story he was still himself, still the person who took the job he was learning. The prisoner, on the other hand, is presented as calculating his own interest by selecting the new officer precisely for this—presumably very visible—innocence. The loss of innocence is, at the same time, the acquisition of the front. In an interview I presented in chapter 2, Tony Hollister explained how it was advantageous for a prisoner to show his willingness to fight. As our conversation continued on that theme, he asked me suddenly, "Do you want to see *it*?" When I nodded through the glass he transformed his face into a menacing grimace suggestive of barely contained rage. The moment left no trace except, on the tape, the startled sound I made as he returned to his previous demeanor. Prisoners are explicit that their lives have developed this strong performative dimension. "You're apt to become a different person to survive . . . You might get raped, you know? So you try not to be who you are in front of other people." The different person most prisoners describe is tougher, more masculine, and less accessible emotionally and physically than the weaker self that fears other prisoners. One prisoner sarcastically called his deliberate evocation of this charmed circle of autonomous masculinity "my so-called prison dignity and manhood." Said another, "You have to represent a strong, hard man."[9]

Prison dignity is partly an effect of the dynamics of threat and shame we saw in relation to throwing and violence, but here it is described more self-consciously as something "so-called" that one "represents." Daryl Sanders, who began a long career as an officer when he was in his early twenties, said that as a new recruit he was pushed by his superiors to exert pressure on prisoners—to become, as he put it, a "dog on a chain." Like the prisoner, he said, "You have to put the front up. Do you want to see it?" The next moment he made the same menacing face—a face quite unlike that of the man I knew. "[Prison work] eats at people," he said. "You can see it in the staff. Gratification becomes beating the shit out of somebody who gets stupid. [It's just] sic 'em and boom!" Daryl experienced the expectations on him and his compliance with them as a gradual wearing down of his sense of himself. But eventually, by entering into the same issues of choice and self-management that pervade the self-education materials provided to prisoners, he came to see these alternatives as under his control. " I thought," he told me, "why couldn't I make the opposite [a better self] happen?" The better self, in his view, still has precious little room for expression in the job he is required to do. After reading my description of Kramer's case conference in chapter 3, he said sadly, "This is the kind of thing you just have to look away from or it'll eat you up. You have to be someone you are not."

Daryl's experience of being a dog on a chain is just what the class on verbal tactics is designed to prevent. But these examples show how, once framed as a choice, the learned self—whether the negative "dog," the officer learning to control his body language, or the better self forged in conflict with superiors—can be understood as a kind of mask. Daryl described a moment when, for fun, he put on the face for an inmate he knew well, then smiled and said, "Pretty good, huh?" For a moment, he said, the inmate "thought he'd have to put his front up too!" Beyond the obvious agreement about what the guarded or tough face should look like, these comments and demonstrations suggest—insist, even—that the person under the mask is separate from it. But unsettling questions can develop in an environment that so vigorously requires face and, at the same time, is so attentive to the freedom to choose. What if the person behind the face, who is often described as softer, more real, or more flexible, is also—just another—performance? An officer explained why he did not think that changes in the prison environment could change a prisoner:

> A person is not a liar because he lies, but he lies because he's a liar. The point is, how do we remove the liar out of a person? We can *postpone* lying—we can do it pretty easily—but that does not change the individual.

Taken to its limits, this possibility destabilizes the very idea of a real or truthful self. Under the performance may be only another lie, the self an infinite nesting doll—or even worse, some vacuum the shape of which cannot be found at all. These riddles posed by the performative dimension of self can be merely disquieting for those who, like Daryl, become uncomfortable with the part they are asked to play, or—as here—they can support those who doubt whether a particular inmate can be trusted. But long-term control unit prisoners live on the inside of this issue. If everything they do or say points only to their character as dangerous individuals—if something artificial about their internal constitution is believed to require the mechanical environment in which they live—it becomes almost impossible for them to extricate themselves from the situation of total control.

THE MACHINERIES OF THE SYSTEM

How does the human subject come to inhabit a world
of institutions and social facts . . . that profoundly
matter . . . and how does such a rapport come to
be shattered?

> ERIC SANTNER, *My Own Private Germany*, p. 59

The [control unit] building is a monster that only works
when people do what they are told. It has to work like a
machine.

> CONTROL UNIT OFFICER

I just went through the machineries of the system.

> SAMMY ANDREWS

When Derek Janson described his anger at being digitally searched—a search that occurred after he had already spent some years in control units—he stressed not just that a personal attack had been perpetrated on his body, but that the system failed to use available alternatives.

> [They said] "well, we couldn't rely on the metal detector chair, and we [didn't have] any hand-held metal detectors in the unit at the time." [But] here's the videotape, and you see three hand-held metal detectors right there hanging on the wall in the chain room . . . So I get a letter from the company that makes the chair . . . saying this chair will detect a hacksaw blade . . . secreted anywhere on a person's body. [So] what's the point of them stripping me naked like that and violating me?

Janson believes that he could have been spared the intrusive, feminizing hand of the PA if only the available mechanical means—visible in retrospect—had been employed. He argues, here, from his position at the intersection of many forms of mechanical intervention. The machinelike building that he is accused of trying to outsmart, the electric shield that overwhelmed him, the video camera that recorded the use of force, the hand-held detectors, and the detector chair are all protagonists in this drama. Janson's protest expresses his deep entanglement in the several ways in which long-term control unit confinement presses in on the subjectivity of the prisoner. Most obviously, he is in an intimate relationship—the only "contact" relationship possible to him—with a building and a set of practices. These constitute—in the words of Sammy Andrews, who has also been held for almost ten years in control units—the "machineries of the system."

These machineries are the product of that same fusion of abstract order and material practice evident in food trays and stun belts. Their immediate meaning varies depending on context for, as we saw with the stun belt, they can simultaneously represent both submission and rescue. Here, even as he submits to the building (at least temporarily, for he insists that it is the job of a well-run prison to contain him), Janson wants the impersonal metal detectors to come between his body and his keepers. Both the officers who suspect him and the devices at their disposal are trained on ways to bypass what he says, concentrating on his body as the sign to be deciphered. What is for Janson a surplus—a power that has, unnecessarily, moved in too close—is for them the necessary response to the outlaw. And, entering himself into this cycle of enforcement, Janson projects his response to their behavior into the infinity of time that stretches out before him. "That's all I think about . . . now my only option is to hurt [them]. Twenty years from now, you know . . . I'll be looking for them." When staff on the unit where he is currently held emphasize his trustworthiness, what they mean is that *as* an outlaw he would "let you know" when he might be dangerous.

Machines and truth are intertwined in a different but related way for Sammy Andrews. Sometimes Andrews is able to "maintain" for several years without incident; at other times he receives infractions and further isolation time for threatening or attacking his keepers. He spoke intently through the glass:

> It doesn't make it right but what you've got here [in me] is what the system has created . . . It's too late now, but I don't want to be [like this]—I don't want to be what I've been created into. I do get mad. Sometimes they literally [have] me pulling my hair out . . . to prevent myself from going off but most of the time I want to fight those people that hurt me. And the only way I can fight them is to . . . leave 'em no choice but to come in on me . . . Sometimes it's unavoidable with the games that [these] people play.

Like several other control unit prisoners, Andrews mentioned that he thought a polygraph test might have helped him in various struggles with staff. "They are trained that all inmates are liars. And it *is* hard to believe the unbelievable [things that were done to me]. [But] it's important to me that people *believe* me." Andrews accuses staff of being manipulative:

> They make promises and then don't hold them . . . Instead of making themselves look like a liar they will poke, poke, poke and then I will buckle—and I'm not saying my behavior is justified but then it justifies [theirs] and—it's been that way for ten years . . . They know how to do things to people and get away with it and make it look like the inmate's being a typical inmate and make it all look real good on paper.[10]

These men are embedded in a structure of authority that extends itself into them, into what they are "created into." One aspect of this is bodily, as concrete and intrusive measures of extraction and detection set up a boundary struggle similar to that we saw for throwing. Here, however, that struggle is profoundly bound up with the mechanical routines, practices, and objects that mediate it. The control prison has inserted itself into the thinking of these men (one way of interpreting Figure 21), but not because their minds have been moved to docility. Rather, the preoccupation with control that makes up the texture of the system—its compulsions—becomes as well the compulsion of the prisoner.

Long-term inmates express a sense that they have been undone by these processes and that what they have been "created into" is a different form of being. Pete Owen, thinking back to the period of antagonism we saw earlier in his hearing notes, said that at first he experienced a "stupid hostility." But after a couple of years

> You get a real bizarre second wind, it gets to be a different thing that is *made*—not broken—by the control unit . . . A strong person with a strong will, it's gonna make them into something with a lot of violent potential. For months, years on end, you're in that little box—it comes down to no recognition of your being. And your human dignity becomes immense.

At this point, as he and others described it, the immense human dignity fostered by the insistence that "being"—not just bare need—be recognized congeals into a kind of hyperrationality, a sharpness of thought that precipitates out of this form of confinement. The increased dangerousness of

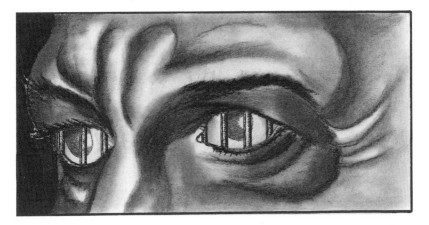

Figure 21. Untitled drawing by Todd (Hyung-Rae) Tarselli. Courtesy of artist.

those who develop this intensified strength of will is a frequent theme of staff as well as prisoners; both use the term "monster" to describe the prisoner who becomes increasingly hardened even as the building he lives in is likewise hardened to keep up with him.

The contraction in space and expansion in time fostered by long-term confinement make the desire for respect that we first visited in chapter 1 "immense." In a prolonged struggle over the coherence of the self—undermined, as we saw there, by this form of confinement—a sense of coherence comes to be located in the very structures that are doing the undermining. One effect of this circularity is, of course, that it becomes more and more problematic to release such a prisoner. Prison officials argue that they owe it to other prisoners and to their staff to take no chances on these men. The notion of risk-based detention—theoretically based on an empirical approach to behavior—unravels in a determination to take no chances at all. Thus unable to influence the future through any actions or words they might produce, long-term prisoners become "violent potential"—simply bodies to be stored. Both the power that holds them and the theories that make sense of using it collapse in on them, making it increasingly difficult to imagine any space of separation between the prisoners themselves, predictive approaches to their characters, and the intensive containment that affirms their dangerousness.

INDIVIDUALIZING DANGER

There are assholes among us.

PRISON PSYCHIATRIST

I'm anti-authority. They call it sociopathic, but I don't like
to put that label on myself. If someone's telling me what
to do, I question their every move, their every policy.

CONTROL UNIT PRISONER

He's a book you'll never get the cover off.

OFFICER OF INMATE

In the 1982 film *Blade Runner,* the cleverly made and dangerous androids
of a grim future world completely resemble humans except for one thing:
having no empathy, they are adept at killing in cold blood.[11] They are being tracked by hunters who use a machine to sort true from simulated humans by examining the emotional reactivity of their eyes. The tension in
the film comes from the fact that as soon as we begin to believe this neat
opposition between natural and mechanical creatures, it is undermined
by ambiguities in the characters of both the humans and replicants. We
begin to wonder whether the ruthless human tracker might actually be a
machine. And some of the replicants reveal empathic depths that raise
doubts about whether they are really nothing but artifacts. *Blade Runner*
plays with the assumption that social beings are not objects and suggests
that objects can perhaps be social beings after all.[12]

The possibility that a person can become an object to another is ever-
present in prison—in the memory of crimes committed, in the routines
of containment, and in the interpretations and risk-assessments that attempt to predict behavior. *Blade Runner* makes the point that there is no
way to know absolutely (until it's too late) whether someone is telling the
truth. For prisoners and staff of course, this fact has practical and sometimes urgent repercussions; just as the film expresses the wish for a technology that might do the job of sorting out the truth, so in prisons architecture, protective gear, and "instruments" buffer any reliance on
words. But this goes only so far; ultimately the possibility of deception
also requires explicit approaches to the uncertainty represented by hidden
motives behind language.

Clearly it is possible, as the officer suggested about lying, to postpone bad behavior—that is, to perform rather than internalize obedience. The long institutional memory that retains some inmates in control units is based on attempts to control for this possibility by relying on history and character rather than recent behavior. In these cases the uncoupling of behavior from character trumps the perspectives on consequences we saw in the last chapter. And although the current *DSM* descriptions of the Axis II disorders rely on behavioral language, they can also be invoked to support this uncoupling because they rest historically on earlier preoccupations with the architecture of character. Antisocial personality disorder is grounded in older diagnoses describing crime and danger as both moral and illness categories; popular diagnoses, psychological instruments, and criminal profiling all dip into the evocative imagery contained in this history.

In a 1999 article entitled "The Criminal Mind: A Challenge to Corrections," James Gondles, the executive director of the American Correctional Association, cites Epicurus's remark that "justice is a compact between men." "How can you have a compact," Gondles goes on to ask, "when one of the parties does not have the . . . ability to conform to the agreement?" Tracing the history of "psychopathology" by going back to a 1913 psychiatry textbook identifying types of "psychopaths," Gondles notes that this term was replaced by "sociopathy" in the 1930s and by "antisocial personality disorder" in the most recent editions of the *DSM*. Gondles reports that these terms all designate a similar set of traits: lack of remorse, dishonesty, manipulativeness, and antisocial behavior. By 1995, he remarks, the focus inside corrections had "shifted to what to test and what to look for in the incarcerated population."[13] An ad for a "Personalized Offender Profile" (Figure 22) offers an interesting glimpse into the strategy of those who market the proprietary psychological tests to which Gondles refers. The assessment and screening instrument is offered here as an "accurate," "fast," and "standardized" technology for "deciding" about an inmate. The advertisers clearly do not feel a need to specify the precise content of such decisions: psychological instruments augment diagnostic systems through specialized forms of knowledge about *who* the offender is—that is, his profile and therefore his placement, as an offender. While the "answer" may not be readily apparent to the prison administrator in need of help, this form of expertise promises to reveal what Gondles is talking about: the truth behind this man's inscrutable face.

Are the terms for antisocial behavior, as Gondles assumes, descriptive

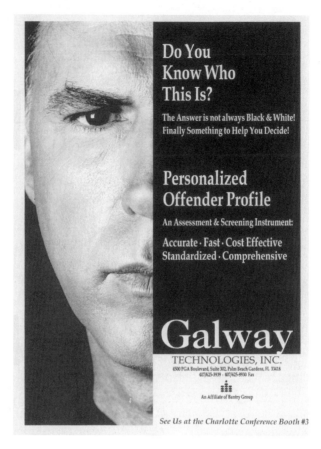

Figure 22. Correctional trade journal advertisement: "Do You Know Who This Is?"

of a natural taxon—a kind of human that can be found in any place or time? Compelling alignments between diagnostic categories and the people in them are certainly evident in psychiatric and penal institutions. Or are these terms descriptive instead of social relations that give some groups, such as clinicians, the power to impose their definitions on others? Scholarly work on many diagnostic categories makes clear that they have genealogies—roots in specific historical moments and cultural preoccupations—and serve social purposes. The philosopher Ian Hacking suggests that putting the issue in this way—as a dichotomy between the natural and the social—oversimplifies the complex ways in which individuals become what they are. He proposes that we ask instead about the dynamic influences that pass between a category and the people who come to be described by it. Through a mutually reinforcing circuit, the available options for how to be a person at a given historical moment interact with that moment's available practices for naming and interpreting human behavior. This "looping effect of human kinds" gives disorders their experiential reality and produces "true, natural kind[s] of [persons]."[14]

We have seen that—not surprisingly—"antisocial" circulates in prisons to create just such loops of interacting, naming, and reacting. Prisoners sometimes say that they or others are antisocial or, like Mullen, resist the description. "I *know* you think I'm just antisocial!" I heard one inmate shout angrily to a mental health worker. Prison workers, as we have seen, may tell a prisoner seeking treatment that he is "just antisocial" or, on the other hand, insist to each other or to outsiders that "they're not *all* antisocial." Thus the term itself—with its everyday entailments of voluntariness and immunity from treatment—becomes a player in situations of mutual shaping that encompass behavior, expectation, and diagnostic practice. Of course this is not to say that prisoners do not behave in harmful ways before they get to prison. But once they are there, these situations are the places where categories and the people in them are further "made up" out of "spheres of possibility" that make some ways of being a person plausible and others simply unavailable.[15]

Antisocial personality disorder and psychopathy, as Gondles points out, are sometimes treated as synonyms and are generally described in terms of a similar cluster of traits. But psychopathy has come to mark off the more defined and culturally resonant territory. In part this is the result of Robert Hare's work in forensic psychology, particularly his development of a quantifiable method for separating out from the mass of antisocial individuals those whose dangerousness is most thoroughly characterological. Hare's "Psychopathy Checklist" of interpersonal and social indicators is widely used in corrections and police work; it includes superficiality, grandiosity, lack of remorse, lack of empathy, impulsiveness, and childhood and adult antisocial behavior. In a popular book recommended to me by several prison mental health workers, Hare says: "Psychopaths are social predators who charm [and] manipulate . . . lacking in conscience and in feelings for others, they . . . violat[e] social norms and expectations."[16] One mental health worker emphasized the characterological basis of predation by telling the story of the scorpion that begs a ride from a turtle and promises not to bite him. When the scorpion does bite after all, he says to the outraged turtle, "I couldn't help it! It's my *nature*."[17]

For mental health workers, psychopathy—when framed as a discrete disorder signifying an essence or nature—offers the strongest possible terms for resisting exposure to those inmates they feel they cannot affect. For example, at a meeting of workers from different prisons an administrator complained that some inmates sent to treatment units were refused admission.

ADMINISTRATOR: (*exasperated*) They look crazy and act crazy, but when they're referred, they're *not* crazy!

MENTAL HEALTH WORKER: Some are psychopaths.

SECOND MENTAL HEALTH WORKER: (*firmly*) Let's call them that . . . Some inmates *have* whatever Hare describes.

What Hare describes is a task of detection that marks some inmates as beyond treatment and suitable only for the tightest control. In this conversation the mental health workers are pushing for an alignment with custody that will make certain prisoners immune to the usual border disputes.

The earliest precursors of what is today called antisocial personality emerged from the same time period as the first penitentiaries when, in the early nineteenth century, the infant discipline of psychiatry extended itself toward the law. In chapter 3 we saw that one aspect of the alliance of the medical and legal was the insertion of psychiatric expertise into the determination of accountability. This expertise in part consisted of eliciting from the criminal the deranged motive that led to his crime, so that, in Foucault's words, "beyond admission," there would be "self-examination [and the] revelation of what one is." At first the emphasis in what was called, later in the century, "moral insanity" was on insanity; even if the criminal had not exhibited signs of madness beforehand, the crime itself was taken as evidence of a deranged mind. By the latter part of the nineteenth century, however, emphasis had shifted to the "moral" and to "a form of justice . . . applied to what one is," that is, to one's "inner will." Once the early prisons had shown themselves unable to effect change on behavioral grounds alone, self-regulation was increasingly located in this interior will— as character—rather than in social habits.[18]

The idea that dangerous behavior could be located in "personality" took on an additional twist in the early industrial context of nineteenth-century America. In an intriguing historical analysis of the personality disorders, Charles Nuckolls explores how antisocial and borderline personality disorders came to be associated respectively with men and women. He argues that these "types" represent the extremes of gender identities that took their modern forms in the nineteenth century; antisocial personality disorder describes an "excessive" or exaggerated independence. It forms the counterpoint and opposite to borderline personality—or excessive dependency—in women. Nuckolls is an agnostic about the extent to which real people inhabit these extremes; in his view the diagnostic descriptions are cultural representations marking off the limits of "normal" gender differentiation.[19] In the nineteenth-century, new spheres of economic possibility based on salesmanship and limited to (white) men opened up new ways of being and, in the process, new diagnostic possibilities emerged. A connection between a pathological use of language and self-promotion was first noted in the 1830s, when James Cowles Prichard, a British physician who served as the commissioner of lunacy, presented a case that "was utterly unlike any other reported in the psychiatric literature up to that point, either in Europe or the United States." The patient "enjoyed the art of lying" and could "convince anyone of anything." Eventually, he made a fortune in real estate. Thus antisocial personality and its older cousin psychopathy developed to describe (mostly) men who are dangerous precisely because they have the elements of success as modern personalities. It is only when self-advertisement is writ too large that it is called a pathological condition.[20]

These diagnostic categories, then—the dangerous individual, moral insanity, psychopathy—are roughly the same age as the modern prison itself. Historically they have not always offered support for punitive individualism; in fact, the persistent bone of contention over the past two hundred years has been the degree to which such conditions are influenced by regimen and susceptible to insight. But regardless of whether they name exactly the same thing at the different moments of their emergence, these terms all incorporate two great modern inventions. One is the industrial machine: the possibility that others may be objects—or even that one may be, oneself, an object—circulates through the same loops that make it possible for the person to be seen as an element in industrial production.[21] The other is the invention of the individual as a repository of hidden motive—the notion that character is written into us, remains partially hidden from view, and has possibly monstrous dimensions. Seen in terms of what they make it possible to say about human nature, these diagnostic categories mark the site of a long-running engagement with the outer limits of modern individualism. When psychopathy is the term chosen—sometimes rhetorically, sometimes in tandem with other, more official diagnoses—it is used to indicate that at these limits we are, as one mental health worker put it, "clear off the end of the diagnostic scale." At that end of the scale the instrumental possibilities of language crystallize into the notion of a mostly masculine hyperrationality.[22] And in a reinforcing and contradictory image, a looping effect with a life of its own, the machine shares this stage with the monster and the animal. Together they constitute the strongest possible phrasing of individual choice as character.[23]

UTILITARIANS WITH WORDS

Our moral values are ornamental
Entombing us in our immorality . . .

FRAGMENT OF A POEM BY AN OFFICER

All of them . . . they're all strange. He sensed it without being able to finger it. As if a peculiar and malign abstractness pervaded their mental processes.

PHILIP DICK, *Do Androids Dream of Electric Sheep?* p. 156

Deviant . . . performances . . . do not exist in a space or time "before" or "outside" of the law they appear to transgress but are rather secretions of the law.

ERIC SANTNER, *My Own Private Germany,* p. 94

Do we need him to be sick to feed us?

MENTAL HEALTH WORKER, OF AN INMATE

An experienced mental health worker, describing how some individuals regard others only as objects, gave this example of a rare success.

I did an empathy test [with the prisoner]. And finally he said, "You know, I just don't get this. I don't know what you are talking about. But I don't want to be a criminal anymore." I tried to come up with some external controls and introduced him to Sister. That worked—he became a Catholic and memorized the rules. He couldn't feel them, but he could follow them.[24]

The point of this story is that the essence of this form of pathology is moral—an aberrant form of social connection. Theories of psychopathy locate the source of this aberration in a pathology of the will that produces antisocial individuals who, as the mental health worker went on to explain, have "no inner voice to guide them," and to whom "people mean nothing."[25] Her story is unusual, however, in its positive ending. She found a way to enlist the characterological flaw in this inmate, appealing, as another prison worker put it, to the "scheming side of the antisocial." The language of predation generally frames lack of empathy in more sinister and permanent terms. At a public lecture Hare played a video of a prisoner he described as his "poster boy for psychopathy," noting what he regarded as self-evident in the man's eyes: "The psychopathic stare is empty. He's staring at you like you are food."[26]

The question of how lack of conscience originates has intrigued generations of clinicians. Developmental perspectives on psychopathy describe children who fail to bond with their caretakers in early infancy and are impervious to punishment.[27] Bonding—described in one account as setting in motion a "magic cycle" that "gives birth to the soul"—is disrupted by abuse or, in some accounts, simply by the child himself.[28] Biological theories suggest that children who become antisocial have an unusual need for stimulation, a "difficult" temperament, or perhaps a brain physiology that causes abnormal language development. Images of a "bad seed" or "savage spawn" suggest both a genetic error and a natural type, like an animal species. These failures of normal genetic and developmental processes produce soulless, morally inert individuals for whom reciprocal human relationships are impossible. Writers on psychopathy express the same ambivalence as prison workers who describe the damaged childhoods of those who, they insist, nevertheless made choices. The deviant developmental process located in childhood is a reversal or stalling of the normal trajectory, often framed as though the child has fallen away from humanity in infancy and is unable to get back.[29]

In fictional and true-crime accounts, dangerous individuals thus created are vanquished once and for all—or at least until the sequel. Prison workers, lacking this option, express a sense of overproximity to individuals whose crimes haunt and sometimes threaten to contaminate them as well.[30] I talked one day with an officer about an inmate we both knew who was young, charming, and—to my delight—described prison life like a sociologist. Later she told me how unnerved she had been to learn that he had raped and murdered a child. "I know we're not supposed to ask this," she wailed, "but you just want to know why—*why?*" Toward the end of our conversation she mentioned that her mother disapproves of her job and often asks, "Why do you *do* that [work]? I think they should all be taken out and shot." She repeated her exasperated, clearly much visited response: "*We're* not the animals for keeping them!" Officers are "not supposed to ask" because they are enjoined to keep a cool distance from the disquieting ambiguity in this kind of situation. This officer is caught between her sympathy for the teenager, her sympathy for the victim—an emotion that both threatens and gives meaning to her work—and the suggestion from the outside world that in dealing with the inhuman one might somehow fall into it. She finds herself positioned between the belief that it is possible to rid the world of the "animals" who are "not us" and the absolute dailiness of her work, with its round of steering, tending, and small talk with perpetrators.[31]

In this environment, empathy is not only a lack in the prisoner but—in these several directions—a hazard for the prison worker. The criminal may come to seem too human, too understandable, and too much like oneself. As one mental health worker put it, "Most people want to believe that people who do horrible things are really different, but these people usually aren't different *enough* to make people comfortable." Prison workers vigorously warn one another against overresponsiveness. One night on a control unit I returned the smile of a prisoner who looked out of his cell as I went along on a tier check. "He's a psychopath," the officers told me. "He has ice in his veins, no feelings at all. That smile means nothing, he'd kill you in a minute." A mental health worker explained: "You have to keep people with rescue fantasies away [from psychopathic prisoners] . . . You need to pick staff who are not caught up in empathy." Later he elaborated, "It is tragic that empathy doesn't work . . . that the bedrock of meeting their needs is *withdrawal.*"[32]

This withdrawal of response entangles prison workers in the same double face of modernity that the prisoners themselves seem to carry. Most obviously, the attribution of pure instrumentality undermines not just the possibility of communication but the very channels through which communication occurs. I attended a group session at which a prisoner had made a fluent, angry case for something he wanted. "[Psychopaths] are opportunists," the facilitator explained later. "They are utilitarians with words." He went on to say of the prisoner's argument, "I tell myself it's not personal . . . It's all about words . . . [He's] not making a [real] connection but using highly charged words that grab us." The liar, in this view, cannot be removed out of the person because the prisoner's language emanates from a false—that is, wholly self-serving—self. Such a false self can, however, pass a polygraph test. One corollary to the instrumental use of words is presumed to be an absence of anxiety that allows the prisoner to calibrate his responses to those of the person administering the test. When I asked a prison official about this, he drew on the temperature imagery common in descriptions of prisoners considered psychopaths. "We call them the icemen," he said. "A stone-cold psychopath, of course he'll pass a lie detector test!"[33]

This comment reflects the view that some prisoners are problematic not because they are irrational but because their very rationality is the source of danger. "[Their] lying" said one mental health worker, explaining how cautious she was with certain prisoners, "it's logical. The logic hooks you into their stream of reasoning." Another explained, "With these instrumental guys, this is their life, this is how they do it." Hervey Cleckley, whose 1982 book on psychopathy, *The Mask of Sanity*, influenced Hare's interpretation, suggests that instrumentality rests on a "counterfeit speech" that is "mechanically" produced; thus "the human being becomes more reflex, more machinelike."[34] In this view language that is seamlessly self-regulated is a mask, a counterfeit character potentially as undetectable—and alien—as *Blade Runner*'s replicants. And of course, since it is undetectable, any seemingly normal account that a prisoner might give of himself can be doubted on these grounds. One prison worker said, "In this context [of prison] you make the assumption that they are lying. *No one* can tell normally."

Paradoxically, then the long-term, "dangerous" prisoner is considered suspiciously able to align himself with the mechanism of his confinement. An officer said of one control unit inmate that he had completely mastered the details of the system—staff days off, delivery times, and all the other minutiae of running the prison.

There is not a single beat that inmate misses. He is kind of scary . . . he's memorized every move we make. I would say that he could eventually come out of a control unit, but not until he is in his fifties.

The prisoner's attention to the order that structures his environment becomes evidence of an excessive rationality that makes it impossible to imagine his release.

Intensive containment, classes on manipulation, and psychological instruments are methods that use the logic of the system to counter the pathological logic of the prisoners. Prison workers also talk, more infrequently, about the value of their own intuitive responses in mirroring back to them the danger represented by the "animal" side of the prisoner. Many mental health workers, in particular, believe that their best defense is that gut feeling corresponding to a diagnosis that we saw in the mental health worker's interview with Mullen. One counselor said, "Psychopaths—you know it on a feeling level. [My intuition] has saved me many times." A mental health worker described her sense that with some prisoners she was "sitting with evil. It's like ice water is running through their veins. I had to have this fortress of goodness around me as I was talking to them." Hardening oneself and guarding against empathic responses ensure that the danger of illegitimate enforcement emanating from the outlaw—that abyss under the law we saw haunting the class on restraints—will not be forgotten in the face of a charming or unnerving criminal.[35]

In comments like these, staff and sometimes prisoners insist that a sense of the uncanny accompanies contact with certain individuals; similarly the literature I have been citing on psychopathic personality dwells, sometimes for pages and chapters, on the uncanny aura that confirms the diagnosis.[36] Often this aura is described in terms of the eerie imperviousness to human connection associated with objectification and hyperrationality—an imperviousness framed as profoundly other and ultimately evil.[37] Certainly a sense of uncanny otherness can be produced by the ritualized forms of containment that distance and isolate certain prisoners. But another source of the uncanny may lie in the historical looping effect we have been exploring. Gordon notes that feeling oneself to be in uncanny, haunted territory is usually understood to suggest contact with something completely other than oneself. She argues, however, that "the social is ultimately what the uncanny is about: being haunted in the *world of common reality*." The aura of danger emanating from certain prisoners may reflect on the conditions of their confinement and on whatever violence lies in their personal history. But it also extends into the future an indeterminate danger that gains energy from the contradictory history of individualism. Gordon, making the point that the uncanny emerges not only from the other but also from the self, describes how in 1910 Sabina Spielrein, a patient of Freud, looked in the mirror and saw a wolf. She wrote "uncannily grim, burning black eyes star[ed] out at me." This monster is timelessly poised between the outside and the inside, both "alien and terrifying" and "lurk[ing] there coldly in the depths"—that is, *her* depths—as a primitive internal "other." Sabina talks to her wolf, an option I will turn to in the next chapter, but the more common response to wolf-eyes is to insist, with the prison workers, that *we* are not the animals.[38]

The loops of historical and psychological influence that tighten around the long-term control unit prisoner reach out, despite this insistence, to snag his keepers in the very things that so disturb them about him: cold logic and lack of empathy. The hardening or reactive armor so carefully described for the prisoner is incorporated into the way prison workers come to see what they do as a hazardous negotiation of the "more and the less 'human,' the inhuman, [and the] humanly unthinkable."[39] At the boundary where this negotiation rests on suspicion—of the prisoners' words, of his humanity, and of his redeemability—the charge that develops suggests a kind of mirroring. No lie detector test, in the view of management, can absolve the prisoner of the assumption that danger lies behind his mask of accommodation to the regime that contains him.

THE FACE OF CONTROL

Some people really aren't human.

PRISON MENTAL HEALTH WORKER

He can't be transitioned to general population. Ever. He's
a psychopath for God's sake!

CONTROL UNIT ADMINISTRATOR

They've built an indestructible prison, not even thinking
you're gonna put human beings in it.

MENTAL HEALTH WORKER

Between me and the state I've lost most of my life.

LONG-TERM CONTROL UNIT PRISONER

A control unit administrator had this argument with a staff member about the long confinement of an inmate:

ADMINISTRATOR:	We have to be careful with guys like you [because that prisoner] is a true manipulator, a psychopath. He can have us [all] under his thumb.
STAFF MEMBER:	He has matured a lot.
ADMINISTRATOR:	He's a danger to the [prison] community. He has those black, solid black eyes. In those eyes you're always a victim. They look right through you. There are only a few people like that. He's cold-hearted, he'll kill somebody.
STAFF MEMBER:	[But] when is enough [punishment, or solitary confinement] enough? When a guy says, I'm ready, I've had enough?
LAR:	He's easy to talk to.
ADMINISTRATOR:	He's *too* easy to talk to. He always has in mind an ulterior motive for his behavior.

This conversation suggests the difficulty of interrupting the fit between this prisoner and the prison that contains him. A complex of mutually reinforcing influences—specific institutional memories, ideas about manipulation, psychological theories, historical resonances—positions him as incapable of reinclusion into general population. The tension hinted at here is indicative of relative degrees of responsibility. The staff member, who knows the prisoner well, argues for a loosening of the sense of inevitability created by the various loops holding him in place. But for the administrator, this prisoner's "maturation" and what he says about himself cannot be safely treated as real—his intentions can be read only from the ulterior motive, the instrumentality that lies behind his presence.

Prisoners like these have received the ultimate call to account for themselves, to hold still as icons of bad behavior. But no matter how many times they are counted and accounted for, they cannot account for themselves because their words are not allowed to "grab" those who contain them. If such a prisoner leaves a control unit, the aura of danger may gradually dispel as he blends into the population. But someone has to take the risk, and it is clear, here, how difficult it is for individual prison administrators and officials to put their signatures on such dangerous authorizations.

The past twenty-five years have seen growing enthusiasm for the profiling techniques and psychological instruments designed to predict antisocial behavior. These are the same years in which maximum security prisons have proliferated and in which the notion that they contain the "worst of the worst" has gained public acceptance.[40] In one sense a prisoner like the one who is the subject of the conversation above is profoundly hidden, and decisions made about him will not enter public discourse unless, as the administrator fears and has experienced before, a crime is later committed. But in another sense these are the most visible of all prisoners. They form the public face of control units, their images merging into others that circulate outside prisons as individual ideal types. Such faces, established in a process parallel to advertising, are "marketed as merely descriptive of what already exists."[41] It is not only, then, that face is cultivated and managed within prisons, but that the prison itself puts forth a face that supports its work. In tours and other contacts with the public, prison workers often describe the most notorious crimes of their charges to drive home the point that their work keeps such individuals off the streets.

But the contradictions that surface in the diagnostic territory we have been exploring emerge as well in the image of the "worst" prisoner. On one hand, for example, in a speech when he was governor of California, Ronald Reagan remarked that the criminal is "a stark staring face: the face of the human predator . . . nothing is . . . more dangerous."[42] On the other hand, as we have seen, a theme of deceptive normalcy pervades descriptions of dangerous criminals. California's attorney general described Kenneth Bianchi, the Hillside Strangler, as utterly ordinary: "This was not a monster but someone who would fade anonymously into all the other people . . . It could have been anybody."[43] The sense of danger here—however contradictory or multifaceted—is not simply emanating like a natural substance from the prisoner himself. This contradictory image of the criminal is at once animal predator and white, middle class, and "normal." In either direction it offers a protean template for the face of danger, opening onto the uncanny underside of the high-tech prison and reinforcing a discourse on crime in which industrial solutions come to seem only right and natural.

If lack of empathy and instrumental speech seem to suggest the specifics of how "dangerous individuals" should be treated, the notion that some people are a different "kind" has broader implications. Descriptions of "inhuman" prisoners tend to imply (without quite saying) that they form a sort of natural species. This suggestion of a species apart makes room for the invocation of seemingly natural rules and sanctions for human behavior—that is, for a bottom to the law that rests on a reiteration that *they*, not we, are the animals. But, regardless of whether individual prisoners are ultimately released from control units, this "they" has room for expansion: Are only the "true" psychopaths a species apart? Or perhaps most or all prisoners? The symbolism of otherness is readily deployed in both diagnostic and racial contexts, and it is perhaps a rather short slide from a criminal class—where at least the answer is not always, as the ad for psychological testing (Figure 22) says, "black and white"—to a criminal species. Mutually reinforcing influences connect the treatment of prisoners in general, the disproportionate racial politics of incarceration, and the potential of diagnostic labels to suggest that a psychiatrically sanctioned, unchangeable nature underlies and legitimates long-term confinement.[44] Permanent exclusion comes to seem a natural and inevitable extension of a character marked by too much inner will. Asks Derek Janson of his own indefinite containment: "I guess their feeling is, I'm a dangerous man . . . But [am I] so dangerous that they can't do nothing but warehouse me?"

Chapter 6 | STRUGGLING IT OUT

I hate stuff that takes years to do. But I will struggle it out.

JOHN LARSON, CONTROL UNIT ADMINISTRATOR

J.-A. MILLER: Given that there are relations of forces, and struggles, the question inevitably arises of who is doing the struggling, and against whom?

FOUCAULT: Certainly, and this is what is preoccupying me. I'm not too sure what the answer is.

"Confessions of the Flesh," A DISCUSSION
IN FOUCAULT, *Power/Knowledge*, p. 207

Seven men are meeting in a neat, carpeted classroom on the other side of the prison from the control unit they manage. John Larson, who administers the unit, his unit manager, Bill McKinley, two uniformed staff, the unit psychologist, and two correctional counselors have gathered to discuss the issue of change.

LARSON: [These control units are] happening everywhere in the country. But you don't hear about those places burning and the problems [they are having] all around the country. You don't get a vision of the inhumanity that comes out of this that we all are aware can occur. There are some things we can do differently to make it better, to make the experience of isolation better. Even though it's not *good*. Trust me, it's the worst thing we can do to people.

MCKINLEY: I [have been] thinking about what we are about. You know most of us didn't set out to be [control unit] people. My feelings were like most staff members, these are bad people and out of sight out of mind . . . [But now] I'm not sure it's reasonable to lock people up twenty-three hours a day . . . Is this the right thing to do? Being locked up in that little room twenty-three hours a day? We *manage* Janson, who's a dangerous individual, but can't we manage him in a less restrictive setting?

LARSON: Policy drives it.

MCKINLEY: But why were they first established? Was it because everything was so out of control—the Marion thing—or what? It's healthy for us to think about it.

CUSTODY SUPERVISOR: I can remember watching inmates deteriorate, being locked up with mental health issues that were not addressed. Deteriorate to where they were just animals, spreading feces everywhere. I think inmates must feel that there's hope. [Before] it was just darkness, hopeless . . . I have experienced that dehumanization.

CORRECTIONAL COUNSELOR: We learned we had to change. I was very defensive [about it]. I had to step back a little. It took somebody coming from the outside [Larson] to say, we have to change.

CUSTODY SUPERVISOR: Sometimes it takes an outsider to say, why are you doing it this way? You're resistive to being changed.

SECOND CUSTODY SUPERVISOR: [Before], the cells were pigeonholes to hold cargo. They had to spend a certain amount of time and then they could go [back to general population]. We didn't offer them anything.

FIRST CUSTODY SUPERVISOR: If we had that same mentality today the place would be rocking and rolling like it did before.

MCKINLEY: We could have gone the other way.

Four years before this conversation, the unit in which these men work was "rocking and rolling" with the kind of upheaval I have described in earlier chapters. When Larson became associate superintendent—after a career spent at other prisons in the state—he began an effort to transform the negative conditions that had taken hold at the prison. In the first stage of the project the unit was renovated to make it harder for prisoners to throw, fish, and make weapons. Renovations also included a general improvement in the appearance and cleanliness of the unit, including a vigorous effort to remove racist graffiti. Staff were confronted with new expectations and training; a few were asked to leave. At the time of this conversation, administrative staff walk the tiers once or twice a week talking to inmates and addressing problems; an education program enables prisoners to take classes together. Four years after the initial transfer of authority to a new administration, the unit has a dramatically lower incidence of violence and use of force. Inmates for whom indefinite confinement had seemed inevitable have now left the unit and are living successfully in general population.[1]

In this chapter I explore the issue of reform as it is "struggled out" by those attempting it. This attempt involves specific practices that challenge but do not overturn the economy of attention we have explored thus far. In an article the unit staff had read before their meeting, Hans Toch notes: "Each new supermax prison adopts rules and regulations from its precursors, who acquired them from prior supermaxes. No one along the line has been tempted to second-guess or revise received wisdom."[2] The changes I describe here are the result of such a second-guessing, in which the relationship between plans and their realization is opened to reflection and the seeming inevitability of practices questioned. In the process some of the common practices of confinement that unit staff took for granted, such as the avoidance of prisoners by administrative staff and the refusal by staff to apologize to inmates for mistakes, have been exposed as arbitrary.

It has become a truism in critical writing on the prison that "reform" is a recurring element in the perpetuation of institutions, both shoring up the existence of particular institutional structures and holding out an ever-receding goal of order. Reforms have historically formed a sort of moving threshold that invokes the past only to plan a better future; they carry forward, often in unconscious ways, the very past that is to be changed. For many critics—in a view that minimizes the agency of individuals and stresses the resilience of structure—reform works to do something other than what it seems by holding in place what it attempts to ameliorate.[3] In practical writing for institutionally based audiences, on the other hand, proposals for improvement—remarkably similar over decades and even centuries—continue to offer better classification systems, more efficient management, and more effective and professional approaches to the placement, movement, and control of inmate populations. The question in this literature is "what works?"—to manage better, to improve bad conditions, or to make a system more functional.

I consider here how a specific change is neither a plan or proposal nor a completed, historical event, but rather an ongoing, problematic, and fragile effort at the local level. At this level the attempt to change a control unit involves people in processes of questioning and resistance that cannot be fitted into either of these broad general interpretations. Instead of making an either/or case in which the terms—better policies on the one hand, a broad economic and political critique on the other—are framed in incompatible languages, I want to reframe the issue in terms of an ongoing narrative reinterpretation. The terms of this process are expressed by the supervisor who says that during the "before" of the unit, there was "darkness, hopelessness" and that "inmates must feel there is hope." He is speaking of the inmates, but also of the staff. How does hope itself become a protagonist in an environment as totalizing and dehumanizing as a supermax unit?

To ask the question in this way is not to resolve the issues raised by this form of confinement, though I believe that the practices described in this chapter can alter the experiences of at least some prisoners and staff. To ask the question in this way is also not to solve the contradictory effects of the ways in which efforts at solution tend to be framed. Instead I want to show how these questions are being "struggled out" by those who live and work within them. Struggling it out is not a framework or plan— though it involves planning—but a pragmatic and fractured work of local change.[4] Whether it will lead to larger changes, and whether it will last, remain to be seen. Those questions are subordinated, here, to the ways in which hope can—through an admittedly mysterious process—attach itself to a larger questioning of the arbitrariness of institutions.

CHANGE

Without a story of re-inclusion . . . there are now no
models of the corrected life and fewer linkages, however
tacit or implied, between keeper and kept upon which to
build common ground.

CHARLES BRIGHT, *The Powers That Punish,* p. 317

It's hard to believe how much the place has changed for the better.

The immediate history of the unit—sharply delineated by staff and inmates as its "before"—was a period of tension and violence following on years of neglect. Prisoners attacked officers, destroyed parts of the physical plant, and threw feces on staff; staff used force on a daily basis and were involved in incessant grievances.[5] Injuries and contamination were frequent. McKinley, the unit manager, describes how his work at that time was grounded in an implicit theme of masculine power:

> Seems like every day I would come to work and see my . . . co-workers dressed in battle gear, sweating, agitated, and wet from doing a cell extraction. This was normal, I didn't realize it bothered me. We were proud that we could handle these situations with these inmates . . . We thought we were in control . . . We couldn't back down and let *them* win, could we?

A prisoner describing that time reflects the focus of both staff and prisoners on the physical environment.

> [We were] protesting the conditions of our confinement. And the only way was to destroy property. The upper brass . . . started saying, "Why are you all destroying thousands of dollars of our property?" [We] said, "It's the conditions that we're living under. You treat us like we're less than people."

Both the preoccupation with "normal" control expressed in the first quote, and this inmate's comment on being "less than people" describe a narrowing of attention to a matter of mere handling. As Larson said of that time, "The only way [the inmates] could get attention was to destroy."

Despite the primarily visual forms of control that shaped routine unit management, staff could describe their workplace as "out of sight, out of mind." McKinley said, "You could go in your office, close the door, and as long as you did the paperwork and stayed out of the way, everyone was happy [with you]." Desks were always invisible under piles of grievances, infractions, and incident reports. Describing the time when he took over administration of the unit, Larson said, "I had inherited a monster. It had just continued that way forever—they could never catch up or get out of their offices. Incidents, grievances, and infractions continued to pile up. I saw I would be stuck in my office." The atmosphere was one of stagnation, a dead end in which bodies (as "cargo") and paper were handled day after day but almost no movement—save that fueled by aggression—actually occurred. What was at stake in changing the unit, then, was not only a reduction in the level of violence but a shift in emphasis to frame it not as a permanent or semi-permanent place of punishment, but as a passageway through which an inmate in trouble could reconstitute himself as a candidate for reentry into the general population.

Officers and inmates describe the current unit as almost unrecognizably different. The administration began the process of change by addressing problems with the physical environment, especially weaknesses in the design of cells. To support staff safety, explained an administrator, "you need to make that cell firm and hard and make the staff feel secure."[6] Officers were expected to respond to this attention by changing their tone and behavior. Inmates described the difference:

> You look at this unit [before]. The staff were suited up twelve hours a day in riot gear . . . I've been back here . . . for over a year now and I've not seen one incident where I've seen a staff member in [riot gear].

> If you got a yard coming, they give it to you. When it comes time for chow, they give you your food tray. They don't spit on your food tray. They don't dump your food tray on the floor of your cell when they open your cuffport. They don't write you bogus infraction reports.

One officer described how the change had affected him:

> We are not here to punish them anymore. Punishment is their being in this building. [If] you come here being a real hardnose and stuff you will force yourself out.

This reframing of the logic of the control unit surprised the inmates. One man described what happened when he arrived from another prison and was admitted onto the unit late in the day.

They made someone give me food, my dinner, and they said, "Here you go, sir." And "Thank you." They're real respectful . . . and that's a real big thing, someone that treats you like a human being. You're going to be cool.

To the surprise of staff, experiences like this led this prisoner and others like him to exert pressure for good behavior on their peers, thus contributing to the general improvement in the unit's atmosphere. One important difference from the past, for at least some staff, is a more open acknowledgment of the inmate's situation. McKinley says:

We say to inmates, this is a terrible place for you to live. We don't want you here. We are going to work with you to get out of here. No one has ever said this to them. I never thought about it before, it never mattered to me. I never personalized what it would be like in that little cell. Now I do take it personally. It's wrong. It's wrong for human beings to lock them in these little cells.

I have described throughout this account a logic of choice that makes placement in a control unit the mark of perverse forms of autonomy. To take the unit's effects personally is to unravel this assumption. The inmates' situation comes to be seen as embedded in more complex influences than those offered by the disciplinary system alone. This is not to say that inmates and staff are any less subject to the rules of the disciplinary system. But the efforts of unit staff foreground those elements of discipline that are susceptible to being taken personally—that is, that recognize the person who is the target of discipline—thereby bringing into focus the possibility for the "human" to become the ground of their work.

THE WAREHOUSE MISSION

Every attempt I ever made to distance myself from the subject, to criticize it, even to question its very right to exist, has only got me more involved in its inner life.
STANLEY COHEN, REFLECTING ON HIS CAREER AS
A CRITICAL CRIMINOLOGIST, "Social-Control Talk," p. 8

Discussions of reform are often framed in terms of the disparity between "promise and practice."[7] The promise is usually a plan or theory about criminality: Bentham's prison, for example, with its utilitarian theory of motivation, or the prisons of nineteenth-century America with their dream of civil order reflected in architectural projects. The promise is often described as foundering on the inertia of prison bureaucracy, the pressure of unanticipated social change, or architecture that cannot be shifted from its routine use. Accounts of these failures question how good intentions were compromised and what larger historical forces bore down on those who failed. Some take for granted that reform of institutions can be framed only in terms of the reform of individuals.[8] Others, however, insist that reform is incidental to the historical creation of the individual as its target.[9]

In the nineteenth century the idea that some sort of orderly process could turn (mostly lower-class) boys and men into "Christian gentlemen" was wildly popular. The reformatory movement and other prison reforms rested on the dream of a docile citizenry and an orderly institutional life in which disciplined work reflects and creates social order in general.[10] But within this seductive vision is an assumption so basic as to be almost invisible. The point of these reforms was that through a process of exclusion prisoners would ultimately be included—or reincluded—in civil life. Whether or not this actually happened, the rhetoric of reform revolved around the possibility. When abuses were brought to light, they were a scandal because inhumanity to prisoners suggested that they were no more than animals or slaves. Thus in reform "the criminal becomes simultaneously the 'other' (a byproduct of damage, disorder or difference) and yet potentially 'like us' (wanting the same things, thus reformable, but needing useful strategies for conformity, skills for survival . . .)."[11]

The problem under discussion by John Larson and his staff is not that reform is being mindlessly repeated in the current prison complex. It is that the purpose behind reform—the idea that drove prison regimes to experiment with treatment or the medical model or any of the methods that have come and gone over the years—has itself taken on the air of scandal that once attended the exposure of abuse. As we have seen, it becomes increasingly difficult for prisoners in control units to be seen as wanting what others want or as capable of absorbing any strategy.[12] Writing in 1983, Peter Scharf speaks of what was then a recent atmosphere in which the "rejection of any purpose for corrections" was palpable in prisons that had abandoned all "experiments in new forms of correctional treatment." The warehouse model that resulted from this change—and has become increasingly overt over the ensuing years—entailed a failure of imagination in which "virtually no form of redemption [is] possible."[13] The stagnation of this absolute form of exclusion is the backdrop to the staff's description of "pigeonholes for cargo" in which deteriorating inmates merely waited out their time.

We have seen that absolute exclusion creates a form of control in which the will of the individual prisoner becomes the only proper target of the law. Two complementary constraints then make up the dead end of the control unit: either the inmate must be exhorted toward completely "free" choice, or he must be defined as irrational enough to escape into the stigmatizing respite of the therapeutic. In the numerous regimes of reform since the nineteenth century, the project of individual reshaping could be framed in terms of "industrial discipline" or "therapeutic techniques"; either could "provide a plausible account of what ought to work."[14] Given today's image of the control prisoner, however, the question becomes less whether these efforts really do work than whether some alternative to warehousing can be imagined at all.

Although the language of choice can become wholly punitive, it also suggests possibilities for inclusion. One young officer expressed his frustration with what he felt was a general indifference to these possibilities:

OFFICER: Coming into prison bureaucracy and politics was difficult. I'm getting to the point where I'm frustrated . . . because I'm losing some of my optimism. It's set into reality [for me that] staff can make this a very negative environment. There's always this feeling that you don't have any input in anything, you don't have any power. [But] this is a *correctional* facility. Aren't we supposed to be correcting behavior? How much correcting do we do? I believe that we should be correcting behavior, not warehousing people. Because if these guys leave here and move into my neighborhood I want something productive out of them. Let's have them get a job and pay some taxes, you know.

LAR: So in your vision of correction what would it look like?

OFFICER: Well, I think we're on the right track, and I think every method's been tried. This job just repeats itself in a pattern.

The confusion of this last remark expresses something many prison workers imply: a feeling that some unfilled promise is mysteriously just out of reach. Correction seems to this officer something that ought to work but that is not, in fact, even being tried.

The men who are talking about change on their unit frame it as "challenging the warehouse mission" they feel has been given to them. The horizon of that mission is composed of those limit-cases that most clearly mark the warehouse: the mentally ill who go down in a tangle of prison rules they cannot follow, and the "bad" who are not to be believed. These limits are at once the limits of the human and the terms of a situation from which there is no exit. The questions of the unit's staff reflect a struggle to find some sort of counternarrative in which prisoners figure as, in their way of putting it, potential citizens and taxpayers. Thus they ask: Why does it have to be like this? What kind of humanness is possible here? Like earlier reformers, they have embarked on the double mission of reforming the prison by reforming the prisoners. Unlike many of them, they must start by insisting that the prisoners are capable of reform in the first place.

MCKINLEY: Is what we're doing the right thing? I know we're progressing but are we doing enough? In effect what we're doing is continuing that punishment thing. What's the reason? The reason is because that is what we were taught, that's what we did in the old days.

LARSON: Because policy prescribes . . .

MCKINLEY: But maybe that's wrong.

COUNSELOR: But you've got to take baby steps, because if you just totally change things people can't buy into it.

MCKINLEY: I'm just talking about right and wrong.

The problem of the unit, then, is how to rehabilitate rehabilitation in an environment of punitive individualism. The baby steps of changes that may be—but certainly are not guaranteed to be—acceptable to the system occur not as radical departures from the known world, but within the available horizon, in terms that everyone can recognize if not agree with. I describe here two specific changes—tier walks and education booths—that have become pragmatically and symbolically central to the unit's practice and to the self-definition of its staff and inmates.

Both of these practices are classically governmental: methods of management and control that also individualize. But they do so in way that has a texture best described as "effervescent."[15] No one should read this to mean that the environment of this prison is not oppressive. But even a slight loosening of the grip of "what we were taught" suggests questions about how those who wield disciplinary power might also "go off the designated path" in unexpected directions.[16] Going off the designated path—the path of the warehouse—involves the unit's staff in narratives and practices that both use and push against the available intersections of power and knowledge. These efforts do not produce closure but instead unsettle the terrain on which business as usual has proceeded.

I WANT SOME OF THAT TALK

Whatever her fear . . . she nonetheless listened to the wolf.
    AVERY GORDON, OF SABINA SPIELREIN, *Ghostly Matters*, p. 50

This is the best. The way people treat you, talk to you,
with mutual respect. They treat you with respect. It's more
personal, they come around and talk to you and help you.
    CONTROL UNIT INMATE

Attention makes inmates feel that someone hears them,
not that they are rewarded for bad behavior.
    JOHN LARSON

The small group of people gathering one morning outside the control unit gates for the weekly "tier walk" includes Larson and McKinley, both wearing suits and ties, two uniformed supervisors, the classification counselor in his jeans, and me, my steno book and pen under my arm. We pass by the sergeant's office and through an additional set of doors, nod hello to the officer in the control booth, go through one more set of doors and out onto the tiers. Starting at one end of the unit, we walk slowly up and down, gradually dispersing as the inmates call out to talk with us. The unit is quiet. Some men are asleep, and some read or watch television in their cells; some stand at their windows in their underwear.

The staff gather at the door of a man who talks for a long time about how his TV headphone cord has broken and the sergeant has not responded to his kites. The group listens soberly, leaning forward to hear. When the others move on, McKinley says to the inmate, "Why didn't you come to me? Why didn't you write me a kite about this?" "I try to go up the chain of command," says the prisoner, "You know, follow the chain." McKinley says, "Yes, I understand, but you and I know each other. I should know about this." Out of earshot of the inmate, Larson hands the old cord to a counselor and says, "Would you go right now and get a new one and give it to him?" As he moves on down the tier a young man—still a teenager—calls out to him. He explains anxiously that he has been trying to call his mother during his yard, but cannot get through. Larson takes a small piece of yellow paper from his jacket pocket and writes down the number, promising to call her.[17] Moving in this way through the unit, the staff takes up the minutia of dependence—the cold food tray, the lost property, the dirty shower stall. They stand still outside the inmates' doors, listening intently. As Larson explained to an inmate who expressed anger about something he had not mentioned when it happened several weeks earlier, "We do [the tier walks] so you don't [have to] hang on to [things]. We don't want to leave your cell if a problem is still on you." This is one of the primary purposes of the practice, and it is clear that many inmates have already had a chance to address problems and can simply ignore the group. One of the prison workers kids a young man who is watching Jerry Springer, "Pretty soon you're gonna sue the state for rotting your brain!"[18]

Many conversations during tier walks are to support the goal of getting inmates out of the unit. "How are you doing?" Larson asks one man. McKinley, standing slightly behind him, says, "We need to get out you out of here." The inmate says that he's now on level three. Good, say the two administrators, you'll go out as soon as you are on level four. A couple of doors down a man wants to talk about an infraction he has received. He's upset that the officers have restricted him. "I can understand some of the factors in your behavior," one of the staff members says. "Doesn't make it right, but it's understandable." As the captain comes over to discuss with him whether he can get some of his property back, another inmate calls to me from down the tier. He is twenty years old and says he's getting out of prison soon. Like others upon hearing that I am a college professor, he wants to talk about the books he is reading—Freud and Jung—and wonders whether I have any idea how he could go to college. He reminds me of a prisoner I talked with on a different day who enthusiastically began a conversation about books and then, as though suddenly in mid-sentence remembering where he was, laughed, "Smart as I am, and some of the things I do are so stupid!"

Down on the lower tier I stop to talk to a man who brushes off the approaches of the staff and says to me, "I hate these cops with a passion. I've got staff assaults." He has been locked in control units for four years, and it is clear from our conversation that he has, in a phrase common on the unit, "burned his bridges" and will be hard to place back in general population. Like another prisoner who said, "I don't like talking to [staff] . . . because that'd be like talking to my worst enemy," he is unimpressed by the tier walk. Another man talks for a long time to the counselor, and when he moves on I go up to the prisoner's window. He is small, his jumpsuit falling several inches below his ankles. Smiling, holding a bright red apple in one hand, he begins demonstrating with the other how "space particles" collide and form waves that are the basis for time travel. Einstein and Darwin understood this, he says, his mind seeming to bob among imagined stars; Darwin too was dyslexic. It is easy to imagine how he got here—unable to read, unlikely to understand the rules—and hard to imagine how he will get out.

A few steps down the tier an older prisoner, his gray hair in a long ponytail, calls me over to volunteer,

> What's going on here is the most positive thing I've seen in years, [Larson] coming and talking to people. If you put a man in here and he's in total isolation he's gonna start acting out. Before, it was real hard to get out [of here], even with good behavior.

Like many on this unit, his stay will be short as he moves quickly up the levels and out to a general population unit. But at the cellfront of Janson, Larson is walking a thin line between reassurances that he won't be in a control unit forever and making clear that permission for transfer depends upon higher authorities.

LARSON: We need to work together on [this]—you can tell us what is happening [to your emotional state], we can tell you [how the decision process is going].

JANSON: If this is gonna be my fate . . .

LARSON: (*firmly*) There's really no reason for that. It's taking a commitment from both of us to make it work.

JANSON: I'm doing what you tell me to do.

LARSON: You are, we can't ask for more. I respect that composure that you have.

JANSON: I'll tell you where I'm at. You know I'll tell you the truth.

After Larson moves on, I talk to Janson for a bit, like the others leaning against the door in order to hear. He tells me he's been reading Dyer's *The Perpetual Prison Machine,* a book that describes the recent growth of prisons. "It's kind of a repetitive circle, isn't it?" Janson says. "I didn't know what a big industry this is. If I was out, I'd buy stock in prisons!" He asks me how my book is going, and I anxiously describe the differences among possible audiences. I am thinking of the many ways this very moment can be read. "You can't please everyone," he says, "You gotta just do the best you can." As I catch up with the group, an inmate calls out to Larson:

> I know when thanks are due and they are due here. I've been in prison for twenty years and never seen anything like this. The way this place is ran, you guys are doing a heck of a job.

Two hours after the tier walk began, the unit has gradually emptied of staff. Down on the lower level, the counselor is moving away from a voluble man to whom he has been listening for fifteen minutes. He motions to the booth officer. Not wanting to hold things up, I hurry to leave with him. As we pass through the door, the prisoner he has been talking to calls out to me, "But what about *me*? I want some of that *talk*!"

The institution of walk-arounds is a radical move in the context of contemporary control unit regimes.[19] The same staff now engaged in questioning other aspects of their work vigorously resisted it, and it is considered "nuts" by other workers at this and other prisons. Tier walks interrupt the hierarchical order according to which it is the officers who have direct contact with inmates; the man who had a problem with his television headphones and felt he should follow the chain was expressing common practice. Walk-arounds also interrupt the conventional economy of attention with its parsimonious distribution of interaction and suspicion of language. They create a kind of middle distance, neither hierarchical removal nor the dangerous intimacy so often feared. In this context words, not feces, are the medium of exchange. "If I don't talk to them, how would I know them?" asks Larson. "If you are listening to the offender, he is saying something." Some of the discussion between administrators and inmates addresses this directly; Janson's situation is brought up and discussed (as it is week after week, with frustration voiced on both sides), or a prisoner is encouraged not to hold back. This process is not the same as therapeutic encirclement, which is suspect or impossible in this space. Talk here dwells on conditions and strategies, as much diagnostic of problems in the system as in the individual. Prisoners are understood to be active, but not autonomous, participants in these problems.

The nature of the interruption created by tier walks is understood by many staff through an imagery of abandonment. This is often framed in the animal/human terms we have seen throughout. Thus, for example, Larson believes that custody staff in training should be locked up as "inmates" to find out what it is like.

> All of a sudden, you're locked up in a little cell. We don't want to talk to you; we want you to leave us alone. We need to realize what we are doing to each one of those offenders. They are dependent 100,000 percent. If we don't get them for their yard, why is it gonna kill us to say we're sorry? We don't realize what we've done.

He expanded on this point at the meeting with his staff.

> If you really want to know what we are doing—I don't know if I can ever communicate this the right way—but if you go out and look at a dog pound and try to translate that into what we're doing to people you'll get a little sense. Now they have multiple cell dog pounds and they have single cell dog pounds and they have people that like some of the dogs and they have people that don't like some of the dogs and they have dogs that don't like some of the dogs, and they have dogs that don't like the people that work with them. When I walk through a pound I get a sense of, what are we doing? How can these dogs be happy like some of them show and pretend to be when someone comes in? And those pens are *open*, they can *see* their neighbor and they can socialize with them. The one that bothers me is the

little dog that sits back in the corner and acts like he's gonna get beat up and he's scared to death and he shakes. What happens to him? I believe people are people. We've got some bad bad people, some not-so-bad people, and some people that have done some bad things but that doesn't make them bad. But how do you weigh these things in a sensible way that is individualized enough to make an impact on a person? I'm not trying to make it look like we are running a dog pound. But anything that comes close to it turns me off. We need to take whatever steps it takes.

Like the pound, units like this extend a condition of abandonment from which—by implication—the only exit might be death. The dog that cowers and can't "show himself to be happy" is the one no one will take—the one too abused to respond. To refuse attention, in this metaphor, is inhumane at the most basic of levels. "People are no different caged," Larson continues, "They want attention. They demand it, even negative attention; they do stupid actions to get a reaction." This perspective, transmitted to the rest of the supervisory staff, insists on persevering with prisoners who are hostile or avoid contact. The results can be understood in pragmatic terms, as indicated by the inmate who said that dealing with problems regularly tends to lessen acting out. But the gesture is also framed as "human"—it is human to be available, to listen, not to walk away from a cellfront when the person on the other side is in the middle of a sentence.

We have seen throughout this book that the "other than human" haunts the prison. On the one hand the irrational—the psychotic or the behavioral—cannot be assimilated to the structures of rules and policies that stabilize the prison as governable. On the other, too much rationality is read as a condition of inhuman disconnection. These opposites have great symbolic weight in marking the abject status of the other and making sense of intensive confinement. But neither can be entirely metabolized within the actual regime of the control prison. As symbols, the prisoners who embody these opposites threaten staff with difficult questions about the humanity of the project in which they are engaged; as people, their continued "storage" threatens to make the prison nothing more than a dangerous warehouse.

The tier walk both upholds and challenges the fundamental premise of custody that uncertainty is to be avoided. By talking to prisoners frequently and dealing with specific problems before they are magnified in solitude and anger, the staff avoids surprises like withheld meal trays and sudden fits of rage. The calm atmosphere that sometimes attends walk-arounds has developed over time as prisoners learn there will be future opportunities to talk to responsive staff. Speaking critically in the context of a different prison, one officer said of escalating situations, "The machine doesn't care why [the inmate] intends his behavior. But if you *see* that [indifference of the machine] you can figure out why he does it. Is he afraid of others? Does he want attention?" Wanting attention—asking for it—structures the walk-around, but as a routine that does not stigmatize the wanting itself.

The walk-around has an open structure that does not control either the length or the content of interactions. Prisoners bring up whatever they want and talk for as long as they want. Sometimes the atmosphere is tense, as they complain about staff or vent their frustration at events in prisons from which they have just been transferred. This way of handling problems has begun to set a precedent for dealing with trouble on a larger scale. Larson insists to his staff that:

[When we fight the inmates] they are the only ones who lose. We're always gonna win, we're always right. There's no way that they're gonna win. Is that the right way to manage people?

This perspective was put to the test during an incident in which several inmates barricaded themselves in their cells. The emergency response team was called, but asked to wait outside. As the leader of the team explained, "We don't 'go get him' without negotiations. No reason to be in a hurry." In this case negotiations involved a prolonged discussion of what was bothering the inmates; supervisory staff remained on the unit all night. The prisoners demanded: "Why are you doing it like this? Why don't you come in and get us?" Finally, the next morning, they left their cells peacefully. An emergency response team member summed up the incident:

It was cool because before it would have exploded through the whole tier. It was a good ending, no one got hurt, but they lost their levels and had to do restitution for what they broke. Line staff thought they got off too easy. [But there's] gotta be some gray areas. Strict security, there's no gray there.

Difficulties that are interrupted in this way make certain premises visible—such as the mutual investment in "war" that both staff and inmates can develop. As Larson put it, "I had to spend hours explaining it to both shifts; I wouldn't let none of it happen so they were all mad at me." The prospect of less trouble threatens some staff and inmates because of the way control is understood as a matter of "hard" versus "soft." "If we don't have any problems with our inmates," McKinley explains, "we'll be seen as 'powder puffs,' and 'a bunch of sissies.'" Those who demand "their pound of flesh" are, in his view, trying to avoid this perception of being "not manly." Addressing problems before they erupt or responding flexibly when they do "doesn't give you credit, it labels you as weak." A uniformed staff member in a different part of the prison complained:

> Guys out on the deck orchestrating undermine the authority of officers. You should not traverse that terrain [of the tiers]—you don't *want* inmates to know you. The goon suit, the mask keeps them from seeing your face. It is better for them not to know the people in authority.[20]

Within the prison, criticism for tier walks comes almost entirely from this custodial direction, which sees them as suspect for reasons of softness. One person who had left correctional work had this to say, though, when I described the practice to him.

> It doesn't appear to be brutal, but the reality is you're forcing prisoners into a position where it's just as cold and brutal as it ever was, 'cause they're locked up and they're *less than*, and they take that on . . . You still achieve the same end. You're still destroying people . . . you're still building more prisons.

I have a similar question, which I pose to Larson: Isn't there a danger that if these changes succeed in pacifying and calming, making this place "better," they will make change in the larger system (particularly in the proliferation of these units) less, rather than more likely?[21] Larson holds one hand up at eye level to represent "real humanity" and holds the other, at the level of the table where we are sitting, to show "where we are now." He moves the bottom hand up a couple of inches to indicate the level he feels he can reach with the changes he is making.

> We do not get our full humanity until these people go out into a normal situation. We aren't even close. It doesn't take a genius to tell what we're doing to each other [in prisons]. And there's no danger that we can even

get close to making it truly right. There is a risk [of perpetuating these units] but what's the value of the risk? This damage of demeaning and isolating conditions is happening *now*. We need to have no fear of doing the right thing—the inmates will respond and then they won't be here.

In other words, Larson insists, we cannot expect to find our full humanity in this situation, only to recognize that we don't have it. Inhumanity comes to be located differently: less often is it primarily in the prisoners— it has begun to threaten "us."

In the conversation with Jeremy Roland with which I began this book, I asked him whether the changes happening on this unit could perhaps be used to support the continued use of these prisons. He thought I was coming back to the public response to any effort to help inmates. "That is just ignorant," he said. "They're thinking [you should] beat us with whips and chains." I tried again, but my question made no sense—in fact it seemed almost cruel. "I try to keep my hopes up," he said. "That's all you have, is hope."

STRANGE AS IT SEEMS

If we treat a psychopath as less than a person, are we then not doing exactly what we criticize him for?

GWEN ADSHEAD, "Psychopaths
and Other-Regarding Beliefs," p. 43

We can't give up on nobody even if they are a psychopath.

JOHN LARSON

We should have more social experiments. I mean, this thing doesn't appear to be working! I'd be willing to pay more taxes for some experiments. You can't just say nothing works. That's so defeatist, so negative.

PRISON ADMINISTRATOR

Imagine yourself sitting in a phone booth for a couple of hours. It's uncomfortable, but it's worth being uncomfortable two or three times a week.

INMATE, OF EDUCATION BOOTHS

About two years before the conversation that opens this chapter, I first heard about one of the new projects for the unit: "education booths" that would allow prisoners to take classes together. Under the policies that gov-

Figure 23. Lecture in the auditorium of Fresnes Prison, France. Reproduced with the permission of the Ecomusée de Fresnes.

ern the operation of these units prisoners can never be in the same room together; no group events ever happen. Education offerings on the unit were limited to high school equivalency (GED) tutoring in the visiting booths. The booths under construction in the inmate welding shop would be made of steel, with windows on three sides so that prisoners could see and talk with one another and a teacher.[22] The unit's glass-walled hearing rooms, which at the time contained only tables with cuff rings, would have enough space to line five booths against one wall.

The next time I went to the prison I took a drawing that shows prisoners in small wooden booths like telephone booths. The date is 1832, the place the auditorium of a French prison. This illustration in *Discipline and Punish* is a visual trope for Foucault's argument that the combination of power/containment and knowledge/normalization is the central dynamic of the prison. A more recent drawing (Figure 23) shows the same scene. "We haven't come very far, have we?" said Larson, studying the illustration I gave him. On my next visit I found that the picture had been framed and placed on a shelf in his office.[23] In the meantime, as the booths were gradually finished and installed on the unit, their sur-

Figure 24. Building education booths in prison welding shop. Photo by Lorna A. Rhodes.

real aspect was apparent to everyone (Figure 24). Walking away from watching the welders one day, Larson said, "I know it is easy to ridicule this." On the day the booths were put in, he wrote me the news and added, "I just want you to know that I know that this is barbaric." Unit staff described the booths as heavy, medieval, and strange (Figure 25). Inmates joked about them, and some on the first day of class climbed all over them, testing for strength. The teacher, too, said, "I had my doubts about the booths, it's like putting guys in a can. At the first graduation we took pictures—it's impossible to say, that's my class, because it looks so weird."

Why build the booths then? The primary reason is that they resist or evade the rule of absolute separation. Instead of being confined to individual instruction, inmates can take classes in anger management and victim awareness that are premised on interaction in a group.[24] But, just as important, the booths make this possible in a way that cannot be faulted on security grounds. "Barbaric" or not, the stronger and more escape-proof they appear, the more acceptable they are to custody staff, prison officials, and a public seemingly intent on removing all "frills" from prisons. As the

Figure 25. Education booths in the control unit. Photo by Lorna A. Rhodes.

teacher pointed out, "The booths are not pretty, not warm and inviting. They look really solid. And the inmates are happy with them, they understand that the public can't think we're being too warm and fuzzy." The staff view is that building them solidly reduces the possibility of an incident and secures their project. Paradoxically, then, the booths are seen to increase the chance that inmate-students will be considered fit for eventual interaction in the general population; if someone were to get hurt in a less extreme solution, groups and classes would be "all over."

One day a statewide meeting at the prison coincided with a graduation ceremony for inmates who had successfully completed a victim awareness class. Some fifteen administrators and mental health workers were invited onto the unit and crowded into the room with the booths. Two men who had completed the course sat next to each other in the middle of the row, one in jeans and the other in the unit's white jumpsuit.[25] The unit manager stood in front of the booths and addressed the gathering: "Strange as it seems," he said, "these steel structures signify hope. The efforts these inmates have made to bring about change is really a progressive thing." He praised the inmates for completing the difficult class. Larson then stood in front of the two men, turned his back on the room, and addressed them directly. "I know this [class] has been hard for you. These booths are not what we prefer, but they give us the opportunity to do this. We're here recognizing that you've done something that's to your credit."

After the teacher spoke briefly, someone in the audience said, "Maybe the inmates want to say something!" The younger of the two men spoke first:

This is really a good thing, advantageous to everyone. I know there's a lot of zero tolerance out there, but rehabilitation can happen. When you become cognizant of the victims and all the debris you leave [from your actions] you get your humility back. It made me feel better about change.

The second man, edgier than the first, said:

I've been sitting in a cage the last five years due to my own stupidity and ignorance. I never would have taken this class without [the staff here]. It puts a value on life that I didn't see and made me more aware of what I've done to people. Without these type of classes people in these cages are never gonna learn right from wrong.

The teacher handed each prisoner a certificate through the door of the booths and everyone clapped. Cookies and juice were on the table with the cuff ring, and someone handed them in to the inmates through the cuffports. I went up to talk with the younger man, whom I knew from walking the tiers. "I always considered myself just a hustler, a drug dealer," he said, expanding on the theme of his brief speech. "I never thought about someone dying, I'd never been to a funeral. I didn't think about how my actions might have peripheral damage."

As people began filing out, I realized that the younger man was wearing jeans because he had left the unit and no longer had to wear the white suit of the maximum security prisoner. In fact, he did not have to be in cuffs at all anywhere else in the prison; as soon as the officers had escorted him back through the unit's outermost gate, they simply took the cuffs off and allowed him to return to his living unit. He left to the words of the unit manager, "Now if you are having any trouble over there, tell the sergeant right away and let us know right away. No one's perfect, we don't expect perfect, but you let us know. We know you can make it." The way this prisoner's brief control unit visit was handled signified—though so routinely no one noticed—how maximum security acts as a kind of "warp" within which even a medium custody prisoner must wear cuffs and be confined in a booth. The booths are both acquiescence and resistance to this fact.

The aspect of the victim awareness class that most impressed inmates and staff was a visit by a woman who had lost her eighteen-year-old son to a brutal murder. In an unusual concession, she was allowed to bring in her son's ashes, pictures of him as a child, and the crime scene and autopsy photos taken after his death.[26] These she took up to the booths and showed, individually, to each prisoner. This was what the staff at graduation referred to when they said that the class was difficult—two of the students wept despite the presence of the other prisoners. Jeremy Roland explained that he had lost a cousin with whom he had been close. When he took the class, he said, "It made me feel human again, to see her compassion and her emotions, to see the hurt in her. I can relate to it." Later in the class the teacher showed videos for a section on "Hate and Violence."

> I showed them a video of Byrd in Texas . . . and one about Matthew
> Shepard.[27] It was very difficult. We talked about how people hate *them*.
> I don't know whether it made a difference [but] to a couple of guys I would
> say yes, it did. Even if they are faking it, that's fine. If they learn to fake it
> good enough it will just become part of them. We've tried everything else,
> haven't we? We're still building more prisons and making harder laws. If it
> hasn't worked, maybe we should try something else.

The victim awareness class stirred up a conversation among the unit staff that gets to the heart of their project: is there any point in having such a class for lifers who will never get out of prison? As the teacher presented the argument, "Does it do good for guys who will be here for years? Yes, it does. It makes them human, it's good for them." Jeremy's sense of being made human is echoed by staff who say that their own humanity is at stake in these efforts. I asked the teacher what the notion of the human meant to her:

We are saying we want them to understand other people and look outside themselves. We all need to look at other people and make that connection, [to see] that all feel the same kind of things . . . I don't necessarily think there's some [one] moment of epiphany but I think if we give them enough of those moments of connection there's more of a chance. There is for all of us. I think those ed booths give those opportunities, to make that connection with me, or each other or one of the officers.

"Making them human," being human, and humanizing oppose the "animal" and the "inhuman." But the booths also raise the question of *who* connects, of what development of feeling or sense of self can be called forth into this connection from men otherwise excluded from it. The issue here is the same we saw earlier in the program materials that encourage inmates to think of themselves both as ultimate choice-makers and as "written on" by their lives. Prisoners described the classes raising questions about what kind of self they have and what they are capable of.

[The class] is quite beneficial. The inmates can talk about things they would do in [in anger-provoking situations]. Some guys will tell the truth. They can't talk to the officers [because] it's prison common law. In class people tried hard to be themselves, or sometimes if there were hard questions that would reveal their true self they just wouldn't speak. People in prison are pissed off—it's good when this guy [the teacher] comes in who's willing to argue with these [prison] norms. He is part of the prison but he's pretty slick. It's a double standard, but he has an exception. The officers are the side of the enemy.

For this prisoner the class offered a moment of relief from the performance of toughness and a space in which a staff member—despite his power—could be seen as an ally.

Other inmates spoke of the social experience provided by the booths. The man who returned from general population to attend his graduation had explained earlier, while he was still on the unit:

I did sixty days with nothing [at a different prison], nothing to read, just looking at the wall. You go crazy; it messes with your brain. [Being in the class] was different. It's nice to be able to *see* who's next to you. I'd rather have been in a regular class, but [in the booths] you can talk to the person next to you, you don't have to yell . . . it's neat.

Jeremy Roland described an initial skepticism, but said, "Once I got there I realized it did help me . . . I can be real opinionated sometimes and she [the teacher of the victim awareness class] was able to open my eyes up to a different perspective."

The possibility of a false self hovers in the background of some of these conversations. After the graduation ceremony one prison worker who had been in the audience raised the issue directly. He began with a guarded acknowledgment that the booths might be a good idea, but added: "You have to watch out, because you can get a psychopath in there who is just pretending." As the teacher's comments about those who "fake it" suggest, unit staff are faced with all the objections we saw in the last chapter. If a "true self" does not in fact exist, those trying to address it may be simply deluded. Given the ubiquitous nature of this issue, it is inevitable that worries about manipulation surface and are made the more acute—at least at times—because here the extreme distance from inmates fostered by the environment has been problematized.

Larson voices doubt about the ethical basis and stability of the category of psychopathy. One inmate had received a psychological report that recommended indefinite detention in maximum security; the report noted that a "hypothesis" of "psychopathy" should not be "discounted" despite a less than definitive score on the Hare checklist. Larson said angrily, "They used his criminal history to write this, so of course it comes out this way! It makes it hard for us. What are we supposed to do?" Of a different inmate he said,

It is hard to define a psychopath but easy to define commitment based on the contacts I've had with someone. If someone tells me something, I want to believe 'em. Sometimes *they* believe something they're saying [even if not true]. Diagnosis leads to labeling, and that leads to a self-fulfilling prophecy. "I must be one, so here's what I'm gonna do." We don't know when a psychopath is ready to change. We have to try. You can't *make* people change, but you can make agreements with them. Lots of times the antisocial label isn't warranted.

The tier walks and education booths, premised on listening and talking, assume that who someone is depends at least in part on the context in which they live. Larson describes incoming inmates as "angry at the system and at themselves and at what's happened to them . . . you have to see who they are." The unit's staff allow for the possibility of faking. But they also try to "listen to the wolf," the threatening other on the other side of the bars. Larson said of one prisoner who had been described by some staff as psychopathic when he first came onto the unit, "His eyes are not as dark [now]—he seems more of a human being. He said to me, 'I've changed.'" By not foreclosing on this prisoner, he insists that the abnormal will is subject to social mediation. "We're not reaching into their brain and making them a good person. The first thing is treating them with respect."[28]

It is a desire to convey this interpretation to inmates and official visitors that makes the graduation ceremonies important to the staff. Jeremy complained of his graduation that "I know what an animal would feel like at the zoo, people coming in looking at the monkeys in the cages . . . it's society seeing you at your worst." But the staff know that the audience of other prison workers is the one that counts if their charges are to be regarded as fit to move back into general population. At graduation the inmates' pending or completed departure from the unit is framed in terms of their capacity for authentic responsiveness. Seen as responsive, they can be provided with the minimal social capital for reentry into the larger system or the outside world.

The education booths have seemed uncanny to me ever since I recognized in them the echo of Foucault's historical illustration. They fascinate in part because they so concentrate the uncanny surplus of power that pervades the prison in general. But they are also a strategy to repair the image of rehabilitation by engaging that very surplus and using it to circumvent the scandal that currently clings to any engagement with prisoners. The possibility that haunts the education booths and many of the unit's inmates is an absolute exclusion in which isolation signifies that no "reform" is possible or can even be proposed. Arguments about psychopathic inmates who must not be given up on and lifers who can be humanized are ultimately about the possibility for reinclusion—into general population, perhaps into society, but in the face of narrowed possibilities, at least into the human.

The picture of the booths in *Discipline and Punish* is meant to make the point that these cellular arrangements create an efficient and homogenized individuality, with education and religion the supplemental shaping aspects of a power that is primarily architectural. The education booths can be read in this way, too. But they can also be read, as inmates and staff seem to, as an attempt to make inmates "individual" *enough* to be recognized at all.

UNIT MANAGER: Should we increase our attention to each inmate and develop an individual plan for *each* guy?

COUNSELOR: If [only] we could spend twenty minutes a day with each guy . . .

LARSON: It goes back to numbers.

The only way "rehumanizing" can happen under these conditions, as many staff and some inmates see it, is to *locate and display* the individual's availability for compassion, connection, and learning—to mark his accessibility to a conversation that proceeds elsewhere, without him. This is the paradox of the booths, at once an absolute extension of confinement and an exit strategy.

Both classes and tier walks position issues of crime and accountability in more complex social and narrative frameworks than those available in the more cursory interactions that are usually possible—the exhortations, infractions, and hearings where choice is flattened into those forks in the road that cannot be explored in their complexity. But they must do so in the context of the failures—supposed and real—of the many treatment regimes that in the current climate seem too dangerous and liberal. Jeremy, in prison for life after his third strike, was saying—as became clear in the rest of our conversation—that redemption into the "human" world is his deepest wish. The feeling of being in a zoo in which society could see him at his worst was shameful—and could be shameful—only because of this possibility. A similar impulse toward inclusion, however strange its shape, was expressed by the teacher:

I like the booths because I can go right up to [the inmates], and I feel like we are more equal because we're just all in there together. And I'm in my own kind of a cage because I can't get out [of the room or unit] without somebody letting me out either! They feel like they are in cages all the time. [In the booths] they feel like they are out—because they're all together. They look at it as a real opportunity.[29]

Thus the ceremonial gestures of progression and reinclusion made possible by the booths offer staff and inmates a way to express their awareness of the intangible audience of "society." Society in the form of legislators and taxpayers may object to the booths as frills, society looks down on these men as the lowest form of life, society is where victims have been harmed and most of the inmates hope someday to return. The politics of the prison becomes the politics of *these* faces. Jeremy said, "I don't know what you do to educate the public that this is positive, this is good." When the inmates stand formally in the booths for their GED graduation photo, they radiate the hope that their surroundings can be undone, if only momentarily, by the caps and gowns they wear. The teacher expresses her hope that they can be seen, in this way, as citizens.[30]

> That's why I like having people come and visit . . . [to] understand better that these guys go back and live next door to us.

WE AGAINST THEM

> The system runs by itself. You could take everybody out, and it would still run.
>
> MENTAL HEALTH WORKER

> This [the warehouse, the dog pound] is not the way you're gonna help people change. You're doing this, they're doing that—that's a war, we against them.
>
> JOHN LARSON

> LAR, OF PRISONS: People have such complex positions on things.
> CONTROL UNIT TEACHER: It's kind of hopeful, isn't it?

McKinley is talking with Larson about a young inmate who was transferred into the unit the week before.

MCKINLEY: He has a juvenile history. He's angry, he got threatening last week. He won't talk to anyone, doesn't like anyone, doesn't like me . . . I don't mind us moving toward him, but . . .

LARSON: He needs a program [plan] . . . I want to transition him [out].

MCKINLEY: (*to LAR*) We almost always agree, but on this one we don't. (*To Larson*) I disagree. I don't think he has any control.

LARSON: He'll be like [a notoriously violent long-term prisoner who was sent to prison for only a few years initially] who killed two people in prison. This guy is trying to be tough, trying to prove himself.

MCKINLEY: I don't know what to do with him.

LARSON: I can tell you what it will be in twenty-five years [if we don't do anything]. We can talk to him each week about it, let him think each week.

MCKINLEY: I hope so. [Right now] we don't have any cooperation from him. He wrote a kite today: Is this another deception, are you gonna goon me and transfer me out to [another control unit]?

LARSON: See, he don't trust nobody. I don't know what happens to someone like this in juvenile [to make him like this]. *He* has to do it [control himself enough to be able to leave]—we can't do it for him. But we have to give him the opportunity.

These administrators are positioned between the two chronic hazards of their work. On one side is the prisoner himself, angry, hurt, suspicious, and out of control. He reminds them of others they have known who later exploded into murderous rage. Without some impulse toward self-regulation, this man will be lost, and his future deeds will come back to haunt them. They recognize the damaging environment he comes from and the harm of his current situation; they can draw on few remedies except the hope that "thinking" while under constraint can enlist him in his own salvation.

On the other side of this conversation is the hazard of the prison system itself with its complex of related agencies and, somewhere upstream, the social violence and neglect that feed it. Frustration with the system is a common theme among unit staff, both because of the way inmates are sent in, and because transfers out are not under their control. "It gets frustrating" one of the counselors says, "when you sit here and see guys sitting here and [their release] gets put off, and they hear the same things over and over and they get frustrated." Every day the staff encounters evidence that the system as a whole—without anyone seeming to intend it—can keep their own best intentions from realization. Larson explains,

[Inmates] are recommended for release [from maximum security] but they [staff/administration at other prisons] don't send in the paperwork. Nothing happens. Nothing is happening to reduce the control unit population. No one will listen to me.

Dealing with conditions on the unit—at what may seem to be the very basic level I have described here—diminishes the intense preoccupation with the emotional and bodily aspects of abjection that we saw in the first chapter. But this in turn brings to the fore the larger dilemmas within which the unit exists. Some of these are structural: waves of new prisoners crowding into the system, lack of psychiatric treatment, and obstacles to releasing prisoners from the unit. A second dilemma is the one we have seen throughout: how to address the prisoner's will—his capacity for change—while acknowledging, in a system in which such acknowledgment is suspect, that both his past and his present environment may have something to do with his behavior. And a further dilemma surrounds the question of how to make changes stick. The more they can be turned into policy, congealed, and made firmly part of the system, the greater their purchase under changing administrations and conditions. But it is clear from the fate of other change efforts that the firming up of plans can turn today's good idea into tomorrow's policy albatross; classification itself, with its injunction to attend the needs of individuals, came into being through just such historical routinization.[31]

The staff of the unit have become increasingly reflective about these issues. In part this results from a growing confidence that they might, in fact, succeed in making their changes stick. The "before" fades from memory, and fewer of the older staff remain. When I ask a question about something in the past, McKinley says, "The way it used to be seems like a thousand years ago. Even though it isn't that long ago, it seems so different." The result—change in the inmate—is the proof. McKinley continued, "Now we *expect* inmates to change. And we don't care who we get—we'll take the ones that other places don't want because we know we can work with them." The changes that have occurred seem to him solid and permanent. "When you adopt this philosophy and live it, it is against your nature to violate it. We own it now. The inmates expect it. We train for it."

Some remain doubtful, however. Many officers continue to locate trouble firmly in the inmates and see a disturbing harbinger in what they regard as their loss of control of the tiers. The teacher, on the other hand, sees change as tenuous in the face of the overall politics of corrections and the larger society.

> I think it's good but I'm not optimistic about it lasting. It's terrible it could happen, but if any of the people change [all this] will just fade away. I hate to sound like one of the inmates, but it's also political and so not about human beings . . . I don't think it's inmates that are going to make it not happen. I think it's *us*.

Sorting out how the seeming inevitability of control prisons nationwide reflects larger national imperatives is difficult even for many analysts outside the prison system. On the inside the emphasis on individual choice as the basis for punishment makes it difficult for people to ask how individuals are connected to one another, let alone how economic and political influences intersect in complex ways to produce the current system. Many prison workers, perhaps less constrained on this point in conversations with me than with their co-workers, were quite able to place themselves imaginatively in the position of the despised or threatening other. But sustaining the practices that support this possibility is another matter. The specific content of the changes I have described is probably less important than their interruption of the value placed on the withdrawal of attention. Speaking of what is right and human permits this interruption by providing a way to talk about "us" as well as "them." These efforts resist the tendency to make the inmates nothing but willful bodies, frame attention in antimechanical ways, and redirect focus onto language. They push against the abstractions of taxonomy and policy on the one hand and the concrete restrictions that prevent inmate contact and transition on the other. As the staff are the first to say, these efforts are also incomplete, tenuous, and a struggle.

I certainly did not imagine this chapter on the day I first visited a control unit and saw Jamal Nelson striking his arm against the implacable wall of the exercise yard. With the reform I describe here still in progress, supermaximum prisons around the country still under construction, and prison conditions and costs receiving increasing national attention, I cannot end with a neat package of conclusions as to what it means. Historians seem to have an easier time ending their books, for they can point to the "larger forces" that they know, in retrospect, either carried forward or overwhelmed the long-ago struggles they recount. But for an ethnographer, those struggles are too immediate and compelling—and more than that, far too located in specific individuals—to surrender to the forces of history however they may be understood.

I feel a kinship here with other recent writers chronicling the specifics of institutional life in the United States. At the close of a bleak account of the educational conditions that contribute to the imprisonment of black youth, Ann Arnett Ferguson asks, "Are [the] alternatives . . . either quick hopeless fixes or paralysis because small changes cannot make a difference in the long run?" But she cannot end with a question mark. "Allowing ourselves to imagine the possibilities . . . is an indispensable first step."[32] Discouraged by the failure of a court-ordered change in a juvenile prison, M. A. Bortner and Linda Williams end their book, "Change is essential to nurture youthful hopes and to rekindle our own."[33] Clearly these authors find themselves, at the end, somewhat at a loss. Themes of hope and imagination seem necessary emotionally but ungrounded; one senses that their purpose is to enable both writer and reader to put the book down and, somehow, move on. Echoing Jeremy, whose situation is without any apparent solution, they say, "Hope is all we have."

But I wonder whether it is possible, instead of drawing on hope primarily as a last resort, to locate it a little more sharply within these environments where it seems least likely. It seems to me that the staff and inmates of the setting I have described here are stubbornly enacting a hope constructed out of the historical specifics of their situation and, having once been largely without it, they do not want to give it up. They engage a governmentality that itself is effervescent—offering possibilities because, not in spite of, its tendency toward incongruity and making do. They draw on the fact that an institution, as we have seen throughout this account, is inhabited by a multitude of positions and voices. On close inspection neither alliance nor enmity is quite as simple as it seems, and individuals can almost always tell more than one story, sometimes contradictory, about themselves. Failures of imagination, then, may be failures to see how many imaginations are at play and how they might, in fact, "struggle it out," for if we cannot escape our history, we might at least make better use of it. I am not willing to give up the hope suggested by these efforts. They represent the possibility that we might be able to imagine and work for something else, to interrupt the terms we have been given. Surely that imagining—which both uses and pushes against the frameworks we already have—is the only way that these places and those consigned to live and work in them can be thought otherwise.

GLOSSARY OF PRISON TERMS

CELL EXTRACTION: Forcible removal of inmate from cell.

CELLIE: Cellmate.

CELL WARRIOR: Prisoner who acts tough only because he is locked down.

CHAIN: 1) Prisoners being transported; 2) chain of command, hierarchy of custodial authority.

CLASSIFICATION: System that sorts prisoners according to level of security.

CODE: Social rules among prisoners; for example, no snitching on another prisoner.

CONTRABAND: Items prisoners are not allowed to have.

CONTROL UNIT: A maximum security unit in which prisoners are locked into solitary cells for twenty-three hours a day and allowed out only under restraints and escort.

COUNSELOR, CORRECTIONAL: Person who has responsibility for classification and other aspects of inmate management.

COUNSELOR, MENTAL HEALTH: Person with mental health counseling credentials who may work in a treatment unit or in other settings.

CUFFPORT: Opening in door through which maximum security prisoners receive meals, clothing, and mail and are handcuffed for removal.

CUSTODY LEVELS: Degrees of security precautions ranging from maximum (solitary cells, total surveillance), close (tight perimeter security), medium, and minimum (camps, dormitory-style facilities).

DING: Mentally ill prisoner.

FISH (N.):   New prisoner.

FISH (V.):   To use clothing threads like fishline to pass notes and other contraband under cell doors to other prisoners.

GENERAL POPULATION: Prisoners who live where most prisoners live, or settings in which most prisoners live, as opposed to segregation units or special residential units.

HARDEN: Change the physical features of a cell or facility to improve security.

HOLE: Segregation or isolation; may or may not be the same as control unit.

HOUSE: Cell.

INFRACTION: Violation of prison rules.

JACKET: Label.

KITE: Note used for communication between prisoners and staff.

LEVELS/STEPS: Progressive privileges gained through good behavior.

LOCKDOWN: Condition in which prisoners are kept in cells all day.

MAIN LINE: Meal service or chow line; more generally, where general population prisoners live.

MAXIMUM SECURITY: Can refer to control units or to the security level of an institution containing general population inmates.

PROTECTIVE CUSTODY: Segregated housing placement to protect an inmate whose safety is threatened.

PRUNO: Wine made from fruit.

RAT: Prisoner who provides information to the administration about other prisoners; snitch.

SEG: Segregation; may or may not be the same as control unit placement.

SEPARATEE: Inmate housed separately from another inmate to ensure no contact between them.

SHANK: Prisoner-made knife or other sharp weapon.

SNITCH: Prisoner who provides information to the administration about other prisoners; rat.

SUPERMAX: Sometimes refers to any control (maximum security) facility, sometimes refers only to the larger free-standing ones.

YARD (N.):   Exercise area for inmates.

YARD (V.):   To go to yard or to be sent to yard.

APPENDIX: NOTE ON RESEARCH

PRISON POPULATION
IN WASHINGTON STATE

As of mid-2003, Washington State had a prison population of approximately 15,000 with 400 control unit beds and four psychiatric inpatient units with approximately 450 beds (about 200 inpatient beds were added in 2002). In our study of the state's control unit prisoners my colleagues and I found that 71 percent were white, corresponding to their proportion in the prison population as whole; the state's population is 85 percent white. Control units had a lower proportion of African Americans (18 percent versus 23 percent) and a higher proportion of Native Americans (7 percent versus 3 percent) than the general prison population. At the time of our study, out of 232 inmates, 20 had spent over five years in control unit confinement (some of it discontinuous) and 5 had spent over eight years in control units. Washington has 765 women in prison, 7 percent of the total incarcerated population; there are a few segregation beds for women but no control unit.

STUDY BACKGROUND

The University of Washington/Department of Corrections Correctional Mental Health Collaboration was created by legislative mandate as a response to the large number of mentally ill prisoners entering the prison system. The project was funded by the Department of Corrections, first under the leadership of Chase Riveland and later under Joseph Lehman. It was based in the University of Washington School of Nursing under the direction of David Allen, with David Lovell as full-time investigator.

The UW/DOC Correctional Mental Health Collaboration carried out a number of projects between 1993 and 2002, including clinical case consultation, policy planning, and the development of a medium security psychiatric unit. In 1994–96 David Lovell and I developed a "mobile consultation team" that brought together prison workers from different disciplines and facilities to address difficult custody/treatment situations.[1] Beginning in 1998, I worked with David Allan and David Lovell on issues involving the state's control units; this project included research on inmates and staff which we conducted as a team as well as my ethnographic research. Research procedures were approved by University of Washington and Department of Corrections Human Subjects Review Committees.

METHODS

The material on which this account is based falls into two main types: the ethnographic material I gathered through participant observation, and more formally obtained material from semi-structured (ethnographic) interviews. I attended meetings, classes, hearings, and prison events and talked with staff—sometimes at length over many meetings—individually and in small groups. I usually spent full days or sometimes two or more consecutive days on visits. In a few places I describe events in which I participated with David Lovell or other members of our group. My contact with prisoners included twenty hour-long taped interviews with control unit inmates (part of our larger study), follow-up interviews with several inmates that took place either in control or general population units, and numerous conversations at cellfront. I took notes at the time of the event in most cases or wrote down what I remembered later. The quotations in this book are taken either from tapes or from notes made as people spoke. In several places I have used material from taped interviews conducted by my colleagues. A number of prison workers at all levels commented on earlier versions of the manuscript, and I discussed specific issues and passages with several prisoners.

I gained general understanding of prisons from some events that are not directly described here, such as several days job-shadowing an officer, a day-long training session with special emergency response and hostage negotiation teams, visits to maximum security prisons in other states, and participation in therapeutic workshops for prisoners. Obviously, participating directly in the lives of prisoners was not an option, especially for a woman studying all-male institutions. Workers' and administrators' security and privacy concerns also governed what was possible. Thus some things that are important in prisons—for example, violent incidents, relationships between prisoners, everyday life in general population units, and the handling of staff misbehavior—were beyond my ability to directly observe.

The study of control unit inmates that we began in 1999 had three components in addition to the ethnographic. One was a medical records review of 122 inmates conducted by Kristin Cloyes, David Allen, and David Lovell.[2] The second was the administration of the Brief Psychiatric Rating Scale (BPRS) to all prisoners we interviewed. This is a small set of observations and questions about mood, sleep, and cognitive disturbance that we felt could help demonstrate the effects of intensive confinement on inmates.[3] Finally, David Lovell, David Allen, and Kristin Cloyes and Cheryl Cooke (both graduate students in the School of Nursing), and I conducted interviews in three of the state's control units. The 87 prisoners we interviewed represent 30 percent of the total number in maximum confinement at the time. Control unit staff first distributed a description of the project to 131 randomly selected prisoners; the 87 who agreed to be interviewed (66 percent) were brought by officers to visiting booths. Interviews were taped and later transcribed and coded. Our questions were primarily about the situations that brought prisoners into the unit, the experience of living in intensive confinement, and their expectations for return to general population. Interviews with the 40 staff who volunteered were conducted on all shifts, privately in offices or in a few cases in control booths, and similarly taped and transcribed.

NOTES

NOTE: All names of prisoners and prison staff in this book are pseudonyms.

INTRODUCTION

1. See the appendix for a description of how interviews were conducted and other aspects of the research on which this book is based.
2. In the end Vincent was transferred to a psychiatric facility. The staff expected that had they been forced to take him to an emergency room, he would have been referred from there to a hospital psychiatric unit. Such a solution would likely have been temporary.
3. The generic terms I use to describe those who work in the prison system replace specific titles for most workers other than officers. "Prison worker" refers to prison staff in all job categories. "Mental health worker" refers to all noncustodial staff providing psychological treatment, including psychologists, social workers, and a variety of others with counseling credentials. "Custody supervisor" refers to uniformed staff above the level of officer: sergeants, lieutenants, and captains. "Administrators" manage specific prisons; "officials" are in charge of the regional or statewide correctional organization. Glossing job categories in this way sacrifices some of the texture of prison work in order to protect the confidentiality of

individuals. Throughout this account I mention escorts or companions; these were almost always prison workers whom I already knew. The extent to which I could move about unescorted inside prisons depended on the circumstances.

4.	The analysis I present here is not intended to minimize the fact or the effects of serious crime but to question how we understand and respond to crime in general. The vast majority of prisoners will return to what is called (often euphemistically) the "community" or (more realistically for many) the "streets." For discussion of the effects of incarceration in reinforcing violence, see John P. May and Khalid R. Pitts, eds., *Building Violence.* More than half (1.24 million) of local, state, and federal prisoners have committed nonviolent offenses in which there was neither harm nor threat of harm to a victim (Judith Greene and Vincent Schiraldi, *Cutting Correctly,* 3; also see John Irwin, Vincent Schiraldi, and Jason Ziedenberg, "America's One Million Nonviolent Prisoners").

5.	Exceptions include Charles Bright, *The Powers That Punish,* and Patricia O'Brien, *The Promise of Punishment,* both of which describe the complex social life of prisons in the past, and for contemporary prisons C. Fred Alford, "What Would It Matter?" and Stephen Duguid, *Can Prisons Work?*

6.	Allen Feldman, "On Cultural Anesthesia."

7.	Angela Y. Davis, "Race and Criminalization."

8.	See Don Sabo, Terry A. Kupers, and Willie London, "Gender and the Politics of Punishment," on prison language and classification. Willie London, a prisoner who is one of the coauthors, differentiates the "prisoner," who is "always thinking of freedom, held against his will"; the "inmate," who "will do anything" and "has no individual will"; and the "con," who tries to "get over on anyone in any way possible" (9). Many prisoners I talked with used "inmate" and "prisoner" interchangeably, as I do here; "convict" was used more infrequently. To many prison workers the term "offender" has come to seem more acceptable than "inmate." In keeping with the recent trend toward long sentences, it seems to indicate a permanent rather than temporary status.

9.	The figure of over two million is from Fox Butterfield, "Prison Rates among Blacks" (A11); for a slightly earlier figure see Greene and

Schiraldi, *Cutting Correctly* (9). The number of people in the corrections system as a whole (including probation and parole) was 6.6 million in 2001, according to Allen J. Beck and Paige M. Harrison, *Prisoners in 2001*. Excellent studies have been done on the recent growth in prisons and on connections between race and the criminal justice system. See, for example, Alfred Blumstein and Joel Wallman, "The Recent Rise and Fall of American Violence"; Michael Tonry, *Malign Neglect;* Elliott Currie, *Crime and Punishment in America;* James Austin and John Irwin, *It's about time;* Marc Mauer, *Race to Incarcerate;* Steven R. Donziger, ed., *The Real War on Crime*; Alfred Blumstein and Allen J. Beck, "Population Growth in U.S. Prisons: 1980-1986"; Theodore Caplow and Jonathan Simon, "Understanding Prison Policy and Population Trends"; and David Cole, *No Equal Justice.* Irwin, Schiraldi, and Ziedenberg note, in "America's One Million Nonviolent Prisoners," that prisons and universities both target young adults; between 1987 and 1995 state expenditures for prisons went up 30 percent while support for universities went down by 19 percent. See the appendix for information on Washington State's prison population.

10. Over 90,000 women are incarcerated nationwide, with a rate of imprisonment that grew by 88 percent between 1990 and 1998 (Beck and Harrison, *Prisoners in 2001*; Greene and Schiraldi, *Cutting Correctly*, 9). Studies of women's imprisonment include Joanne Belknap, *The Invisible Woman;* Pat Carlen, *Sledgehammer;* and Barbara Owen, *In the Mix.* Owen gives a helpful account of her ethnographic work in a women's prison; Adrian Howe's *Punish and Critique* and Ngaire Naffine's *Feminism and Criminality* offer feminist analyses of imprisonment and criminal justice more generally. Washington's prison for women was not part of the study on which this account is based, and the dynamics I describe should not be assumed to hold for women.

11. Greene and Schiraldi, *Cutting Correctly,* 1.

12. There is debate about whether prisons help rural areas as much as promised, and about the extent to which prison labor is a factor in the global economy. See, for example, Ruth Wilson Gilmore, "Globalisation and U.S. Prison Growth," and Christian Parenti, *Lockdown America.*

13. See Katherine Beckett and Bruce Western, "The Penal System as Labor Market Institution," 45–50.

14. See Joseph T. Hallinan, *Going up the River;* Parenti, *Lockdown America;* and Sasha Abramsky, *Hard Time Blues.* My "Toward an Anthropology of Prisons," provides a review of literature on prisons. For a concise summary of issues at the height of the prison boom, see Eric Schlosser, "The Prison-Industrial Complex." Two books coedited by Paul Wright, a prisoner in Washington State, offer essays on the political economy of prisons and the criminal justice system more generally (Daniel Burton-Rose, ed., *The Celling of America;* Tara Herival and Paul Wright, eds., *Prison Nation*).

15. Avery F. Gordon, "Globalism and the Prison Industrial Complex," 147; Angela Y. Davis, "A World unto Itself: Multiple Invisibilities of Imprisonment."

16. An additional element here is an intensified public representation that crime and criminals are a central social problem. Crime was a staple of nineteenth-century pamphlets and newspapers. But the recent increase in crime stories and rising fear of crime dates in general from the 1960s and more specifically from the early 1980s. Katherine Beckett suggests, in *Making Crime Pay,* that media portrayals of crime danger and drugs are organized into thematically coherent "interpretive packages" that not only "frame" social problems but also highlight certain issues *as* social problems.

17. A recent report from the Justice Policy Institute describes public, political, and correctional support for cuts in prison spending; for a sense of the numbers involved, consider that California's incarcerated population decreased in 2001 by 3,557 inmates to 159,444 (Greene and Schiraldi, *Cutting Correctly,* 3). Also see Fox Butterfield, "1% Increase in U.S. Inmates Lowest in Three Decades." Overall prison population has continued to grow, however, despite these decreases, for some states, in rates of incarceration (Beck and Harrison, *Prisoners in 2001;* for a comprehensive discussion of U.S. prison policy see Craig Haney and Philip Zimbardo, "Past and Future").

18. A "New Penology" in the early 1980s emphasized rational management and scientific risk assessment; see John J. DiIulio, Jr., *Gov-*

erning Prisons; DiIulio, "Understanding Prisons"; Beckett, *Making Crime Pay;* and Austin and Irwin, *It's about Time.*

19. Some studies of prison work are by researchers who took jobs as officers. Of these the most recent is *Newjack,* journalist Ted Conover's compelling account of a year working at Sing Sing. James W. Marquart's "Doing Research in Prisons" and Mark S. Fleisher's *Warehousing Violence* were written in the 1980s. Little has been written about the women who have entered correctional work since the 1980s, but see Lynn E. Zimmer, *Women Guarding Men.*

20. As will become clear throughout this book, security concerns are primary.

21. Mental health also involves risk assessment, largely conducted through psychological testing, a topic to which I will return in chapter 5.

22. Conover, *Newjack,* 282–283. There are probably a number of reasons for the discrepancy between reports of abuse from prisoners and comments from many who have worked extensively in prisons that most guards are not abusive (for example, Robert Johnson in *Hard Time).* One is that prisoners reach out to the courts and human rights organizations specifically as a result of bad treatment. Second, differences among prison systems and prisons result in wide variations in tolerance for and reporting of abuse. Third, there are subtle forms of abuse that occur under the radar of either internal or external observation. And, finally, abusive officers are the least likely to talk to observers, and their peers may follow a code of silence. In our interviews with prisoners we found that most differentiated carefully among staff members, who were described as ranging from abusive or indifferent to professional and helpful.

23. The relationship of the Correctional Mental Health Collaboration with the corrections department developed in complex ways over a long period of time and involved numerous individuals, many changes and shifts in direction, and multiple perspectives and interests on both sides. The question of what, precisely, we "collaborated" with varied during the course of our work. We supported projects of change or resistance inside the system—as described in chapter 6—but whether it is possible to effect long-term change through such efforts remains in question.

24. Jimmy Santiago Baca, "Past Present," 363.

25. Norval Morris, "The Contemporary Prison," 203. Johnson writes: "Most prisoners attempt to carve out a private prison world composed of niches or sanctuaries, offering sheltered settings and activities that insulate them from the mainline prison . . . Prisoners who use this environmental diversity to create niches live not as role types . . . but as individuals . . . who treat their peers and officers [with] a measure of respect and even affection" (*Hard Time*, 66). For prisoners' social/psychological interactions in various prison environments see Hans Toch, *Living in Prison;* Hans Toch and Kenneth Adams, *Coping;* and Hans Toch and Kenneth Adams, *The Disturbed Violent Offender.* Among the many prisoners' accounts of life in prison—or, more accurately, of a variety of different lives—*Undoing Time,* edited by Jeff Evans, and *Prison Writing in 20th-Century America*, edited by H. Bruce Franklin, offer a wide sweep of perspectives. Earlier sociological literature on prison life is reviewed in my "Toward an Anthropology of Prisons."

26. Several recent commentators believe the image of incessant brutality and rape in contemporary prisons to be overdrawn. Wilbert Rideau, a long-term prisoner at the Louisiana State Penitentiary, notes in *Life Sentences* that electronic surveillance has reduced the amount of inmate-on-inmate violence. Conover concluded from his year working at Sing Sing that rape is relatively rare (*Newjack*). On the other hand, see Don Sabo, Terry A. Kupers, and Willie London, eds., *Prison Masculinities*, for several articles describing rape in prison as well as discussion of larger issues of masculinity and violence. A number of men we interviewed mentioned or hinted at fear of rape as a reason for the actions that put them into segregation.

27. I was least able to spend time with prisoners and do not attempt to present coherent narratives or representations of their lives. Prisoners have written and spoken extensively about themselves; in addition to the work mentioned above, some journalists and researchers who have taught in prisons explore prisoners' narratives and perspectives. See, for example, C. Fred Alford, *What Evil Means to Us;* Patricia E. O'Connor, *Speaking of Crime;* and Drew Leder, *The Soul Knows No Bars.* Leder's book includes lively discussions of social theory with his inmate-students.

28. For descriptions of the panoptical prison see John Bender, *Imagining the Penitentiary;* Robin Evans, *The Fabrication of Virtue;* Michel Foucault, *Discipline and Punish;* and Michael Ignatieff, *A Just Measure of Pain.*

29. Avery F. Gordon, *Ghostly Matters*, 134. Gordon argues for attention to forms of disappearance, as in Argentina and during slavery, that haunt and shape the present. I have been influenced by her work throughout this book, particularly her insistence on the complexity of social and historical personhood and her evocation of the uncanny elements in modernity.

I. CONTROLLING TROUBLES

1. Control prisons across the country differ in the amount of time prisoners are actually out of their cells; twenty-three hours of confinement per day (or, often, for five days a week, with twenty-four hours a day on weekends) is the standard. They also vary in design, population, and intensity of conditions from state to state. Descriptions of other states' regimes can be found in Human Rights Watch, *Cold Storage*, Leena Kurki and Norval Morris, "Purposes, Practices, and Problems," and in a recent judicial decision on the housing of mentally ill inmates at Wisconsin's Supermax Correctional Institution in Boscobel, Wisconsin (*Jones'El v. Berge*, 164 F.Supp.2nd 1096 (W.D. Wis., 2001)). See Marilyn D. McShane and Frank McShane, *Encyclopedia of American Prisons,* 420-27, for a general discussion of security issues; Margo Okazawa-Rey and Gwen Kirk, in "Maximum Security," provide a critical examination of the notion of "security" embedded in prison practices. Prisoners in control units differ among themselves in status (in terms of privileges earned), custody level (their classification in the prison population as a whole) and whether they are held in disciplinary or administrative segregation. Unless these differences are relevant to a specific example, I simply use the terms "control inmate" or "control prisoner." I have chosen a middle path, here and throughout, between the specifics of Washington prisons and more general descriptions of correctional practice.

2. There is little definitive information on the total numbers incar-

cerated in control unit housing nationwide. In 1997, the National Institute of Corrections published the results of a survey of supermax housing. The survey found "at least" 57 supermax facilities nationwide, with ten corrections departments "pursuing the development of approximately 3,000 additional supermax beds." Thus, for example, in 1977 Connecticut had 504 beds in one institution; Louisiana had almost 900 supermax beds at the state penitentiary at Angola; Texas had sixteen control units, with a total of more than 13,500 beds. The supermax prison at Pelican Bay in California houses 1,500 prisoners in 22 control units and an additional 1,600 maximum security prisoners in slightly less restrictive conditions (National Institute of Corrections, *Supermax Housing*, 1). A more recent figure for prisoners in administrative segregation and protective custody (and therefore likely to be housed as I describe here) is 42,000 (Camille Camp and George Camp, eds., *The Corrections Yearbook 2000*, 26). An excellent general piece on control units that discusses the issue of population is Leena Kurki and Norval Morris, "Purposes, Practices, and Problems." Also see Roy King, "The Rise and Rise of Supermax," Chase Riveland, "Supermax Prisons," Craig Haney and Mona Lynch, "Regulating Prisons of the Future," Fay Dowker and Glenn Good, "The Proliferation of Control Unit Prisons in the United States," and Austin and Irwin, *It's about Time*, 117–38.

3.   In some prison systems officers carry guns routinely. On abuse of guns at a Virginia supermax prison, see Dan Pens, "Abuse of Force at Virginia's Supermax." In most cases, however, guns are considered a liability for line staff, and reliance is placed on armed men in the towers to prevent escape and SWAT teams to maintain order.

4.   Officers share with prisoners a preoccupation with time, fighting to wrest from the job the shift they want or weekend time with their kids. Education and medical care that prisoners receive may seem unfair to officers not able afford them for their own families. In some states, however, strong unions have lobbied successfully for good pay and benefits for prison work.

5.   Leon (Whitey) Thompson, *Last Train to Alcatraz*, 12–13. See the glossary for clarification of prison terminology. Some prisons with newer control units continue to maintain a separate unit for

shorter-term "seg." The differentiation of these units from control units—either may be called "the hole"—is clear in the context of any specific prison, but not across prisons. The trend nationwide suggests that control units tend to drive out aging segregation units.

6. Human Rights Watch, *Cold Storage,* 18.

7. Sundiata Acoli, a member of the Black Liberation Army imprisoned since the early '70s, describes one such early crackdown: "At Trenton State Prison they created a control unit overnight by rounding up two hundred-fifty prisoners . . . within a month . . . they had let everyone else out except for about fifty or sixty of us who were more politically inclined" (Bonnie Kerness, ed., *Uses and Effects of Control Unit Prisons,* 1–2). Accounts of the invention of the control unit vary. Marion had isolation sections called control units in the 1970s, and some writers consider earlier maximum security institutions, like Alcatraz, to be a form of control prison. However, it is the condition of maximum control initiated at Marion in 1983 that has led to calling the proliferation of these units the "marionization" of confinement. See Bonnie Kerness, "Permanent Lockdown in the United States," for a short history and discussion of the racial and legal implications of the crackdown; McShane and McShane, *Encyclopedia of American Prisons,* 317–18; and Bill Dunne, "The U.W. Prison at Marion, Illinois," on Marion Penitentiary. Craig Haney says of control prisons that they are "unique in the modern history of American corrections . . . [they] represent the application of sophisticated, modern technology dedicated entirely to the task of social control, and they isolate, regulate and surveil more effectively than anything that has preceded them" ("Infamous Punishment," 3). Tom Wicker describes the political struggles that preceded Marion (*A Time to Die*); also see Bert Unseem and Peter Kimball, *States of Siege,* on the prison violence that occurred during the 1970s and '80s. Christian Parenti, *Lockdown America,* and Peter B. Kraska, ed., *Militarizing the American Criminal Justice System,* discuss the larger context of changes in policing and criminal justice that have occurred over the past twenty-five years.

8. I am influenced here and throughout this book by Eric L. Santner's *My Own Private Germany.* Santner writes about Daniel Paul Schre-

ber, a psychiatric patient who lived in Germany in the second half of the nineteenth century and was the subject of Freud's theory of paranoia. Santner is interested in the way Schreber's illness suggests certain paradoxical aspects of modernity, some of them prefiguring later events in Germany. He is especially concerned with how institutions are subject to "secretions" of effects—such as madness, excessive uses of force, and perverse knowledge-systems—that expose their internal contradictions.

9.   The literature on control prisons focuses primarily on the negative effects of sensory deprivation and is largely based on interviews conducted as a result of legal action or the work of human rights organizations. See Stuart Grassian, "Psychopathological Effects of Solitary Confinement"; Stuart Grassian and Nancy Friedman, "Effects of Sensory Deprivation in Psychiatric Seclusion and Solitary Confinement"; Haney, "Infamous Punishment" and "Mental Health Issues in Long Term Solitary and Supermax Confinement"; and Human Rights Watch, *Cold Storage*. One Canadian study that found no detrimental effect from sixty days of segregation has been criticized on methodological grounds (see Michael Jackson, *Prisoners of Isolation;* Julian V. Roberts and Robert J. Gebotys, "Prisoners of Isolation"; and Ivan Zinger, Cherami Wichmann, and D. A. Andrews, "The Psychological Effects of 60 Days in Administrative Segregation"). In "Out of Sight," Human Rights Watch provides a set of guidelines for improving conditions in supermaximum security. Also see Fay Dowker and Glenn Good, "The Proliferation of Control Unit Prisons in the United States."

10.   "Institutionalized" is a term used by prisoners and staff and refers to inmates who have become dependent on various aspects of incarceration. See McShane and McShane, *Encyclopedia of American Prisons,* 357–63, on an earlier literature about "prisonization."

11.   The other person in this exchange was my colleague David Lovell. While noise characterizes most control units, a few shut inmates behind heavy, soundproof doors. Grassian, a psychiatrist, explains that both conditions have similar effects. "It isn't a lack of sensory stimulation but a lack of perceptually . . . meaningful . . . stimulation that is really of importance . . . white noise [produces] psychiatric disturbance much more quickly [than silence]" (Bonnie

Kerness and Holbrook Teter, eds., *Survival in Solitary*, 65). Grassian reports: "Experiences described by . . . prisoners included hearing voices—often saying frightening things to them—but usually the prisoners had no means by which to corroborate what they thought they heard . . . Prisoners report that noises take on increasing meaning and frightening significance: 'I hear noises, can't identify them—starts to sound like sticks beating men. But I'm pretty sure no one is being beaten . . . I'm not sure'" (Grassian, "Psychopathological Effects of Solitary Confinement," 1452).

12. Kerness and Teter, eds., *Survival in Solitary*, 33, 21. Depending on their "level" or privileges, prisoners may order books through the mail. I have seen Joel Dyer's *The Perpetual Prison Machine,* Terry Kupers's *Prison Madness* and Parenti's *Lockdown America* in control unit cells. Some prisoners mentioned corresponding with the American Friends Service Committee.

13. The "stonewall" quote is from Kerness and Teter, eds., *Survival in Solitary*, 33. Prisoners who insist that they are "strong-minded" may be embarrassed to admit weakness and may not anticipate the later ill effects of this adaptation. Craig Haney writes of the withdrawal of human contact from control unit prisoners, "Human identity formation occurs by virtue of social contact . . . when our reality is not grounded in social context, the internal stimuli and beliefs that we generate are impossible to test against the reactions of others . . . Some [prisoners] . . . lose the ability to initiate behavior . . . Apathy and lethargy set in . . . In extreme cases, a sense of profound despair and hopelessness is created" ("Infamous Punishment," 4–5).

14. Andrei Moskowitz, "Self-Sufficient Isolation," 27. I cannot do justice here to the complexity of Moskowitz's concept. The design includes provision for family visits, the possibility of occasional social contact with other prisoners, and "maximum creative autonomy" among the prisoners so housed. The individual units are not intended to accommodate the highest security levels. In his patent application for the design Moskowitz writes: "Assuming that the criminal is to be confined, can we devise a system that, as its guiding principle, incorporates many of those positive aspects of confinement that contribute, in the ordinary citizen, to the improve-

ment of his life . . . while dispensing with those aspects . . . that are pointlessly destructive of life and spirit? Can prisons be designed so that confinement leans more toward the quality of discipline rather than torture?" (Patent No. 5,351,450 [10/4/94]). Andrei Moskowitz can be reached at 265 West 72nd Street, New York, NY 10023 (212 721–2280). The notion of a small, governable, and somehow manly domain, so expansively expressed by Moskowitz, can shrink in a control unit to the size of a Bible, regarded by some prison workers as all an inmate needs to lift himself into emotional and spiritual discipline.

15. David J. Rothman, *The Discovery of the Asylum.*

16. Gustave de Beaumont and Alexis de Tocqueville, *On the Penitentiary System,* 72. Contemporary reports suggest that some of the "silent" prisons did succeed in enforcing silence through thick walls, masks, and whippings (Lawrence M. Friedman, *Crime and Punishment in American History,* 79). But preventing what was then called "evil communication" was apparently a constant battle (Robin Evans, *Fabrication of Virtue,* 6).

17. Bentham believed that men were motivated purely by pleasure or pain, and that his prison would rehabilitate because it allowed inmates to avoid pain through their own actions; this calculation of benefit was supposed to extend beyond the individual to the social whole. The utilitarian influence can be seen in Beaumont and Tocqueville's comment that although the penitentiary may not produce "radical reformation" it nevertheless creates "habits of order" that the convict follows on release (*On the Penitentiary System,* 90*).* "The prison was an 'inexorable and inescapable . . . remoulding process by which evil-doers were to be . . . re-formed into industrious and obedient utilitarian citizens" (Douglas G. Long, *Bentham on Liberty,* 218). This is a materialist psychology, a re-forming that cannot come only from the outside. The prisoner's own will is appropriated by the regime in which he is confined, forcing him to calculate how his own interest can be served by his obedience. Later versions of the Panopticon had a smaller central chamber available to a variety of observers and a more complex surveillance hierarchy (Evans, *Fabrication of Virtue,* 438, 198–202).

18. Friedman, *Crime and Punishment,* 155–59.

19. Several commentators on the control prison have drawn a connection to the silent prisons. Although Foucault speaks of the "swarming" of prison discipline into society as a whole in the nineteenth century, providing an illustration of a twentieth-century prison, his work precedes the currently increased popularity of the design in the United States (*Discipline and Punish*).

20. The advertisement is for Aramark Managed Services. Depicting a food tray juxtaposed with the instruments of business management—calculator and account books—the ad points to the juxtaposition of administrative plans and the bodily needs of inmates.

21. Ignatieff, *A Just Measure of Pain*, 9.

22. Beaumont and Tocqueville say that solitary confinement is insufficient and dangerous; "many prisoners . . . only left the solitary cell to go to the hospital" (*On the Penitentiary System*, 163). On corporal punishment in prisons see McShane and McShane, *Encyclopedia of American Prisons*, 115–16.

23. Beaumont and Tocqueville, *On the Penitentiary System*, 44.

24. See Kraska, ed., *Militarizing the American Criminal Justice System*, and Parenti, *Lockdown America*, on the increasing use of such methods across all forms of enforcement.

25. As Kurki and Morris note, "Extractions in a supermax have the quality of an organized test of force, defined in immediate time, to prove who has authority, when that issue is not really in doubt" ("Purposes, Practices, and Problems," 418). Santner suggests that the circularity in play here has, as one of its elements, a conflation of closeness and distance. The institutional power exerted by those in authority exhibits both a profound removal from and an "obscene over proximity" to those who are subject to it. Thus "sites and resources of legitimation"—institutions, hierarchies—"secrete a kind of uncanny surplus of power and influence" (Santner, *Private Germany*, 52, 6).

26. Exceptions are grievances filed internally, which may or may not influence an inmate's treatment, and legal action against the prison system; many changes in prison management have come about through lawsuits.

27. Peter J. Boyer, "Genius of Death Row," 75. This prisoner inadvertently reveals the enmeshment involved in such activity when he

speaks with relish of inmates' expertise at throwing, then immediately complains about their food being contaminated by the filth on the unit.

28. Jarvis Jay Masters, *Finding Freedom,* 40–41. Masters's initial surprise at encountering this behavior suggests how it is passed on from one generation of prisoners to another.

29. Feldman makes a similar point in the context of prison rebellion in Northern Ireland, "To understand the symbolic systems of the H-Blocks . . . it is . . . necessary to abandon the view of symbolization as a purely expressive activity . . . and to take up the notion [that it is] a determining material performance" (Allen Feldman, *Formations of Violence,* 165).

30. Ray Luc Levasseur, "Trouble Coming Every Day," 7.

31. William Ian Miller, *The Anatomy of Disgust,* 51. Miller's argument is inspired by and indebted to Mary Douglas, whose classic *Purity and Danger* proposed a connection across societies between bodily pollution and social boundaries. "When something disgusts us we feel tainted, burdened by the belief that anything that comes into contact with the disgusting thing also acquires the capacity to disgust" (Miller, *Anatomy,* 12).

32. I draw here on the work of Julia Kristeva, who calls the person or thing on the other, contaminating, side of a boundary—that is, the side away from the self—the "abject." Abjection, in her sense, is intimately tied to social life, a condition both outside the human and too-human. "It is . . . not lack of cleanliness or health that causes abjection but what disturbs identity, system, order" (Kelly Oliver, *Reading Kristeva,* 232). Elizabeth Grosz notes that for Kristeva, "Detachable, separable parts of the body . . . retain something of the . . . value of a body part . . . there is still something of the subject bound up with them—which is why they are objects of disgust, loathing and repulsion" (*Volatile Bodies,* 81).

33. As Miller notes, "Those who . . . are . . . insensitive to the disgusting we think of as belonging to somewhat different categories: proto-human like children, subhuman like the mad" (*Anatomy,* 11).

34. Santner calls this turn the "literalizing tendency of institutions." Exploring the intersection where institutional power meets its

object, he writes that social "facts" are necessarily maintained through a repetition of bodily practices and experiences. "The repetitive demand to live in conformity with the social essence with which one has been invested, and thus *to stay on the proper side of a socially consecrated boundary*, is one that is addressed not only or even primarily to the mind or intellect, but to the body" (Santner, *Private Germany*, 12, emphasis in original).

35. Chase has been the subject of a *Sixty Minutes* segment as well as a story in the *New York Times Magazine* in which this drawing originally appeared (Bruce Porter, "Is Solitary Confinement Driving Charlie Chase Crazy?"). Thanks to Charlie Chase for his help.

36. He went on to note a diminishing of injuries since the introduction of pepper spray. "Pepper spray is the best thing we've ever had." The threat of its use creates pressure against defiance from other inmates nearby who don't want to be exposed to it.

37. Kerness and Teter, eds., *Survival in Solitary*, 23.

38. "Younger" here refers to boys and men ages eighteen through early twenties, "older" to men in their late twenties through mid thirties. This prisoner was about twenty.

39. James Gilligan, *Violence*, 114.

40. Gilligan, *Violence*, 132, 111. Gilligan's is one of a number of recent works supporting, if somewhat indirectly, prison officials' perception of increasing numbers of disturbed young men. In *All God's Children* Fox Butterfield describes the historical matrix within which succeeding generations are incarcerated at ever earlier ages. Similarly, Richard Rhodes's *Why They Kill* describes how individuals respond to a social context that "coaches" them to believe that insults must be redressed regardless of the consequences. Parenti's *Lockdown America*, while offering a blistering critique of police and prisons, also describes larger economic and political forces—particularly changes in the labor market—that contribute to social pathology of all kinds. For related perspectives on early experience and violence, see Dorothy Otnow Lewis, *Guilty by Reason of Insanity*, and Robin Karr-Morse and Meredith S. Wiley, *Ghosts from the Nursery*. Kurki and Morris, taking the position that the proliferation of control unit prisons is largely political, doubt that they rep-

resent a real increase in violence. "Have prisoners become more violent, more dangerous? The data do not so suggest. Have the politics of punishment changed? Probably" ("Purposes, Practices, and Problems," 385–86). As Chase Riveland notes, "these prisons have become political symbols of how 'tough' a jurisdiction has become" (*Supermax Prisons*, 5).

41. Sandra Lee Bartky, *Domination and Femininity*, 84.

42. Michael Ignatieff, *The Needs of Strangers*, 50.

43. Of course, each of these things can be distorted—polluted air, contaminated food, indifferent medicine. These then become one basis for protests and legal action based on rights, the only route open.

44. Ignatieff, *Needs of Strangers*, 13, 50.

45. More subtle forms of abuse include teasing and baiting, withholding or delaying needed items or activities, spitting in prisoners' food, and ignoring requests for aid. Many accounts and court cases attest to abusive behavior; prisoners at Clinton prison in upstate New York, for example, have won numerous court cases over excessive use of force by guards (Matthew Purdy, "An Official Culture of Violence Infests a Prison"). The Stanford Prison Experiment, conducted in 1971, is often cited as an example of the situated nature of prison brutality. In the experiment, college students randomly sorted into "guards" and "prisoners" rapidly took on extreme versions of their roles, resulting in such disturbed behavior that the experiment had to be terminated. Johnson questions the generalizability of the Stanford experiment, since the students were "implicitly encouraged to play out stereotypical conceptions" of their roles and, in fact, the majority of the "guards" did not become abusive (Robert Johnson, *Hard Time*, 12). See Mark A. Henry, "Unethical Staff Behavior," for a correctional perspective on managing staff misbehavior.

46. See David Lovell, Kristin Cloyes, David G. Allen, and Lorna A. Rhodes, "Who Lives in Supermaximum Custody?" for a description of Washington's control unit population. Writing of the federal prison at Florence, Colorado, Robert Perkinson says, "[The Bureau of Prisons] offer[s] mostly anecdotal evidence [that these are the 'worst of the worst'], emphasizing details of proverbial prisoner brutality rather than case studies of statistical data. The *Denver*

Post, for example, introduced the ADX with mug shots of Manuel Noriega, John Gotti, and assorted neo-Nazis and serial killers . . . Contrary to [these assertions] shipment to an ADX requires less than grisly stardom. In fact, the designation of a prisoner's security level is an arbitrary process . . . there is no judicial oversight in determining who will be sent" (Perkinson, "Shackled Justice: Florence Federal Penitentiary and the New Politics of Punishment," 123). An article in the *New York Times* about this prison does give statistics, though their source is not cited: "Of the men sent here . . . 35% have committed murder in prison, 41% have tried to escape and 85% have committed assaults in prison" (Brooke, "In 'Super-Max,' Terms of Endurance," 30). See Jackson, *Prisoners of Isolation*, for a brief but thoughtful discussion of the effect on prisoners of the perceived justice or injustice of their detention.

47. From an interview entitled "A New Perspective Warden" in the *Newsletter* of Minnesota Correctional Facility—Oak Park Heights, Nov./Dec. 2001, 4.

48. The reason for changed behavior, however, may be only indirectly related to the fact of detention, as when a prisoner who is being threatened in general population gets into a fight to prove he can defend himself. He will go to "the hole" having made his point and may not need to fight again when he gets out. In that case, has the discipline itself taught him not to fight?

49. See Adam Jay Hirsch, *The Rise of the Penitentiary;* Friedman, *Crime and Punishment;* Angela Y. Davis, "Race and Criminalization"; and Angela Y. Davis, "From the Convict Lease System to the Super-Max Prison." Friedman notes that corporal punishment of slaves was called "correction" (*Crime and Punishment*, 85).

2. THE CHOICE TO BE BAD

1. Charles Stastny and Gabrielle Tyrnauer, in *Who Rules the Joint?* quote an unpublished 1977 paper by John P. Conrad and Simon Dinitz: "The phrase *lawful prison* . . . refers to a prison that both conforms to the law as prescribed by the courts and maintains an orderly regime" (7).

2. Robin Evans, *The Fabrication of Virtue*, 6. A shared "common

sense" is rooted in a common European and specifically Enlightenment history. I do not mean that everyone shares equally in this inheritance or that it doesn't have different meanings depending on one's social positioning. But even prisoners of widely varying backgrounds must contend with these assumptions, because they are built into the operation of the prison itself and shape the context within which differences are negotiated.

3.   Tom Wicker, *A Time to Die,* 46. Wicker, a journalist, was invited into Attica as an observer by the prisoners who had taken it over; he became heavily invested in the ensuing—and eventually failed—negotiation. He writes of himself in the third person throughout the book.

4.   In a commentary on Walter Benjamin's 1920 essay, "Critique of Violence," Jacques Derrida notes, "The word 'enforceability' reminds us that there is no such thing as law that doesn't imply . . . the possibility of being enforced" ("Force of Law," 5). The German word in Benjamin's essay translated as "violence" (*gewalt*) means both violence and authority, and Benjamin is concerned to unpack the relationship implied in their conjunction. This is a different project from that which seeks to determine the boundary between proper and improper use of force (as in, for instance, John Irwin, *Prisons in Turmoil*). Eric Santner, to whom I owe this interpretation of law, points out that because it is impossible to say whether the first imposition of force was legitimate (because no legitimacy preceded it), the law has a performative dimension that threatens to break through its apparent solidity. "At its foundation, the rule of law is sustained not by reason alone but also by the force/violence of a tautologous enunciation—'the law is the law'—which is for Benjamin the source of a chronic institutional disequilibrium and degeneration" (*My Own Private Germany,* 9–10). Compare Thomas Hobbes in 1651: "covenants, being but words and breath, have no force to oblige, contain, constrain or protect any man but what it has from the public sword" (*Leviathan,* 145).

5.   That these instruments tend to retain the aura of this moment can be seen in the frequency with which cuff motifs are displayed in law enforcement catalogs in the form of tie pins, key chains, and other personal items. One administrator proudly wore a handcuff tie pin

given him by one of his supervisors. Going over my thinking here with him, I described the idea that such items fetishize the way force underpins law. "That's right," he agreed. "Too bad it's not based on something else, like maybe books."

6. This point is similar to that made by Charles W. Nuckolls in the title of his book: *Culture: A Problem That Cannot Be Solved.*

7. There are three layers to the sense of agency I am talking about here. One is simply the capacity to act; the second is self-awareness of one's acts—a feeling of being the person in charge of them; and the third is the question of whether and how much one's felt choices are really submission to the enforced or internalized demands of others. Prisoners obviously have reason to struggle with issues of agency. But for prison workers also the imposition of force has a dynamic of inevitability, a logic that can take them over as well. This is one reason they insist that the inmates are in control of whether or not force is applied.

8. David A. Ward, "Supermaximum Custody Prisons in the United States," 31.

9. An interesting aspect of this discussion is that the author is referring to an old study of a "special group" of Alcatraz prisoners to justify the proliferation of the new, rather differently designed supermax prisons. No studies have been done of how well prisoners released from these contemporary prisons actually do, although see Ivan Zinger, Cherami Wichmann, and D. A. Andrews, "The Psychological Effects of 60 Days in Administrative Segregation."

10. I draw here on Charles Taylor's history of the Euro-American self and particularly on his discussion of autonomy and disengagement as important components of that self. As he observes, "If we follow the theme of self-control through the vicissitudes of our Western tradition we find a very profound transmutation, all the way from the hegemony of reason as a vision of cosmic order to the notion of a punctual disengaged subject exercising instrumental control" (*Sources of the Self,* 174). This control is generally framed as a masculine ideal, a point that has been thoroughly unpacked by feminist scholars. My point is not only that a historically grounded vision of the ideal male self is at work here, but that prison workers and prisoners are engaged in self-conscious enactments of this

ideal—or in some cases in counter-performances that play on its terms (cf. Judith Butler, *Gender Trouble*). As James W. Messer-schmidt, writing about prison masculinities, puts it: "Gender is accomplished systematically, rather than imposed on people or set-tled beforehand, and it is never a static or finished product. Instead, people construct gender in specific social situations—different mas-culinities emerge from practices that utilize different resources" ("Masculinities, Crime, and Prison," 68).

11. This is not a suicide threat expressed specifically to me, but a description of general despair of which everyone involved, includ-ing the unit psychologist, is aware.

12. This is also true, of course, of religious materials readily available to prisoners.

13. The differences between Janson and Tuttle on the dimension at issue here emerge from their use of distinct but related technologies of self-making. Janson represents what Nikolas Rose calls the "ethics of enterprise" in which the self is enlisted in a project of "competi-tiveness [and] boldness." Tuttle, on the other hand, takes up the more therapeutic and less entrepreneurial approach of personal growth through self-reflection. Both prisoners reflect a "responsibi-lization" of the self that gives a central role to choice (*Inventing Ourselves*, 157).

14. This method of controlling prisoners has a long history. See Mar-ilyn D. McShane and Frank McShane, *Encyclopedia of American Prisons*, 87–95, for an overview of classification.

15. Some of the major infractions have parallel minor (or "general") infractions, e.g., deliberately causing an inaccurate count versus failure to comply with count; refusing to work versus failure to show up for work. This gives hearing officers some flexibility in their decisions. Some major infractions, of course, are crimes that lead to sentencing in the courts. Others result in loss of good time and longer prison stays without outside adjudication.

16. This man explained: "You know, they call 'em fishes, people who are rookies . . . People do get raped. There's people that get beat up and get all their stuff took."

17. Cell extractions must be videotaped and are postponed until tap-ing begins; a prison worker speaks to the camera describing events

to that point. Requests for the prisoner to comply are recorded. However, during entries the camera is necessarily behind and at times blocked by the team that goes into the cell.

18. The reference to a witness is about the role of officers in backing one another in hearings.

19. Some prisoners speak of the political implications of efforts to make them into "model persons" compliant with mainstream expectations.

20. As in the criminal justice system more generally, "in order [for the criminal] to be held responsible, the essence of [his or her] act can only . . . be captured in its *author*" (Sara L. Knox, *Murder,* 57).

21. Igor Primoratz, *Justifying Legal Punishment,* 34. Primoratz adds, "When dealing with animals, or with the insane, or with children, we normally go by other standards."

22. This officer had worked in a control unit but wanted to transfer to a less restrictive setting because "there [the inmates] have more choices, it's like the real world. In the control unit, you're just catering to 'em."

23. One prisoner responded this way to my question about whether he, like his keepers, thinks that he is in the control unit by choice. "Any choice you make puts you into certain situations and certain situations escalate to other situations . . . it is half and half . . . sometimes it just escalates out of nothing. Aw, man, I don't know! To say that I want to come here, that I made these choices? Oh no, believe me, that is out of line!"

24. In a recent textbook in criminal justice, Don M. Gottfredson places a definition of rationality prominently near the beginning: "A rational decision is the choice, among those possible for the decision maker, that makes it most likely that the objectives of the decision will be achieved." The connection between this emphasis on the volitional nature of misbehavior and recent criminal justice policy is clear: "The view of the criminal in the public mind has transformed into a more volitional, more willful actor . . . If offenders choose crime, after all, then rehabilitation as a response seems less appropriate than severe sanctions designed to tilt the equation in favor of choosing a legitimate alternative" (Don M. Gottfredson, *Exploring Criminal Justice,* 13 and 19, quoting Timothy Flanagan,

"Community Corrections in the Public Mind," *Federal Probation* 60 [3]: 9). Calling this orientation "punitive individualism," Elliott Currie notes, "To some conservative critics, acknowledging that certain social arrangements are more likely to breed crime than others is tantamount to excusing the behavior" (*Crime and Punishment*, 112).

25. Michael R. Gottfredson and Travis Hirschi, *A General Theory of Crime*, 11.

26. The period of prison disruption that led to the development of control units also led to other increasingly governmental approaches to managing behavior; John J. DiIulio's *Governing Prisons* is a classic in this genre and one that was recommended to me early on by a prison official. As Katherine Beckett describes this approach: "'Administrative' or 'managerial' criminology . . . is technocratic, behaviorist and 'realist' in tone and is primarily oriented toward devising new and better techniques for managing the crime problem" (*Making Crime Pay*, 8). The technical preoccupations I describe here are one element in this project; for discussion of this emphasis in law enforcement more generally see Christian Parenti, *Lockdown America*, and Peter B. Kraska, ed., *Militarizing the American Criminal Justice System*.

27. I use "technologies" here to refer to the material means of control. Clearly these are related to technologies in Foucault's sense—that is, to practices of control that produce the subject position of inmates (*Discipline and Punish;* cf. Rose, *Inventing Ourselves*).

28. Prison workers vary, however, in how much investment they are willing to make in the training and attention required by security. Some enthusiastically perfect their marksmanship and train on emergency teams; others regard all such exercises as window-dressing required by distant administrators. One officer mentioned that membership on a team, with its special uniforms and training days, can inspire resentment from peers.

29. Indeed, a couple of years later fishing through the modified doors had resumed.

30. I am not attempting here to offer a picture of how these devices are actually used in prisons. Probably nothing could be less visible to an outsider. My aim is the more modest one of considering how an

extreme or limit-case can bring into sharp relief the question of the relationship between total control and the prisoner's will.

31. Julia Lutsky, quoting from Stun Tech's literature, in "Amnesty International Calls for Stun Belt Ban," 6. The company's name for the belt is "Remote Electronically Activated Control Technology" or "REACT."

32. This comment seems to be an echo of the company's training literature. To my knowledge none of the officers I spoke with about the belt had actually seen a prisoner shocked with it. Amnesty International's report on the stun belt emphasizes the pain and suffering caused by the shock delivered by the belt, the fear induced by its prolonged use during transport, and its use, in some states, to control prisoners during court appearances. They also express concern over the export of these devices to countries in which torture is routinely practiced. They recommend that "federal, state and local authorities ban the use of remote control electro-shock stun belts by law enforcement and correctional agencies, prohibit the manufacture, promotion and distribution (both within and from the USA) of such stun belts [and] suspend the manufacture, use, promotion and transfer (both within and from the USA) of all other electro-shock weapons, such as stun guns, stun shields and tasers, pending the outcome of a rigorous, independent and impartial inquiry into the use and effects of the equipment" (Amnesty International, *Cruelty in Control? The Stun Belt and Other Electroshock Weapons in Law Enforcement.* [1999], available: http://www.amnestyusa.org/rightsforall). Amnesty does not suggest, nor do I, that American prisons routinely use deliberate torture. Nonetheless, the arguments made by Amnesty, Human Rights Watch, and the American Friends Service Committee strongly suggest that we consider how the use of electrical devices—even when they are not "activated"—enters into close proximity to torture. "While some of the more overt forms of physical torture . . . employed by repressive governments and paramilitary groups are not authorized or practiced in the United States at either the federal, state or local levels, there are a number of criminal justice policies and practices that constitute 'cruel, inhuman or degrading treatment or punishment'" (Mark Sher-

man, Bonnie Kerness, and Laura Magnani, *Torture in the United States,* 1).

33. I draw here on Santner's description of institutional disequilibrium and emergency in which he suggests that at the "bottom" of the force underlying the law—on its underside, so to speak—lies torture. The abjection produced by torture can be seen as a "substance" that stands in for a lack of substantial foundations to which the institution might appeal for final and ultimate legitimation (*My Own Private Germany,* 42–43; cf. Michel de Certeau, "The Institution of Rot").

34. One female officer said, "If you want a career in corrections all that stuff [the classes on technical skills] plays into it. In the good old boy system, who are they gonna go for [for promotion]? The guy who's trained in [pepper spray], electric, all of it. It's a bit Rambo."

35. Hugh Gusterson, *Nuclear Rites,* 117. Thus workers in both cases enact, in a very physical way, a form of "freedom from bodily determination . . . and the very materiality of the body" itself (Gusterson, *Nuclear Rites,* quoting Susan Bordo, "Material Girl," 653). Robert Romanyshyn's discussion of the "abandoned" modern body in *Technology as Symptom and Dream* is also helpful in this context.

36. Cf. Elaine Scarry, *The Body in Pain.*

37. The rationale for electroshock devices was expressed by one worker who explained that they are so effective in frightening inmates into compliance that they reduce cell entries, reduce inmate and staff injuries, and avoid uses of pepper spray that cause all inmates in the unit to experience discomfort. He described an incident in which a group of inmates were refusing to leave their cells; he dimmed the lights on the tier and held up the crackling electric shield to one of the "leaders." "His eyes got huge . . . we didn't have a single cell entry that night." This worker had conducted dozens of transports with the belt in which no prisoner had ever "tested" it—in his view a persuasive rationale.

3. THE ASYLUM OF LAST RESORT

1. These men are coming into prison from county jails, which do not operate on the same classification and behavioral systems as pris-

ons. But for many, of course, this is not their first induction to prison.

2.   There are other women in the room who go about their tasks indifferent to the semi-clothed men around them. The officer's warning is delivered in part for my sake as a visitor, but it also points to the prevailing assumption that attention calls forth undesirable behavior.

3.   This is a reference to research on psychological assessment and risk management.

4.   He will be sent to a crowded reception unit where prisoners are housed together without consideration of their crime or behavior; vulnerable prisoners like this one may be harassed or assaulted before they receive the help promised by the screening process.

5.   The expression "get stupid" has connotations that will be explored in the next chapter.

6.   On our way over to the building, the mental health worker mentioned Erving Goffman's study of the psychiatric hospital as a totalizing institution. "Remember *Asylums*?" he asked. "You'll see how dehumanizing works." Goffman's classic description of the ritual stripping of clothes and identity upon entry into an institution does indeed fit this situation (*Asylums,* 14–35).

7.   The screening instrument was adapted in 1996 by Ron Jemelka from the *Referral Decision Scale* developed by Linda Teplin for the Cook County Jail (Chicago). It notes on the first page that the federal courts consider failure to identify and treat psychiatric conditions and suicide risks as denial of medical care and therefore an instance of "cruel and unusual punishment."

8.   It is important to note that I do not address the specifics of mental illness itself, the accuracy of psychiatric diagnosis, or the validity, from a psychiatric perspective, of any particular diagnosis of an individual. I am interested in how diagnosis enters into the prison as a taxonomic project and how the results of this project affect the way prisoners' behavior is understood. Thanks to David Allen for helpful comments on the shaping of this chapter.

9.   This phrase is from H. Richard Lamb and Linda E. Weinberger, "Persons with Severe Mental Illness in Jails and Prisons."

10.   An article in *Corrections Today* describes this situation as "Orwel-

lian": "Imagine that our government deliberately began to cut funding for the chronically mentally ill. Instead, prisons and jails were built to provide public psychiatric care" (Chris Sigurdson, "The Mad, the Bad, and the Abandoned," 70). Changes in the way we define criminal intent and in the laws governing treatment in prison have contributed, along with deinstitutionalization, to the fact that at least 10–15 percent of those in prisons are mentally ill (Lamb and Weinberger, "Persons with Severe Mental Illness," 486). See Fox Butterfield, "Prisons Replace Hospitals for the Nation's Mentally Ill"; Mary L. Durham, "The Impact of Deinstitutionalization on the Current Treatment of the Mentally Ill"; Terry Kupers, *Prison Madness;* E. Fuller Torrey, *Out of the Shadows;* and Theodore Caplow and Jonathan Simon, "Understanding Prison Policy and Population Trends," 68–71. Marilyn D. McShane and Frank McShane, in the *Encyclopedia of American Prisons,* provide a general discussion of issues in prison treatment (320–25). Of one hundred new admissions to Washington prisons in 1988, 8.4 percent were diagnosed with schizophrenia, bipolar illness, or mania; 1.9 percent with schizophreniform disorder; and 10 percent with depression (Ronald Jemelka, Eric Trupin, and J. A. Chiles, "The Mentally Ill in Prisons"). Often prisoners themselves have attempted to find or retain psychiatric care before the crime that leads to their incarceration (Michael Winerip, "Bedlam on the Streets"). As Caroline Knowles points out in "Bedlam on the Streets," many psychiatry-centered accounts fail to show how little psychiatry actually does for mentally ill people who have been relegated to marginal or nonexistent "community" treatment (5).

11. For example, abusive language directed to a staff member can be infracted only if "the inmate knew that the statement was abusive"; tattooing or self-mutilation only if "the inmate knew, or should have known, that his behavior was inappropriate." Leaving aside the ample room for interpretation here, it is clear that an "insanity defense" is built into the system at the level of policy.

12. "Mental illness" is such a standard term that it may seem simply inevitable. But it carries certain unspoken assumptions that have effects on both workers and inmates. In most of psychiatry there has been a strong impulse, over the past forty or so years, to highlight

biological features of the major mental illnesses such as schizophrenia and depression. These conditions are increasingly seen as diseases with predictable symptoms that can be treated with medications. See T. M. Luhrmann, *Of Two Minds,* for a discussion of the split in contemporary psychiatry between biological and psychodynamic approaches, and Allan V. Horwitz, *Creating Mental Illness,* for an overview and critique of diagnostic practices in psychiatry.

13. For a description of how hidden weapons and cell alterations contribute to a successful escape see Joe Jackson and William F. Burke, *Dead Run.*

14. The context for this concern is that officers may need evidence for hearings or—more rarely—for prosecution.

15. One source of time pressure is that each shift has a defined set of tasks that they are not supposed to leave for the workers on the next shift.

16. Kramer represents a worst-case situation of falling through the cracks, resembling other cases of neglect in group homes, home care situations, and psychiatric hospitals. Situations like this are widely described in the news, in accounts by prisoners, and in the human rights literature. Overwhelmed jails are often unable to care adequately for mentally ill inmates; Kramer was sent to this prison not because his sentence required it, but because the unit described here was credited with providing decent psychiatric care.

17. I take the terms "encirclement" and "dilution of punishment" from Jacques Donzelot, *The Policing of Families.* Donzelot describes juvenile treatment in France as a merging of normalization and policing. The system he describes is far more centralized and systematic than psychiatric care in the United States; I give the notion of encirclement a somewhat more positive interpretation than his.

18. Hans Toch, *Mosaic of Despair,* 41, 52. See also Craig Haney, "Mental Health Issues" and the decision in the Boscobel case barring mentally ill prisoners from Wisconsin's supermax prison (*Jones'El v. Berge,* 164 F.Supp.2nd 1096 (W.D. Wis., 2001)).

19. Edward M. Podvoll, *The Seduction of Madness.*

20. Tillich is in prison on a fairly minor drug offense. He says of his fear of general population, "My life was being threatened . . . I came here with the hope and trust that [the corrections department]

would protect me and . . . the whole system betrayed me . . . I arrived at [receiving] depressed and worried, very worried." Tillich's chart says that he "malingers to gain special treatment and gets relief from boredom by being 'at war' with the staff."

21. Louis A. Sass, in *Madness and Modernism,* argues that there are more than coincidental similarities between the phenomenological world of schizophrenia, which often involves a dissociative strangeness, and the modernist evocation of alienating spaces and dislocated objects. This connection suggests, perhaps, that nothing could be worse for mentally ill individuals—other things being equal—than the harsh interiors of modern prison buildings.

22. A control unit inmate described a mentally disturbed neighbor: "You can hear him in there sometimes, when he is talking to himself—he is just lost in a sea of images."

23. Nick Mansfield notes, in *Subjectivity,* "The ownership of the clean and proper body is merely the most intense and emotional example of the orders of law and laws that produce a controlled and manageable subject." The firm boundaries and tight logic of the law are contradicted by the signs of "internal ambiguity and uncertainty" emitted by unkempt, disheveled bodies (85).

24. Elizabeth Lunbeck, in *The Psychiatric Persuasion,* points out that in these discourses the "normal" is a shadowy presence, not actually available but always invoked. This is more so in prison where all are by definition deviant in some way.

25. Most prison units do not have "staffing" meetings at which all or most workers are able to talk together on a regular basis; many mental health units do provide this opportunity, and it is one way in which the differences described in this chapter are sustained.

26. "Decompensation" is a common term in psychiatry meaning to deteriorate into a psychotic or disorganized state; for custody workers it is synonymous with "losing it" or "tweaking."

27. Borderline personality disorder describes extreme difficulties with identity and the regulation of emotion. See Marsha Linehan, *Cognitive-Behavioral Treatment of Borderline Personality Disorder.*

28. Some inmates have been taking medications for years; recent improvements in psychiatric medication have made these effects less likely for those on newer drugs.

29. The process is aided by some inmates' acceptance of help. "The people who declare war on the system are not mental health," explains one counselor. "The mentally ill don't necessarily have a hate thing for the system, it's more normal for them."

30. Some prisoners take an enthusiastic approach to medication management. One young man requested a specific antidepressant during his unit's brief visit from a part-time psychiatrist. "I can see when I'm going off mentally and my mind's getting stirred up. I need to go back to that balance. I want to take it [the antidepressant] at night. Then, if I have a crazy dream I won't wake up with a mood disorder." The psychiatrist gave him the drug he requested and explained in detail the rationale for his regimen of other medications.

31. Therapy in mental health units—of any kind—is often interrupted and difficult to sustain over time. For some inmates, however, contact with sympathetic others, quieter living space, protection, and medication are enough to make a major difference in their experience.

32. Tillich's description of himself could be interpreted as a kind of domestication or pacification, as his resistance is reinterpreted as symptoms and he is diverted from his attacks on the prison system. In the larger sense this may well be true. But in the context of the options available to him, resistance served only to keep him in the control unit while the diversion offered by treatment interrupted what had become a precipitous physical and mental decline. It should be noted that the administrator who got him transferred to the mental health unit was also resistant to "the system," insisting that holding him to further time for infractions was an inappropriate and punitive response to his behavior.

33. Lunbeck describes the psychiatric case as it developed in the early twentieth-century hospital as the product of a "relentless, if uneven, scrutiny." Because it did not work on the tangible physical symptoms of the medical case, this scrutiny required the cooperation of patients; it is "fragments of behavior and experience" that are shaped into the coherent description of a psychiatric illness (*The Psychiatric Persuasion*, 133, 142).

34. Hans Toch ("The Life of Lifers," 8) notes that a parenting model

is common in prisons and takes the form of typical transactions such as "I want, you can't have" and "You must do what I tell you, why should I have to?" "Child-Parent transactions are invariably asymmetrical," in Toch's view, and it is true that mental health units are organized around relationships that are already defined as asymmetrical and authoritarian. I am arguing here that for staff, parenting can provide less authoritarian ways of relating to those seen as having diminished psychological maturity.

35. Some prison workers are skilled at providing coherent therapy based on one or another of these techniques. My purpose here, however, is to provide a general sketch of approaches that are held in everyday as well as expert versions. Both the developmental and behavioral perspectives have the effect of "psychologizing" authority and framing it in terms of the best interests of those subjected to it (Nikolas Rose, *Inventing Ourselves*, 93).

36. Suzanne R. Kirschner, *The Religious and Romantic Origins of Psychoanalysis,* 108. Kirschner, who offers a historical overview of the developmental assumptions underlying a variety of Euro-American religious and therapeutic narratives, notes that this tragic dimension includes antisocial tendencies and the inherent human limitations on both connection and autonomy (109).

37. On the relationship between early experience and criminal behavior see, for example, Robin Karr-Morse and Meredith S. Wiley, *Ghosts from the Nursery;* Dorothy Otnow Lewis, *Guilty by Reason of Insanity;* and, for prisoners' accounts, Jeff Evans, ed., *Undoing Time.*

38. Lonny R. Webb, "Addressing Severe Behavior Problems in a 'Super-Max' Prison Setting," (10). The point, according to one prison worker, is to "catch them being good." This benign interpretation is easily lost in settings where swift and inexorable punishment ("consequence") can be framed in behavioral terms.

39. Cognitive behavioral programs are a more sophisticated version that includes work with inmates' thought-processes.

40. One mental health worker pointed out that the logic of this mode of obedience can entangle both prisoners and staff: "The only reward we can offer is also the goal, to be able to come out [of their cells] and be prosocial. If they demonstrate the ability to do that

they are allowed to do it. It folds back on itself." An earlier discussion of behaviorism is in my "Panoptical Intimacies."

41. The person who told me this story referred me to its source in Buñuel's 1961 film *Viridiana*. Interestingly, in the film the scene does not include the broad sweep or rescuing gesture he remembered.

4. CUSTODY AND TREATMENT AT THE DIVIDE

1. This was a theme in interviews with staff on both control and mental health units who felt that they themselves needed support.

2. "Tentative and shifting alliance" is from John Ransom, *Foucault's Discipline* (21). Foucault defined power not as sheer force but as "action on action" with diffuse effects that cannot be separated from those of knowledge. Ransom argues that Foucault is often misread as saying that therefore power and knowledge are in a purely repressive relation of identity, a reading easily made in light of his use of the prison as his example. Ransom says, "On the one hand, by bringing these two terms [knowledge-power] close together, Foucault dismisses the idea that some form of knowledge (of our true nature, true interests, and so forth) can act as the platform from which we can denounce power. On the other hand, by refusing to collapse them into one big ball of domination, he points to the oppositional possibilities present in the tentative and shifting nature of their alliance" (21). I make use of this interpretation here in approaching the complex ways in which custody and treatment—in their earlier incarnations the very power and knowledge of *Discipline and Punish*—relate to each other in the contemporary prison. In the next chapter I turn to an example of power-knowledge alignment, and in the last chapter, to a situation where they move further apart.

3. Writing of Sing Sing in 1932, Warden Lawes says, " The State of New York, under the able and liberal prompting of its Governor, Franklin D. Roosevelt, [is] hard at work to provide an early method of segregation. But who can guess at the numberless lives that have been shattered and the bodies that have been wrecked by the neglect and indifference of a hundred year old penal policy?" (Lewis E. Lawes, *Twenty Thousand Years*, 176).

4. Correctional counselors do not do therapeutic counseling—the title dates back to the period when they had a more global responsibility. Today, with large caseloads and much paperwork, counselors have little time to spend with individual inmates.

5. From inside prisons this is regarded as a simple fact of life. The siting of prisons, however, is influenced by political and economic forces that converge to place inmates in rural areas far from the cities many of them are from.

6. While it is true that "classification is a main mechanism for creating simplicity and order out of the diversity of most inmate populations," it does not produce the kind of closure the policies and procedures themselves suggest (Michael Tonry, "Prediction and Classification," 328). The impulse to separate inmates from one another and to define them in relation to norms was fundamental to the early prison, at first depending only on architecture to separate individual prisoners from each other. This method quickly proved impossible to sustain. Nineteenth-century Europe and America saw a flowering of classificatory logic, with the "new penology" of the 1870s initiating an early classification phase. Nevertheless the prisons became crowded, chaotic places in which order was maintained by sheer force (David J. Rothman, "Perfecting the Prison," 112; Edgardo Rotman, "The Failure of Reform," 156; Lawrence M. Friedman, *Crime and Punishment*). A wave of reform in the 1920s is responsible for the first version of the classification systems used today. "Case work" was incorporated into a therapeutic model emphasizing diagnosis and "individualized design . . . responding to each offender's needs" (Rotman, "Failure of Reform," 164). But efforts to bring in teams of professionals to test, interview, and plan therapeutic regimens poorly withstood the "capricious environment" of the prison. James Austin and John Irwin describe the rehabilitative enthusiasm of the 1950s and include a devastating prisoner account of resistance to "group therapy" in a California prison (*It's about Time*, 45). Austin and Irwin offer a clear description of types of classification (99–100); see Marilyn D. McShane and Frank McShane, *Encyclopedia of American Prisons*, 87–96, for a brief history.

7. Some prisoners remarked that "ordinary" fighting should not be

infracted, suggesting that the energy spent on penalizing it was unnecessary. One said, "They're gonna fight until they get tired . . . I mean, sure, you have to prove yourself to somebody and get beat up, but what's a black eye, a broken nose? That ain't nothing . . . usually an ass-whippin' will get you over . . . It's a different world in here."

8. For examples, see Julian V. Roberts and Robert J. Gebotys, "Prisoners of Isolation"; Rothman, "Perfecting the Prison"; and Rotman, "Failure of Reform."

9. John Irwin, *The Felon*, 52, 53. This suspicion corresponded to an increased politicization and an increase in alliances between prisoners and the outside world that occurred at that time (Irwin, *Prisons in Turmoil;* Tom Wicker, *A Time to Die*).

10. Austin and Irwin, *It's about Time*, 97.

11. While the seriously mentally ill have to be treated under the law, that grab bag of treatment described by Irwin would today be called "frills." Other changes have also contributed to the narrowed sense in which treatment is used today. One is that psychiatry itself has changed a great deal since the days of those "solutions to psychological problems" in the California prisons, becoming more medically and biologically oriented. Custody has changed in the direction of professionalization and bureaucratization, with centralized classification systems and procedures based on "ostensibly valid scientific methods or knowledge" (Austin and Irwin, *It's about Time*, 98).

12. American Psychiatric Association, *Diagnostic and Statistical Manual—Fourth Edition,* 273. The diagnostic manual has taken on increasing importance because of its use as the basis for insurance claims. See Donald M. Lowe, *The Body in Late Capitalist USA,* for a critical discussion of how psychiatric categories and professionals have entered into many institutional arenas.

13. A version of this story appears in my "Taxonomic Anxieties."

14. I met Mullen again a couple of weeks after his admission. He explained that he was frightened to go into general population and concerned that his anxiety would be apparent to stronger inmates.

15. In the period since the treatment era described by Irwin, which

relied on a variety of "therapeutic"—often developmental—orientations, psychiatry went through a classificatory revolution that is represented by changes in the succeeding volumes of the *DSM*. Early editions were based on a medical model of mental disorders and included theories of causation, while the two latest editions (III and IV) are primarily behavioral and descriptive. Descriptions of the history, current use, and theoretical implications of the *DSM* taxonomy can be found in Atwood Gaines, "From DSM-I to III-R"; Allan V. Horwitz, *Creating Mental Illness;* Mitchell Wilson, "*DSM*-III and the Transformation of American Psychiatry"; and Allan Young, *Harmony of Illusions.*

16. American Psychiatric Association, *Diagnostic and Statistical Manual-IV*, 629; Lowe, *Body in Late Capitalist USA*, 157. The other three axes deal with physical conditions, psychosocial stressors, and assessment of functioning. The *DSM* taxonomy is mostly context-free: "stressors" and "vulnerabilities" are mentioned, but the individual is the target only as a collection of features. The effect is to naturalize the categories so that they "take on the look of something . . . not made by human hands" (Wilson, "*DSM*-III," 408). Critics of the *DSM* within psychiatry point out that this approach encourages clinicians to minimize the patient's story in order to "look *for* the symptoms needed to make the diagnosis" (Gary Tucker, "Putting *DSM*-IV in Perspective," 160). Or, as one prison mental health worker put it, "The trouble with diagnosis is tilting the patient to it."

17. As many observers and patients note, chronic mental illnesses such as schizophrenia do in fact become entangled with self-identity. For a compelling discussion of this point, see Sue E. Estroff, "Identity, Disability, and Schizophrenia."

18. T. M. Luhrmann, *Of Two Minds,* 14, 115.

19. This officer gave as an additional example an inmate snitching on another and not thinking that "if you get caught ratting you can get hurt."

20. There's an interesting slip of the tongue in this remark—"any other welfare inmate." The outside provision for "need" here blurs with that inside; the inmate with the "penitentiary stink" cannot escape being framed as needy and damaged in either case.

21. For example, a prisoner who had been in a control unit for several

years described how, when placed back in population, he tried to get his "stupid" cellie to do his share of chores.

22. This issue is similar to what is called "secondary gain" in psychiatry—that is, the benefit derived from an illness. Thanks to David Lovell for pointing out this connection.

23. If one asks about the rule lying behind this discussion—"Does the disciplinary process trump diagnosis?"—prison workers often answer, as this one did, "Yes. Especially if a guy's high enough functioning to be out in main line . . . then we expect that he has the skills to face these [difficult] situations and deal with them." In other contexts, however, the same people may speak of intervening in a variety of overt and covert ways to help or sympathize with vulnerable prisoners.

24. This is true of the major psychiatric medications, which are generally recognized to be difficult for patients. Note that the providers of meds are a "they"—this aspect of treatment is most remote from the officers, taking place to some extent behind the veil of medical confidentiality. Custody workers are sometimes sharply critical of minimal or incompetent treatment, as seen in this comment by an officer, "Right now they have [that inmate] way over-drugged. It scares me because it is to the point where he can't keep his balance. Always stoned out, yeah."

25. The deal was a trip to the day room. This is typical of the seemingly small and very concrete stakes in these situations.

26. A larger conflict is suggested in the custody worker's critique. He resents the "school stuff," "writing," and "high and mighty" position of those in mental health who have more education and are more middle class. This sore point is further aggravated by custody workers' sense that even in their own communities, "we're treated funny because we work [in prison]; we're second-class citizens. We get dumped on." In relation to community, management, and treatment, custody workers sometimes feel that "you're the low man on the totem pole, everyone goes around you." These issues come together in the following remark, in which the mental health workers are represented as deluding themselves on the basis of their "expert" knowledge while the custody workers have to do the enforcement and janitorial tasks.

I don't have the schooling to change personality. Sometimes counselors are egotistical and think they can change [the inmates] and we know they don't. We are down in the elbow grease, cleaning up after them; the counselors see them for twenty minutes and the doctors talk to them through the doors. I wish they would spend more time.

27. One officer offered this critique: "There are some [line staff] have never had any authority over anything other than their dog. And now all of a sudden you have the ability to shoot somebody."

5. THE GAMES RUN DEEP

1. No nationwide information is available on the length of control unit confinement. See the appendix for information on Washington State. The reader should bear in mind that issues in states that practice large-scale preventive detention may differ from those explored in this chapter.

2. Avery Gordon, discussing slavery and the connections among profit, accounting, and the counting of humans as property, speaks of "the haunting way systemic compulsions work on and through people in everyday life" (*Ghostly Matters*, 197).

3. As one senior custody supervisor explained firmly to his students, "You gotta talk to [inmates]. We can't just kick ass the way we used to. When I first started, they didn't teach verbal tactical skills. If I told inmates to come out [of a cell] and they told me to piss up a rope, we went in and got 'em out." This emphasis on language as the medium of control is a counterpoint to the assertion that the law is the stable underpinning of the prison. Discussing the Rodney King incident and the insistence by police that the subject of their attack was beyond verbal intervention, Allen Feldman notes, "The subject in logos is the subject in law. The further removed the arrestee is from language, the closer . . . to the body and thus, closer to escalating violence by the state" ("On Cultural Anesthesia," 410).

4. Both white and black "inmates" appear in correctional advertising; however, some ads, like this one, play specifically on themes of racialized menace.

5. Anthony Giddens, in *Consequences of Modernity*, suggests that modernity is characterized by faith in "abstract systems" operated on professional knowledge not available to the layperson. Prisons are such a system, yet one that is not so obviously professional; thus, as we saw in the last chapter, prison staff work to maintain a sense that what they do constitutes a special form of knowledge. One element in this knowledge is, as John Irwin notes, the basic provision that prisoners cannot be trusted (*The Felon*).

6. James Topham, "The Sting," 20. The process of learning to work in prison is more complex than I can do justice to here. Ted Conover writes of his entry into working at Sing Sing that pressure from peers was the most important element in the socialization of officers. "Officers critiqued the permissiveness they perceived in each other more than any other quality" (*Newjack*, 90).

7. The point of the cautionary lessons in training is to prevent seemingly harmless but potentially dangerous connections; involvement with inmates at any level constitutes a form of "getting stupid" for staff. The most obvious instance of breakdown at the boundary is, of course, a sexual relationship between staff member and prisoner; supplying drugs and other contraband is also a temptation. A serious failure to maintain distance is described as a "fall," the same term inmates use for the crime that put them in prison.

8. Topham, "The Sting," 21. Alternative perspectives on manipulation are available in the psychiatric literature. Marsha Linehan, for example, writes of therapy with borderline patients: "Inferring behavioral intent from one or more of the effects of the behavior—in this case, making others feel manipulated—is simply an error in logic. The fact that a behavior is influenced by its effects on the environment ('operant behavior' in behavioral terms) says little if anything about an individual's intent with respect to that behavior" (*Cognitive-Behavioral Treatment*, 17). Many prisoners, turning the tables on their keepers, see both the treatment accorded them in prison and the fact of their incarceration as the intended consequence of larger political manipulations on the part of the corrections department or the government.

9. Don Sabo, in "Doing Time, Doing Masculinity," describes a hier-

archy of prison masculinities that channels prisoners into several different representations or versions of strength (e.g., being tough but also jailhouse lawyering) and weakness (e.g., the role of woman or "punk"). Despite relentless pressure toward the more competitive "masculine" identifications, some prison settings provide resources for prisoners who want to enact other versions of masculinity, including religious and therapeutic groups, friendships with other prisoners, and connections to relatives and friends outside. Sabo and his coauthors stress that masculine identifications are susceptible to change and may be quite unstable in the lives of particular prisoners. We saw evidence in our interviews that younger inmates in particular were considering the various options they felt were available. Several described their recruitment by particular groups and how, in solitary, they were weighing the advantages and disadvantages of membership.

10. Andrews's chart records a tangle of sometimes contradictory diagnoses, including that of "antisocial features," he has received throughout his life. The one that captures his imagination is posttraumatic stress disorder. He remarks on a psychologist's note that he needed treatment for it in childhood: "I could have been an entirely different individual."

11. Some of the material in the remainder of this chapter appears in my "Psychopathy and the Face of Control in Supermax."

12. N. Katherine Hayles makes this observation in *How We Became Posthuman,* discussing the work of Philip Dick, the science fiction writer whose novel *Do Androids Dream of Electric Sheep?* is the basis for the film (169). Thanks to Sarah Elter for helpful comments on *Blade Runner* at an early stage in the writing of this chapter.

13. "What is interesting to me is that between 1913 and today we are still looking for the same traits while having few answers as to why this behavior occurs" (James A. Gondles, Jr., "The Criminal Mind," 6). Thus introduced, the articles in the rest of this issue of *Corrections Today* outline various approaches to personality typing and criminal thinking. Alternative perspectives on this diagnostic territory can be found in Joel A. Dvoskin, "Sticks and Stones," Linehan, *Cognitive-Behavioral Treatment,* and Hans Toch, "Psychopathy or Antisocial Personality." Clinicians and commentators on criminal

behavior differ sharply about whether it can be changed; Gondles takes the position that prisoners should receive treatment despite the fact that their condition is poorly understood.

14. "The looping effects of human kinds" is the title of a 1994 paper by Ian Hacking; "true, natural kinds of persons" is from his *Social Construction of What?* 105. My thinking here is particularly influenced by Hacking's "Making Up People," in which he suggests that psychiatric categories and their objects are related in a "dynamic nominalism" (228). In his work on multiple personality disorder, Hacking argues that "the fact that a certain type of mental illness appears only in specific historical or geographical contexts does not imply that it is manufactured, artificial or in any other way not real" (*Rewriting the Soul,* 12). As Allan Young also points out in his discussion of post-traumatic stress disorder, both psychologically and historically, "the discourse and its object evolve together" (*Harmony of Illusions,* 41), though part of this process is to conceal the fact that it has occurred. Hacking's *Social Construction* and Allan V. Horwitz's *Creating Mental Illness* provide useful discussions of how the "natural" is both an aspect and a product of illness constructions.

15. Hacking, "Making Up People," 236.

16. Robert D. Hare, *Without Conscience,* xi. Psychopathy does not appear as a diagnostic category in the *Diagnostic and Statistical Manual.* Antisocial personality disorder, located on Axis II, is described as "a pervasive pattern of disregard for and violation of the rights of others." The diagnosis depends on and assumes access to police, prison, and hospital records indicative of a criminal history. Hare differentiates psychopathy from antisocial personality disorder: "'Antisocial personality disorder' refers primarily to a cluster of criminal and antisocial behaviors. The majority of criminals easily meet [these criteria]. 'Psychopathy' on the other hand, is defined by a cluster of both personality traits and socially deviant behaviors. Most criminals are *not* psychopaths" (Hare, *Without Conscience,* 25; see also Dennis M. Doren, *Understanding and Treating the Psychopath,* 25, and Grant T. Harris et al., "The Construct of Psychopathy"). Hare's checklist and similar instruments are incorporated into a number of risk-assessment strategies in prisons

although some prison workers complain, in the words of one, that these strategies can be "bastardized and misused" to overextend their reach. Relatively few inmates, however, even in control units, are considered "psychopaths." For discussion of the personality disorders in psychiatric training see Luhrmann, *Of Two Minds;* for a classical clinical approach see Otto F. Kernberg, *Severe Personality Disorders.* For histories of the diagnoses of antisocial personality disorder and psychopathy see Doren, *Understanding and Treating,* and Charles W. Nuckolls, "Toward a Cultural History of the Personality Disorders."

17. The 1989 film *Chameleon Street* depicts a shape-shifting con artist and ends with a variation on this story, the last line of which is "It's my *character.*"

18. Michel Foucault, "The Dangerous Individual," 126, 150. Foucault's point in "Dangerous Individual" is that in the early nineteenth century the relatively straightforward—and primarily juridical—question of whether or not a person was guilty of a specific crime gave way to the question of whether he was "dangerous." It was here that psychiatrists (then called alienists) were called in—and figured themselves as experts—to determine motive or orientation. In Foucault's view, "the 'criminality' of an individual . . . the index of his dangerousness . . . his potential for future behavior . . . can be made to function in a rational way only within a technical-knowledge-system . . . capable of characterizing a criminal individual in himself and in a sense beneath his acts." Foucault considers this access to the "motives" of dangerous individuals one piece in the larger nineteenth-century project to gain control over populations; it was not only a way to control these individuals themselves, but also provided evidence that access to individual motives in general was necessary for social order. Once motives take center stage in criminal justice, punishment comes to bear "on the criminal himself rather than the crime, that is, on what makes him a criminal," and protecting society from danger becomes a matter of producing knowledge about his "inner will." This is a different project from that of the utilitarian prison and creates, as Foucault notes, "the play of [uncertainty] between penal responsibility and psychological determinism [that] has become the cross of legal and medical thought" (144, 140).

19. Nuckolls uses the life of Max Weber as an example of the familial and gendered aspects of personality differentiation.

20. Nuckolls, *Culture,* 151–52; Nuckolls, "Toward a Cultural History," 45. The literature on psychopathy is quick to point out that this personality style is not limited to criminality and may make for success in business and government. In a kind of tongue-in-cheek commentary, a pamphlet for treatment workers at Atascadero State Hospital (a prison hospital) entitled "Profiling and Managing Psychopaths" is illustrated with Dilbert cartoons.

21. Mark Selzer discusses the connections—what he calls the "radical entanglement"—of uses of numbers, mechanized ways of viewing and handling bodies, and industrial capitalism at the turn of the twentieth century (*Bodies and Machines,* 15). Also see Robert Romanyshyn's *Technology as Symptom and Dream,* in which he suggests that modernity has given rise to various paired figures representing its sanitized and shadow aspects.

22. Women are much more rarely described as psychopathic.

23. Susan Bordo uses the term "crystallization" to refer to the way anorexia nervosa connects multiple aspects of personal identity and cultural preoccupation ("Anorexia Nervosa," 139).

24. She went on to describe interactions with such prisoners in which she tried to change their thinking. "When the guys were talking about their crimes, I would correct their terminology, mirror it back to them, try to get them to see that 'I fell in love' was really about lust. [One inmate] would have tears in his eyes—he said, 'You make it sound so bad.' I said, 'It was really *bad*—you changed that woman's life forever.'"

25. Some writers on this topic distinguish between sympathy and empathy, arguing that empathy involves the projection of self into another and therefore is not inconsistent with sadistic forms of crime (see, for example, Roy F. Baumeister, *Evil,* 245). Sympathy and empathy are used interchangeably in prison for fellow feeling, but empathy is most often used in relation to the dangers of manipulation. Prison workers speak of "rapport" to describe good relations with individual prisoners.

26. Robert Hare, Lecture, University of Washington, Seattle, October 30, 1998.

27. Doren, *Understanding and Treating.*

28. Ken Magid and Carole A. McKelvey, *High Risk,* 73; one expert on the treatment of conduct-disordered children warns, "If, at any step, things go wrong, lasting and severe psychopathology may result . . . the results of such trauma are not pretty" (F. Cline, *Understanding and Treating the Severely Disturbed Child,* 27, 129).

29. A large clinical and popular literature discusses child abuse and antisocial behavior. Some writers on psychopathy regard brutal child rearing as necessary (if not sufficient) to produce the condition but others, for example Jonathan Kellerman (*Savage Spawn*) and Hare (*Without Conscience*), insist that "good" parents may produce criminally inclined children for whom there seems to be no environmental explanation (the classic here is Stanton E. Samenow, *Inside the Criminal Mind*). Hare uses brain scans and other tests in an attempt to show that the brains of individuals diagnosed with psychopathy are not responsive to affectively charged words—thus, that these individuals experience all language similarly. "An absence of emotion in the eyes " (J. Reid Meloy, *The Psychopathic Mind,* 71) and a compelling presence (Magid and McKelvey, *High Risk*) are frequent themes in this literature; see also C. Fred Alford, *What Evil Means to Us.* Henry Richards suggests that the "predator" is an archetype with which psychopathic individuals merge through "identification of the actual self with the idealized, destructive self," producing an "inverse conscience" ("Evil Intent," 76). These accounts of a psychologically or biologically deviant developmental process in psychopathy contain an implicit model of what the normal or ideal path through childhood should look like. This model is, in turn, connected to religious and romantic traditions that describe the soul in terms of movement and progress (Suzanne R. Kirschner, *The Religious and Romantic Origins of Psychoanalysis,* 10). See Elliott Currie for a contrasting discussion of the questionable basis and political usefulness of the idea that criminals, particularly younger ones, "cannot change" (*Crime and Punishment*).

30. Some speak of the death penalty not in terms of its larger justification or effects but in terms of what it offers them specifically: relief from the prospect of lifetime engagement with the most problematic prisoners.

31. The full title of Hare's book—*Without Conscience: The Disturbing World of the Psychopaths among Us*—makes clear the us/them separation so central to this discourse.

32. He elaborated this by saying that unconditional empathy was harmful to these inmates and to those around them, but that *conditional* regard had at least a hope of influencing their behavior (though not their "nature").

33. "[Psychopaths] are gamers," a prison worker explained. "Everything they say is nonsense." At a public lecture Hare showed a video interview of a prisoner telling the story of his crime—convincingly, at least to me—and then pointed out the numerous discrepancies between his account and the actual event. He described the watchful psychopath taking a lie-detector test as "like a python ready to strike. [His] relationship with others is that of predator to prey; you are an object [to him]. He's not aroused, but checking how he's doing" (Hare lecture, Seattle, October 30, 1998). Hans Toch points to the circularity of the fact that once the diagnosis is made, all speech is suspect: "Psychopaths by definition [are] manipulators, and anything they [say] about themselves . . . a means to some self-serving (and usually nefarious) end" ("Psychopathy or Antisocial Personality in Forensic Settings," 154).

34. Hervey Cleckley, M.D., *The Mask of Sanity*, 234, 238. Cleckley differs from Hare in assuming, with earlier writers on moral insanity, that the inability to engage in moral reasoning is a kind of illness. "We [are dealing] with a person who has no capacity of distinguishing between what is acting and what is not" (*Mask of Sanity*, 70). In *My Own Private Germany*, Eric Santner describes how at the point where law bottoms out, the haunting possibility emerges that moral agency rests on endless repetition (performance) with no "human" core. He regards this possibility as a kind of secret that is leaked in certain institutional and domestic interactions; similarly in prison, the instrumentality attributed to psychopaths seems to be where a secret about the repetitive and possibly mechanical nature of social performances is touched on (94). Richard Tithecott notes that in the case of serial killers and to some extent criminals in general, a theme of mechanical repetition of crimes recurs and appears uncannily familiar. "How different," he

asks, "are our killing machines from our male machines? . . . it is logical for such machines to regard others as mirror reflections of themselves" (*Of Men and Monsters,* 97).

35. Some descriptions in the literature on psychopathy make heavy use of animal imagery to insist on intuition as an important indicator for the diagnosis. Meloy notes that clinical staff have "counter transference reactions" to psychopathic patients that signify a "primitive, autonomic, and fearful response to a predator"; he suggests that severely psychopathic individuals should be seen, if at all, "only in a highly structured and secure in-patient setting" (*Psychopathic Mind,* 70, 314).

36. One prisoner described another: "He's a really strong person . . . and I think he's a sociopath . . . he's really calculating and intelligent. He reminds me more of a majestic creature, like a shark or a tiger, one of the more solitary cats than he does a human being."

37. See Alford, *What Evil Means,* for a discussion of evil that includes prisoners' comments.

38. Gordon, *Ghostly Matters,* 54, 49, 54, emphases in original. Gordon notes that the uncanny is something that "knocks" for admittance into signification precisely because its outline can be recognized (cf. Freud, "The Uncanny"). "Uncanny experiences are where the unconscious rejoins its animistic and social roots, where we are reminded that what lies between society and psyche is hardly inert empty space" (*Ghostly Matters,* 49).

39. "It is not enough" Judith Butler writes, "to claim that human subjects are constructed, for the construction of the human is a differential operation that produces the more and the less 'human,' the inhuman, the humanly unthinkable. These excluded sites come to bound the 'human' as its constitutive outside, and to haunt those boundaries as the persistent possibility of their disruption and rearticulation" (*Bodies That Matter,* 8). See Piers Benn, "Freedom, Resentment, and the Psychopath," for a debate about the implications of psychopathy that centers on the ethical issues posed by a "less than human" motivation.

40. See Robert D. Hare, "The Hare PCL-R" on the use of his checklist. Robert H. Ressler and Rom Shachtman's account of the devel-

opment of profiling, *Whoever Fights Monsters*, contains themes similar to those discussed by Hare.

41. Lauren Berlant, *The Queen of America* (15). Berlant suggests that over the past two decades the public sphere has become increasingly represented in terms of "faces," with an emphasis on "infantilized," apolitical images such as the child, the fetus, and the immigrant. These citizens are imagined as individual idealized types who "make only particular kinds of national life iconic" (11). In the case of psychopathy, the "superpredator"—popularized in William J. Bennett and John J. DiIulio's *Body Count*—was the iconic image congruent with the prison-growth policies of the 1980s. For a discussion of the complex way in which prison growth, disproportionate imprisonment of minorities, and public perceptions of crime intersect, see Theodore Caplow and Jonathan Simon, "Understanding Prison Policy."

42. Katherine Beckett, *Making Crime Pay*, 47.

43. Magid and McKelvey, *High Risk*, 17; see also Mark Seltzer, *Serial Killers*, on the seeming ordinariness of some criminals.

44. If the imagery surrounding psychopathy prominently included a blatant racial dimension the argument would be a simple one. But in fact it is more subtle in its invocation of race, including both the notion that it is psychologically valid to consider some humans to be a species apart and the assumptions that psychopaths *look* "ordinary," "normal," and, by extension, white. Perhaps this anonymous image—both profoundly "other" and, for the white "majority," eerily "ourselves"—serves to lend an aura of rationality and fairness to incarceration. A study comparing blacks and whites using Hare's checklist supports the possibility that blacks receive higher (more psychopathic) scores. The researchers conclude that "the lack of congruence between ratings of Blacks and Whites . . . raises questions about the appropriateness of using the [psychopathy checklist] with Blacks . . . we cannot presume that our constructs generalize across race" (David S. Kosson, Stevens S. Smith, and Joseph P. Newman, "Evaluating the Construct Validity of Psychopathy in Black and White Male Inmates," 257). However, their work is reported entirely in terms internal to the diagnostic terminology

developed by Hare, and does not address the implications of the fact that Hare's checklist is widely used for black as well as white offenders. While careful clinicians in and outside prisons may be sensitive to these issues, as Christian Parenti points out, "criminal justice . . . reproduces racism in a coded and thus ideologically palatable fashion" (*Lockdown America,* 242). Angela Davis notes, "The current notion that the 'criminals' with which prisons are overcrowded are largely beyond the pale of rehabilitation—that 'nothing works'—is very much connected with the fact [that] . . . 'black' and 'male'. . . have become virtually synonymous with 'criminal' in the popular imagination" ("From the Convict Lease System to the Super-Max Prison," 62). For a critical discussion of race and forensic psychiatry from a British perspective, see Suman Fernando, David Ndegwa, and Melba Wilson, *Forensic Psychiatry.*

6. STRUGGLING IT OUT

1. It is beyond my scope here to describe all of the elements that went into changes on this unit or to explore the complex and shifting relationship it maintains with the rest of the prison system.

2. Toch suggests that these prisons are not likely to be emptied in the near future and argues that fairly simple changes in practice can ameliorate the effects of a dehumanizing technology that treats prisoners as "animate objects" (Hans Toch, "The Future of Supermax Confinement," 11). Toch visited this prison as a guest of our project; later when we received this paper shortly before it was published, I sent it to John Larson, who distributed it to his staff. He began the discussion I've quoted by saying, "[When Toch came here] his sense of vision was too far advanced for me. I didn't agree with him . . . I was kind of naïve; I was defensive. I had no knowledge of the history he portrays."

3. My discussion of reform in this chapter engages Foucault's perspective on historical change, which has been taken up by numerous others to insist that reform can do nothing but perpetuate what is already in place. However, I am influenced by Ransom and by Megill, who both offer more open and optimistic interpretations of Foucault's position. "There is a temptation to derive from Fou-

cault's history of the prison true propositions regarding the actual institution within society that we know as the prison. But it is an error to try to derive from Foucault such propositions as, for example, 'the prison exists in order to foster delinquency and thus to provide a rationale for strengthening the instruments of repression.' Rather, what one . . . finds [in Foucault] are . . . perspectives that may allow us to see more clearly the world in which we live—and may perhaps help us in attempts to alter that world" (Allan Megill, *Prophets of Extremity,* 246; see also John S. Ransom, *Foucault's Discipline*).

4. The narrative of reform is in the background of discussions in earlier chapters of treatment and of earlier historical moments in which changes occurred in prisons. "Reform was the language of narrative coherence in an era when prisons were supposed to rehabilitate criminals" (Charles Bright, *Powers That Punish,* 298). These efforts are now congealed into oppositions such as custody and treatment that have become facts of prison life. In the situation I describe in this chapter, however, the congealing process has not (yet) occurred.

5. Grievances, which can be filed by both inmates and staff, multiply on both sides in a deteriorating environment.

6. This is problematic: as I discussed in the last chapter, both physical and emotional hardening can be part of the problem rather than a solution to violence. From the perspective of prison workers, however, a major source of aggression and violence by staff is insecurity about their own safety. The belief driving the emphasis on the physical plant is that a safe environment allows both staff and inmates to relax and staff to relate more directly to inmates. No inmates we spoke with complained about changes that made it harder to throw feces from cells or to make weapons out of cell fixtures. From the point of view of staff, these changes have the potential to locate hardness in the environment rather than in the staff. Intensified security can also produce increased brutality; I do not assume that what happened in this particular setting is a necessarily expectable result of these measures, but improvement occurred in this case.

7. Alexander W. Pisciotta, *Benevolent Repression,* 62. David J. Rothman

contrasts, similarly, "conscience and convenience" (*Conscience and Convenience*).

8. An exception, and the place where the most trenchant American critique of reform has developed, is the radical reform movements of the 1960s and '70s, which assumed not that the problem lay with individuals (either as crime or as behavior in prison) but that the larger society should abolish prisons as part of a reform of itself (cf. Tom Wicker, *A Time to Die;* John Irwin, *Prisons in Turmoil;* Eric Cummins, *The Rise and Fall of California's Radical Prison Movement*).

9. In *Madness and Civilization* Foucault speaks dismissively of reform as the "incidental music of history"; in later work, however, his perspective on change is more nuanced. His suggestive remarks about "subjugated knowledges," his discussion of the role of chance, and his analysis of power/knowledge and resistance, taken overall, point to the possibility that "vehicles of discipline might go off the designated path" (Ransom, *Foucault's Discipline,* 36).

10. In one description of a particular moment of reform, Pisciotta in *Benevolent Repression* shows that the "reformatory movement" of the late nineteenth century was in fact a moving target of appearance and practice, imitation and conflict. Zebulon Brockway, who created the first Reformatory in Elmira, New York, in the 1870s, proposed a system of incarceration for teenage and young adult men that would "reform" them by providing work, training, and education. The larger impulse behind the reformatory movement is the mid-nineteenth-century shift of focus toward "the criminal, not the crime" discussed in previous chapters. Arguments about making prison life too easy—"one glad sweet song," according to one observer—were arrayed against the notion that criminals were victims of circumstances (128).

11. Bright, *Powers That Punish,* 307. Bright adds that this "apparent humaneness . . . is . . . linked to a guarantee of bourgeois class assumptions about the benign and beneficial nature of progress" (308).

12. Bright's discussion of differences between earlier twentieth-century prisons and the contemporary situation has influenced my thinking in this chapter. He writes that the current project focuses on

"identifying those who do not belong and are to be permanently excluded. Here the illusions of compliance that the prison once sustained are no longer necessary, because . . . inclusion is no longer a goal and willing compliance no longer expected of those with no prospects of access [to social resources]." Bright argues that "a prison that was part of the production of political life and the constitution of moral knowledge was itself constituted by its inmates, who were empowered in historically specific, albeit limited, ways by the redemptive promises of the prison." While "in earlier prison literature, there is always some part of the prison that makes some bond with the inmate . . . [today we see] almost complete alienation [of prisoner from prison and larger society]" (*Powers That Punish,* 317, 316).

13. Peter Scharf, "Empty Bars," 29, 30.

14. Bright, *Powers That Punish,* 316.

15. Anna Tsing raises the possibility that "governmentalities are themselves situated, contradictory, effervescent or culturally circumscribed" ("Global Situation," 340). Effervescence of course makes anthropologists and sociologists think of Emile Durkheim and of the notion that social solidarity depends on emotional moments of group enthusiasm. Though I mean it here in a more general way to point to twists and turns of practices and discourses, it will become clear that "connection" has also become a prevailing theme on the unit.

16. Ransom, *Foucault's Discipline,* 36.

17. He found that the inmate's mother had moved without leaving a forwarding number. A few young prisoners we interviewed volunteered that their families refused their calls and letters.

18. Some readers may find this description of tier walks improbable. The practice does exist at other prisons and has been common historically. My account draws on participation in tier walks at this institution over a three-year period. Some inmates I met on the tiers had already been interviewed by my colleagues or me, and I was able to talk with them further at cellfront. Inmates also told us about this practice in our interviews. Because the group disperses during the process of walking the unit, I had many opportunities to speak with inmates away from staff. I am not arguing here that

this practice is simply an additional form of "order" in the prison—
though it can no doubt become that—but that it disrupts some of
the ways in which the prison is normally ordered. This disruption
shifts some of the work of the staff away from simply cleaning up
after the effects of surplus power (such as throwing) to addressing
it directly.

19. One exception is Oregon State Penitentiary; visits to prisons in
    Oregon and Colorado were one element in inspiring Larson to
    make these changes.

20. For some staff, "undermining authority" is an important element in
    a widely shared theory about how serious prison riots come about.
    The riots of the early 1980s followed a period of extreme disorgan-
    ization within many prisons. Many staff view this as a time when
    "everything" was given to the prisoners, who then simply wanted
    more. At the point where there was no more to give, uprisings
    were inevitable. In this view, attention and privileges are bound to
    run out and the pendulum swing back toward violence. One officer
    complained, "People are believing what the inmates say . . . I've got
    inmates looking at everything I do . . . If you make it so easy [for
    the inmates], you're creating a new monster."

21. Toch in fact ends his paper by suggesting that humanizing supermax
    regimes may help them to survive. Sometime after this conversation,
    Larson made a list of "risks" involved in his project (such as the risk
    of releasing inmates with violent histories into general population)
    that included "risk of saying they work perpetuates them."

22. These were modeled on similar booths at Pelican Bay in California,
    which provided the plans. Some prisons have less restrictive
    arrangements such as desks with chest high dividers to which
    inmates are cuffed.

23. I have been unable to find the original drawing that appears as Plate
    8 in *Discipline and Punish* and have substituted the more contem-
    porary one, which shows exactly the same scene at Fresnes prison.

24. College classes are no longer available, so these limited possibilities
    are all the unit can provide. Even this level of education is threat-
    ened by budget cuts. The content of these courses is based on var-
    ious models of prisoner subjectivity, which are freely mixed by staff.

25. Of the five who had started this particular course, two had been

transferred out of the unit and one had dropped out. The difference in the clothes of the two finishing the course is explained below.

26. The visit was initially problematic both because she brought in unusual items and because the public is not normally allowed on the unit. Officers were uneasy about both the security aspect and the possibility that inmates would be "stirred up" by the content of the class. Supervisors also suggested that officers found it difficult to deal with vivid details of crime while doing their work. After the class was successful, however, the unit's staff became more accepting of it.

27. An African American, James Byrd, Jr., and a gay man, Matthew Shepard, were murdered in brutal hate crimes.

28. He suggests long-term prisoners have a time-limited "window" (perhaps in their late twenties) during which they may be reached. Thus unit staff speculate that some may be beyond their efforts: "I wonder if we're looking to devise a program where the guy will never come back into this environment. There's a guy who doesn't get it in victim awareness. I'm a violent person [he says], they deserved it. There are [some] people like that."

29. The teacher extended this thought to the staff: "The prison is an artificial environment where we all sit down together—we wouldn't be sitting down to lattes at Starbucks."

30. "Discipline displayed to its objects the kinds of 'personhood' that were available and laid out models of behavior for how to become (or seem to become) one of these 'available' people. From the point of view of prisoners these were often ironic iterations, designed to entangle them in various games and deceits . . . But these were also broadcast messages that helped to shape public expectations of what can or should be done to criminals in the name of protecting society" (Bright, *Powers That Punish,* 315). Comments about prisoners living next door do not take into account racial and class divisions in the larger society or their effects in the prison; rather they broadcast a message that legitimates a minimal rehabilitation.

31. Ransom interprets Foucault as saying that this is just how things are. No plan can completely overturn the present order, and no present order is completely based on its own plans (*Foucault's Discipline,* 42).

32. Ann Arnett Ferguson, *Bad Boys,* 235.

33. M. A. Bortner and Linda M. Williams, *Youth in Prison,* 180.

APPENDIX: NOTE ON RESEARCH

1. David Lovell and Lorna A. Rhodes, "Mobile Consultation."

2. David Lovell et al., "Who Lives in Supermaximum Custody? A Washington State Study."

3. Kristin Cloyes, David Lovell, David G. Allen, and Lorna A. Rhodes, "Factor Analysis of the Brief Psychiatric Rating Scale," unpublished paper.

Abramsky, Sasha. *Hard Time Blues: How Politics Built a Prison Nation.* New York: St. Martin's Press, 2002.

Adorno, Theodor. *The Stars down to Earth and Other Essays on the Irrational in Culture.* New York: Routledge, 1994.

Adshead, Gwen. "Psychopaths and Other-Regarding Beliefs." *Philosophy, Psychiatry, and Psychology* 6.1 (1999): 41–44.

Alford, C. Fred. *What Evil Means to Us.* Ithaca: Cornell University Press, 1997.

———. "What Would It Matter If Everything Foucault Said about Prison Were Wrong? *Discipline and Punish* after Twenty Years." *Theory and Society* 29 (2000): 125–46.

American Psychiatric Association. *Diagnostic and Statistical Manual of Mental Disorders,* Fourth Edition—Text Revision. Washington, D.C.: American Psychiatric Association, 2000.

Amnesty International. *Cruelty in Control? The Stun Belt and Other Electroshock Weapons in Law Enforcement.* 1999. Available: http://www.amnestyusa.org/rightsforall.

Austin, James, and John Irwin. *It's about Time.* 3d ed. Belmont, Calif.: Wadsworth, 2001.

Baca, Jimmy Santiago. "Past Present." In *Prison Writing in 20th Century America,* ed. H. Bruce Franklin. New York: Penguin, 1998.

Bartky, Sandra Lee. *Femininity and Domination: Studies in the Phenomenology of Oppression.* New York: Routledge, 1990.

Basaglia, Franco. *Psychiatry Inside Out: Selected Writings of Franco Basaglia*, ed. Nancy Scheper-Hughes and Anne M. Lovell. New York: Columbia University Press, 1987.

Baumeister, Roy F. *Evil: Inside Human Violence and Cruelty*. New York: W. H. Freeman, 1996.

Beaumont, Gustave de, and Alexis de Tocqueville. *On the Penitentiary System in the United States and Its Application in France*. Carbondale: Southern Illinois University Press, 1964 (1833).

Beck, Allen J., and Paige M. Harrison. *Prisoners in 2001*. Washington D.C.: Bureau of Justice Statistics, 2001.

Beck, Ulrich, Anthony Giddens, and Scott Lasch. *Reflexive Modernization: Politics, Tradition, and Aesthetics in the Modern Social Order*. Stanford: Stanford University Press, 1994.

Beckett, Katherine. *Making Crime Pay: Law and Order in Contemporary American Politics*. New York: Oxford University Press, 1997.

Beckett, Katherine, and Bruce Western. "The Penal System as Labor Market Institution: Jobs and Jails, 1980–1995." In *Penal Reform in Overcrowded Times,* ed. Michael Tonry. New York: Oxford University Press, 2001.

Belknap, Joanne. *The Invisible Woman: Gender, Crime and Justice*. Belmont, Calif.: Wadsworth, 2000.

Bender, John. *Imagining the Penitentiary: Fiction and the Architecture of Mind in Eighteenth-Century England*. Chicago: University of Chicago Press, 1987.

Benjamin, Walter. "Critique of Violence." In *Walter Benjamin: Essays, Aphorisms, Autobiographical Writings*, ed. Peter Demetz. New York: Schocken Books, 1986 (1920).

Benn, Piers. "Freedom, Resentment, and the Psychopath." *Philosophy, Psychiatry, and Psychology* 6.1 (1999): 29–39.

Bennett, William J., and John J. DiIulio. *Body Count: Moral Poverty and How to Win America's War against Crime and Drugs*. New York: Simon and Schuster, 1996.

Berlant, Lauren, *The Queen of America Goes to Washington City: Essays on Sex and Citizenship*. Durham: Duke University Press, 1997.

Blumstein, Alfred, and Allen J. Beck. "Population Growth in U.S. Prisons: 1980–1986." In *Prisons*, ed. Michael Tonry and Joan Petersilia. Chicago: University of Chicago Press, 1999.

Blumstein, Alfred, and Joel Wallman. "The Recent Rise and Fall of American Violence." In *The Crime Drop in America*, ed. Alfred Blumstein and Joel Wallman. Cambridge: Cambridge University Press, 2000.

Bordo, Susan. "Anorexia Nervosa: Psychopathology as the Crystallization of Culture." In Bordo, *Unbearable Weight: Feminism, Western Culture, and the Body.* Berkeley: University of California Press, 1993.

———. "'Material Girl': The Effacements of Postmodern Culture." *Michigan Quarterly Review* 29.4 (1990): 653–77.

Bortner, M. A., and Linda M. Williams. *Youth in Prison.* New York: Routledge, 1997.

Boyer, Peter J. "The Genius of Death Row." *New Yorker,* December 4, 1995: 64–79.

Bright, Charles. *The Powers That Punish: Prison and Politics in the Era of the "Big House," 1920–1955.* Ann Arbor: University of Michigan Press, 1996.

Brooke, James. "In 'Super-Max,' Terms of Endurance: Silence, Isolation, and Rigid Control Rule at Alcatraz of Rockies." *New York Times,* June 13, 1999, A30.

Burton-Rose, Daniel, ed., with Dan Pens and Paul Wright. *The Celling of America: An Inside Look at the U.S. Prison Industry.* Monroe, Me.: Common Courage Press, 1998.

Butler, Judith. *Bodies That Matter: On the Discursive Limits of "Sex."* New York: Routledge, 1993.

———. *Gender Trouble: Feminism and the Subversion of Identity.* Ed. Linda J. Nicholson. New York: Routledge, 1990.

Butterfield, Fox. *All God's Children: The Bosket Family and the American Tradition of Violence.* New York: Avon, 1995.

———. "1% Increase in U.S. Inmates Is Lowest Rate in Three Decades." *New York Times,* July 31, 2002, A1.

———. "Prison Rates among Blacks Reach a Peak, Report Finds." *New York Times,* April 7, 2003. A11.

———. "Prisons Replace Hospitals for the Nation's Mentally Ill." *New York Times,* March 5, 1998, A1, A18.

Camp, Camille, and George Camp, eds. *The Corrections Yearbook 2000: Adult Corrections.* Middleton, Conn.: Criminal Justice Institute, 2000.

Canetti, Elias. *Crowds and Power.* Trans. Carol Stewart. New York: Continuum, 1962.

Caplow, Theodore, and Jonathan Simon. "Understanding Prison Policy and Population Trends." In *Prisons,* ed. Michael Tonry and Joan Petersilia. Chicago: University of Chicago Press, 1999.

Carlen, Pat. *Sledgehammer: Women's Imprisonment at the Millennium.* London: Macmillan, 1998.

Cleckley, Hervey, M.D. *The Mask of Sanity*. New York: C. V. Mosby, 1982.

Cline, F. *Understanding and Treating the Severely Disturbed Child*. Evergreen, Colo.: Evergreen Consultants in Human Behavior, 1979.

Cohen, Stanley. *Against Criminology*. New Brunswick, N.J.: Transaction Books, 1988.

———. "Social-Control Talk: Telling Stories about Correctional Change." In *The Power to Punish*, ed. David Garland and Peter Young. Atlantic Highlands, N.J.: Humanities Press, 1983.

Cole, David. *No Equal Justice: Race and Class in the American Criminal Justice System*. New York: New Press, 1999.

Conover, Ted. *Newjack: Guarding Sing Sing*. New York: Random House, 2000.

Cummins, Eric. *The Rise and Fall of California's Radical Prison Movement*. Stanford: Stanford University Press, 1994.

Currie, Elliott. *Crime and Punishment in America: Why the Solutions to America's Most Stubborn Social Crisis Have Not Worked and What Will*. New York: Henry Holt, 1998.

Davis, Angela Y. "From the Convict Lease System to the Super-Max Prison." In *States of Confinement*, ed. Joy James. New York: St. Martin's Press, 2000.

———. "Race and Criminalization: Black Americans and the Punishment Industry." In *The Angela Y. Davis Reader*, ed. Joy James. Malden, Mass.: Blackwell, 1998.

———. "A World unto Itself: Multiple Invisibilities of Imprisonment." Foreword to *Behind the Razor Wire: A Portrait of a Contemporary Prison*, ed. Michael Jacobson-Hardy. New York: New York University Press, 1999.

de Certeau, Michel. "The Institution of Rot." In *Psychosis and Sexual Identity: Toward a Post-Analytic View of the Schreber Case*, ed. D. Allison et al. Albany: SUNY Press, 1988.

Derrida, Jacques. "Force of Law: The Mystical Foundation of Authority." In *Deconstruction and the Possibility of Justice*, ed. Drucilla Cornell, Michel Rosenfeld, and David Gray Carlson. New York: Routledge, 1992.

Dick, Philip K. *Do Androids Dream of Electric Sheep?* London: HarperCollins, 1968.

DiIulio, John J., Jr. *Governing Prisons: A Comparative Study of Correctional Management*. New York: Macmillan, 1987.

———. "Understanding Prisons: The Old New Penology." *Law and Social Inquiry* 61 (1991) 65–75.

Donzelot, Jacques. *The Policing of Families*. Trans. Robert Hurley. New York: Pantheon Books, 1997.

Donziger, Steven R., ed. *The Real War on Crime: The Report of the National Criminal Justice Commission.* New York: HarperCollins, 1996.

Doren, Dennis M. *Understanding and Treating the Psychopath.* Northvale, N.J.: Jason Aronson, 1996.

Douglas, Mary. *Purity and Danger: An Analysis of the Concepts of Pollution and Taboo.* London: Routledge and Kegan Paul, 1966.

Dowker, Fay, and Glenn Good. "The Proliferation of Control Unit Prisons in the United States." In *Prison Crisis: Critical Readings,* ed. Edward P. Sharboro and Robert L. Keller. New York: Harrow and Heston, 1995.

Duguid, Stephen. *Can Prisons Work? The Prisoner as Object and Subject in Modern Corrections.* Toronto: University of Toronto Press, 2000.

Dunne, Bill. "The U.W. Prison at Marion, Illinois: An Instrument of Oppression." In *Cages of Steel: The Politics of Imprisonment in the United States,* ed. Ward Chruchill and J. J. Vander Wall. Washington, D.C.: Maisonneuve Press, 1992.

Durham, Mary L. "The Impact of Deinstitutionalization on the Current Treatment of the Mentally Ill." *International Journal of Law and Psychiatry* 12 (1989): 117–31.

Dvoskin, Joel A. "Sticks and Stones: The Abuse of Psychiatric Diagnosis in Prisons." *Journal of the California Alliance for the Mentally Ill* 8.1 (1997): 20–21.

Dyer, Joel. *The Perpetual Prison Machine: How America Profits from Crime.* Boulder: Westview, 2000.

Estroff, Sue E. "Identity, Disability, and Schizophrenia: The Problem of Chronicity." In *Knowledge, Power, and Practice: The Anthropology of Medicine and Everyday Life,* ed. Shirley Lindenbaum and Margaret Lock. Berkeley: University of California Press, 1993.

Evans, Jeff, ed. *Undoing Time: American Prisoners in Their Own Words.* Boston: Northeastern University Press, 2001.

Evans, Robin. *The Fabrication of Virtue: English Prison Architecture, 1750–1840.* Cambridge: Cambridge University Press, 1982.

Feldman, Allen. *Formations of Violence: The Narrative of the Body and Political Terror in Northern Ireland.* Chicago: University of Chicago Press, 1991.

———. "On Cultural Anesthesia: From Desert Storm to Rodney King." *Amercian Ethnologist* 21.2 (1994): 404–18.

Ferguson, Ann Arnett. *Bad Boys: Public Schools in the Making of Black Masculinity.* Ann Arbor: University of Michigan Press, 2000.

Fernando, Suman, David Ndegwa, and Melba Wilson. *Forensic Psychiatry, Race, and Culture.* New York: Routledge, 1998.

Fleisher, Mark S. *Warehousing Violence*. Newbury Park, Calif.: Sage, 1989.

Foucault, Michel. "The Dangerous Individual." In *Michel Foucault: Politics, Philosophy, Culture*, ed. L. D. Kritzman. New York: Routledge, 1988.

———. *Discipline and Punish: The Birth of the Prison*. New York: Vintage Books, 1979.

———. *Madness and Civilization: A History of Insanity in the Age of Reason*. Trans. Richard Howard. New York: Vintage Books, 1965.

———. *Power/Knowledge: Selected Interviews and Other Writings, 1972–1977*, ed. Colin Gordon. New York: Pantheon, 1980.

Franklin, H. Bruce, ed. *Prison Writing in 20th-Century America*. New York: Penguin Books, 1998.

Friedman, Lawrence M. *Crime and Punishment in American History*. New York: Basic Books, 1993.

Freud, Sigmund. "The Uncanny," in *The Standard Edition of the Complete Works of Sigmund Freud*. London: Hogarth Press and the Institute of Psycho-Analysis, 1919.

Gaines, Atwood. "From DSM-I to III-R; Voices of Self, Mastery and Other: A Cultural Constructivist Reading of U.S. Psychiatric Classification." *Social Science and Medicine* 35.1 (1992): 3–24.

Giddens, Anthony. *The Consequences of Modernity*. Stanford: Stanford University Press, 1990.

Gilligan, James. *Violence: Our Deadly Epidemic and Its Causes*. New York: G. P. Putnam's Sons, 1996.

Gilmore, Ruth Wilson. "Globalisation and U.S. Prison Growth: From Military Keynesianism to Post-Keynesian Militarism." *Race and Class* 40.2/3 (1998/99): 171–88.

Goffman, Erving. *Asylums: Essays on the Social Situations of Mental Patients and Other Inmates*. New York: Doubleday, 1961.

Gondles, James A., Jr. "The Criminal Mind: A Challenge to Corrections." *Corrections Today* February 1999: 6.

Gordon, Avery F. *Ghostly Matters: Haunting and the Sociological Imagination*. Minneapolis: University of Minnesota Press, 1997.

———. "Globalism and the Prison Industrial Complex: An Interview with Angela Davis." *Race and Class* 40.2/3 (1998/99): 145–57.

Gottfredson, Don M. *Exploring Criminal Justice: An Introduction*. Los Angeles: Roxbury, 1999.

Gottfredson, Michael R., and Travis Hirschi. *A General Theory of Crime*. Stanford: Stanford University Press, 1990.

Grassian, Stuart. "Psychopathological Effects of Solitary Confinement." *American Journal of Psychiatry* 140.11 (1983): 1450–54.

Grassian, Stuart, and Nancy Friedman. "Effects of Sensory Deprivation in Psychiatric Seclusion and Solitary Confinement." *International Journal of Law and Psychiatry* 8 (1986): 49–65.

Greene, Judith, and Vincent Schiraldi. *Cutting Correctly: New Prison Policies for Times of Fiscal Crisis.* Washington D.C.: Justice Policy Institute, 2001.

Grosz, Elizabeth. *Volatile Bodies: Toward a Corporeal Feminism.* Bloomington: Indiana University Press, 1994.

Gusterson, Hugh. *Nuclear Rites: A Weapons Laboratory at the End of the Cold War.* Berkeley: University of California Press, 1996.

Hacking, Ian. "The Looping Effects of Human Kinds." In *Causal Cognition: A Multidisciplinary Approach*, ed. D. Premack, D. Sperber, and A. J. Premack. Oxford: Clarendon Press, 1994.

———. "Making Up People." In *Reconstructing Individualism: Autonomy, Individuality, and the Self in Western Thought*, ed. Thomas C. Heller, Morton Sosna, and David E. Wellbery. Stanford: Stanford University Press, 1986.

———. *Rewriting the Soul: Multiple Personality and the Sciences of Memory.* Princeton: Princeton University Press, 1995.

———. *The Social Construction of What?* Cambridge: Harvard University Press, 1999.

Hallinan, Joseph T. *Going up the River: Travels in a Prison Nation.* New York: Random House, 2001.

Haney, Craig. "'Infamous Punishment': The Psychological Consequences of Isolation." *National Prison Project Journal* (Spring 1993): 3–21.

———. "Mental Health Issues in Long-Term Solitary and 'Supermax' Confinement." *Crime and Delinquency* 49.1 (2003): 124–56.

Haney, Craig, and Mona Lynch. "Regulating Prisons of the Future: A Psychological Analysis of Supermax and Solitary Confinement." *New York University Review of Law and Social Change* 23 (1997): 477–570.

Haney, Craig, and Philip Zimbardo. "The Past and the Future of U.S. Prison Policy: Twenty-Five Years after the Stanford Prison Experiment." *American Psychologist* 53.7 (1998): 709–27.

Hare, Robert D. "The Hare PCL-R: Some Issues Concerning Its Use and Misuse." *Legal and Criminal Psychology* 3 (1998): 101–22.

———. "Psychopaths and Their Nature: Implications for the Mental Health and Criminal Justice Systems." In *Psychopathy: Antisocial, Criminal, and Violent Behavior*, ed. Theodore Millon et al. New York: Guilford Press, 1998.

———. *Without Conscience: The Disturbing World of the Psychopaths among Us.* New York: Pocket Books, 1993.

Harris, Grant T., Tracey A. Skilling, and Marnie E. Rice. "The Construct of Psychopathy." In *Crime and Justice: A Review of Research*, ed. Michael Tonry. Vol. 28. Chicago: University of Chicago, 2001.

Hayles, N. Katherine. *How We Became Posthuman: Virtual Bodies in Cybernetics, Literature, and Informatics.* Chicago: University of Chicago Press, 1999.

Henry, Mark A. "Unethical Staff Behavior: A Guide to Identifying and Investigating Staff Misconduct." *Corrections Today* June 1998: 112–17.

Herival, Tara, and Paul Wright, eds. *Prison Nation: The Warehousing of America's Poor.* New York: Routledge, 2003.

Hirsch, Adam Jay. *The Rise of the Penitentiary: Prisons and Punishment in Early America.* New Haven: Yale University Press, 1992.

Hobbes, Thomas. *Leviathan, Parts I and II.* New York: Bobbs-Merrill, 1958 (1651).

Horwitz, Allan V. *Creating Mental Illness.* Chicago: University of Chicago Press, 2002.

Howe, Adrian. *Punish and Critique: Towards a Feminist Analysis of Penality.* Sociology of Law and Crime, ed. Maureen Cain and Carol Smart. New York: Routledge, 1994.

Human Rights Watch. *Cold Storage: Super-Maximum Security Confinement in Indiana.* New York: Human Rights Watch, 1997.

———. "Out of Sight: Super-Maximum Custody in the United States." *Human Rights Watch* 12.1 (2000): 1–9.

Ignatieff, Michael. *A Just Measure of Pain: The Penitentiary in the Industrial Revolution 1750–1850.* London: Macmillan, 1978.

———. *The Needs of Strangers: An Essay on Privacy, Solidarity, and the Politics of Being Human.* New York: Penguin Books, 1986.

Irwin, John. *The Felon.* Englewood Cliffs, N.J.: Prentice-Hall, 1970.

———. *Prisons in Turmoil.* Boston: Little, Brown, 1980.

Irwin, John, Vincent Schiraldi, and Jason Ziedenberg. "America's One Million Nonviolent Prisoners." *Social Justice* 27.2 (2000): 135–47.

Jackson, Joe, and William F. Burke. *Dead Run: The Shocking Story of Dennis Stockton and Life on Death Row in America.* New York: Walker, 1999.

Jackson, Michael. *Prisoners of Isolation: Solitary Confinement in Canada.* Toronto: University of Toronto Press, 1983.

Jacobson-Hardy, Michael. *Behind the Razor Wire: A Portrait of a Contemporary Prison.* New York: New York University Press, 1999.

Jemelka, Ronald, Eric Trupin, and J. A. Chiles. "The Mentally Ill in Prisons: A Review." *Hospital and Community Psychiatry* 40 (1989): 481–85.

Johnson, Robert. *Hard Time: Understanding and Reforming the Prison*. Monterey, Calif.: Brooks/Cole, 1987.

Karr-Morse, Robin, and Meredith S. Wiley. *Ghosts from the Nursery: Tracing the Roots of Violence*. New York: Atlantic Monthly Press, 1997.

Kellerman, Jonathan. *Savage Spawn: Reflections on Violent Children*. New York: Ballantine, 1999.

Kernberg, Otto F. *Severe Personality Disorders: Psychotherapeutic Strategies*. New Haven: Yale University Press, 1984.

Kerness, Bonnie. "Permanent Lockdown in the United States." *Prison Focus* 2.2 (1998): 4–7.

Kerness, Bonnie, ed. *Uses and Effects of Control Unit Prisons: Bonnie Kearness Interviews Sundiata Acoli and Jalil Muntaqim for the National Campaign to Stop Control Unit Prisons*. Paterson, N.J.: P.A.C. Publications, 1996.

Kerness, Bonnie, and Holbrook Teter, eds. *Survival in Solitary: A Manual Written by and for People Living in Control Units*. American Friends Service Committee, 1997.

King, Roy D. "The Rise and Rise of Supermax: An American Solution in Search of a Problem?" *Punishment and Society* 1 (1999): 163-86.

Kirschner, Suzanne R. *The Religious and Romantic Origins of Psychoanalysis*. Cambridge: Cambridge University Press, 1996.

Knowles, Caroline. *Bedlam on the Streets*. London: Routledge, 2000.

Knox, Sara L. *Murder: A Tale of Modern American Life*. Durham: Duke University Press, 1998.

Kosson, David S., Stevens S. Smith, and Joseph P. Newman. "Evaluating the Construct Validity of Psychopathy in Black and White Male Inmates: Three Preliminary Studies." *Journal of Abnormal Psychology* 99.3 (1990): 250–59.

Kraska, Peter B., ed. *Militarizing the American Criminal Justice System*. Boston: Northeastern University Press, 2001.

Kupers, Terry A. "Mental Health Police?" *Readings: A Journal of Reviews and Commentary in Mental Health* (2000): 16–22.

———. *Prison Madness: The Mental Health Crisis behind Bars and What We Must Do about It*. San Francisco: Jossey-Bass, 1999.

Kurki, Leena, and Norval Morris. "The Purposes, Practices, and Problems of Supermax Prisons," in *Crime and Justice: A Review of Research* (vol. 28), Michael Tonry, ed. Chicago: University of Chicago Press, 2001.

Lamb, H. Richard, and Linda E. Weinberger. "Persons with Severe Mental Illness in Jails and Prisons: A Review." *Psychiatric Services* 49.4 (1998): 483–92.

Lawes, Lewis E. *Twenty Thousand Years in Sing Sing*. New York: New Hope Library, 1932.

Leder, Drew. *The Soul Knows No Bars*. New York: Rowman and Littlefield, 2001.

Levasseur, Ray Luc. "Trouble Coming Every Day: ADX—the First Year." *Prison Legal News* 8.7 (1997): 6–9.

Lewis, Dorothy Otnow. *Guilty by Reason of Insanity: A Psychiatrist Explores the Minds of Killers*. New York: Ballantine, 1998.

Linehan, Marsha. *Cognitive-Behavioral Treatment of Borderline Personality Disorder*. New York: Guilford Press, 1993.

Long, Douglas G. *Bentham on Liberty: Jeremy Bentham's Idea of Liberty in Relation to His Utilitarianism*. Toronto: Toronto University Press, 1977.

Lovell, David, Kristin Cloyes, David G. Allen, and Lorna A. Rhodes. "Who Lives in Supermaximum Custody? A Washington State Study." *Federal Probation* 64.2 (2000): 33–38.

Lovell, David, and Lorna A. Rhodes. "Mobile Consultation: Crossing Correctional Boundaries to Cope with Disturbed Offenders." *Federal Probation* 61.3 (1997): 40–45.

Lowe, Donald M. *The Body in Late Capitalist USA*. Durham: Duke University Press, 1995.

Luhrmann, T. M. *Of Two Minds: The Growing Disorder in American Psychiatry*. New York: Alfred A. Knopf, 2000.

Lunbeck, Elizabeth. *The Psychiatric Persuasion: Knowledge, Gender, and Power in Modern America*. Princeton: Princeton University Press, 1994.

Lutsky, Julia. "Amnesty International Calls for Stun Belt Ban." *Prison Legal News* 11.1 (2000): 6–7.

Magid, Ken, and Carole A. McKelvey. *High Risk*. New York: Bantam, 1987.

Mansfield, Nick. *Subjectivity: Theories of the Self from Freud to Haraway*. New York: New York University Press, 2000.

Marquart, James W. "Doing Research in Prisons: The Strengths and Weaknesses of Full Participation as a Guard." *Justice Quarterly* 3.1 (1986): 15–32.

Masters, Jarvis Jay. *Finding Freedom: Writings from Death Row*. Junction City, Calif.: Padma, 1997.

Mauer, Marc. *Race to Incarcerate*. New York: The New Press, 1999.

May, John P., and Khalid R. Pitts, eds. *Building Violence: How America's Rush to Incarcerate Creates More Violence.* Thousand Oaks, Calif.: Sage, 2000.

Mcgowan, Randall. "The Well-Ordered Prison: England, 1780–1865." In *The Oxford History of the Prison: The Practice of Punishment in Western Society,* ed. Norval Morris and David J. Rothman. Oxford: Oxford University Press, 1998.

McShane, Marilyn D., and Frank McShane. *Encyclopedia of American Prisons.* Garland Reference Library of the Humanities, vol. 1748. New York: Garland, 1996.

Megill, Allan. *Prophets of Extremity: Nietzsche, Heidegger, Foucault, Derrida.* Berkeley and Los Angeles: University of California Press, 1985.

Melossi, Dario, and Massimo Pavarini. *The Prison and the Factory: Origins of the Penitentiary System.* Trans. Glynis Cousin. London: Macmillan, 1981.

Meloy, J. Reid. *The Psychopathic Mind: Origins, Dynamics, and Treatment.* Northvale, N.J.: Jason Aronson, 1997.

Messerschmidt, James W. "Maculinities, Crime, and Prison." In *Prison Masculinities,* ed. Don Sabo, Terry A. Kupers, and Willie London. Philadelphia: Temple University Press, 2001.

Miller, William Ian. *The Anatomy of Disgust.* Cambridge: Harvard University Press, 1997.

Morris, Norval. "The Contemporary Prison: 1965–Present." In *The Oxford History of the Prison: The Practice of Punishment in Western Society,* ed. Norval Morris and David J. Rothman. Oxford: Oxford University Press, 1998.

Moskowitz, Andrei. "Self-Sufficient Isolation." *Corrections Forum* 4.2 (1995): 22–27.

Naffine, Ngaire. *Feminism and Criminality.* Philadelphia: Temple University Press, 1996.

National Institute of Corrections. *Supermax Housing: A Survey of Current Practice.* Longmont, Colo.: U.S. Department of Justice, 1997.

Nuckolls, Charles W. *Culture: A Problem That Cannot Be Solved.* Madison: University of Wisconsin Press, 1998.

———. "Toward a Cultural History of the Personality Disorders." *Social Science and Medicine* 35.1 (1992): 37–47.

O'Brien, Patricia. *The Promise of Punishment: Prisons in Nineteenth-Century France.* Princeton: Princeton University Press, 1982.

O'Connor, Patricia E. *Speaking of Crime: Narratives of Prisoners.* Lincoln: University of Nebraska Press, 2000.

Okazawa-Rey, Margo, and Gwen Kirk. "Maximum Security." *Social Justice* 27.3 (2000): 120–32.

Oliver, Kelly. *Reading Kristeva: Unraveling the Double-Bind.* Bloomington: Indiana University Press, 1993.

Owen, Barbara. *In the Mix: Struggle and Survival in a Women's Prison.* SUNY Series in Women, Crime, and Criminology. New York: SUNY Press, 1998.

Parenti, Christian. *Lockdown America: Police and Prisons in the Age of Crisis.* New York: Verso, 1999.

Pens, Dan. "Abuse of Force at Virginia's Supermax: Shoot 'Em If They Step out of Line." *Prison Legal News* 11.2 (2000): 8–9.

Perkinson, Robert. "Shackled Justice: Florence Federal Penitentiary and the New Politics of Punishment." *Social Justice* 21.3 (1994): 117–31.

Pisciotta, Alexander W. *Benevolent Repression: Social Control and the American Reformatory-Prison Movement.* New York: New York University Press, 1994.

Podvoll, Edward M. *The Seduction of Madness: Revolutionary Insights into the World of Psychosis and a Compassionate Approach to Recovery at Home.* New York: HarperCollins, 1990.

Porter, Bruce. "Is Solitary Confinement Driving Charlie Chase Crazy?" *New York Times Magazine,* November 8, 1998, 52–57.

Primoratz, Igor. *Justifying Legal Punishment.* Atlantic Highlands, N.J.: Humanities Press, 1989.

Purdy, Matthew. "An Official Culture of Violence Infests a Prison." *New York Times,* December 19, 1995, A1, A20.

Ransom, John S. *Foucault's Discipline: The Politics of Subjectivity.* Durham: Duke University Press, 1997.

Reiman, Jeffrey. *The Rich Get Richer and the Poor Get Prison: Ideology, Class and Criminal Justice.* 5th ed. Boston: Allyn and Bacon, 1998.

Ressler, Robert H., and Rom Shachtman. *Whoever Fights Monsters.* New York: St. Martin's Press, 1992.

Rhodes, Lorna A. "Panoptical Intimacies." *Public Culture* 10.2 (1998): 285–311.

———. "Taxonomic Anxieties: Axis I and Axis II in Prison." *Medical Anthropology Quarterly* 14.3 (2000): 346–73.

———. "Toward an Anthropology of Prisons." *Annual Review of Anthropology* 30 (2001): 65–83.

———. "Psychopathy and the Face of Control in Supermax." *Ethnography* 3.4 (2002): 445–69.

Rhodes, Richard. *Why They Kill: The Discoveries of a Maverick Criminologist.* New York: Knopf, 1999.

Richards, Henry. "Evil Intent: Violence and Disorders of the Will." In *Psychopa-*

thy: Antisocial, Criminal, and Violent Behavior, ed. Theodore Millon et al. New York: Guilford, 1998.

Rideau, Wilbert, and Ron Wilkber. *Life Sentences: Rage and Survival behind Bars.* New York: Times Books, 1992.

Riveland, Chase. *Supermax Prisons: Overview and General Considerations.* Washington, D.C.: U.S. Department of Justice, National Institute of Corrections, 1999.

Roberts, Julian V., and Robert J. Gebotys. "Prisoners of Isolation: Research on the Effects of Administrative Segregation." *Canadian Journal of Criminology* (January 2001): 85–97.

Romanyshyn, Robert. *Technology as Symptom and Dream.* New York: Routledge, 1989.

Rose, Nikolas. *Inventing Ourselves: Psychology, Power, and Personhood.* Cambridge: Cambridge University Press, 1998.

Rothman, David J. *Conscience and Convenience: The Asylum and Its Alternatives in Progressive America.* Boston: Little, Brown, 1980.

———. *The Discovery of the Asylum: Social Order and Disorder in the New Republic.* Revised Edition. Boston: Little, Brown, 1971.

———. "Perfecting the Prison: United States 1780–1865." In *The Oxford History of the Prison: The Practice of Punishment in Western Society,* ed. Norval Morris and David J. Rothman. London: Oxford University Press, 1998.

Rotman, Edgardo. "The Failure of Reform: United States, 1865–1965." In *The Oxford History of the Prison: The Practice of Punishment in Western Society,* ed. Norval Morris and David J. Rothman. New York: Oxford University Press, 1998.

Sabo, Don. "Doing Time, Doing Masculinity." In *Prison Masculinities,* ed. Don Sabo, Terry A. Kupers, and Willie London. Philadelphia: Temple University Press, 2001.

Sabo, Don, Terry A. Kupers, and Willie London. "Gender and the Politics of Punishment." In *Prison Masculinities,* ed. Don Sabo, Terry A. Kupers, and Willie London. Philadelphia: Temple University Press, 2001.

Sabo, Don, Terry A. Kupers, and Willie London, eds. *Prison Masculinities.* Philadelphia: Temple University Press, 2001.

Samenow, Stanton E. *Inside the Criminal Mind.* New York: Times Books, 1984.

Santner, Eric L. *My Own Private Germany: Daniel Paul Schreber's Secret History of Modernity.* Princeton: Princeton University Press, 1996.

Sass, Louis A. *Madness and Modernism: Insanity in the Light of Modern Art, Literature, and Thought.* New York: Basic Books, 1992.

Scarry, Elaine. *The Body in Pain: The Making and Unmaking of the World.* New York: Oxford University Press, 1985.

Scharf, Peter. "Empty Bars: Violence and the Crisis of Meaning in Prison." *Prison Journal* 63.1 (1983).

Schlosser, Eric. "The Prison-Industrial Complex." *Atlantic Monthly,* December 1998.

Seltzer, Mark. *Bodies and Machines.* New York: Routledge, 1992.

———. *Serial Killers: Death and Life in America's Wound Culture.* New York: Routledge, 1998.

Sherman, Mark, Bonnie Kerness, and Laura Magnani. *Torture in the United States: Prison Conditions and the Treatment of Prisoners.* Report of the Criminal Justice Section, American Bar Association, and Criminal Justice Program, American Friends Service Committee, www.omct.org/woatusa/projects/CATreport/prisons.htm, 1–24.

Sigurdson, Chris. "The Mad, the Bad, and the Abandoned: The Mentally Ill in Prisons and Jails." *Corrections Today* (2000): 70–78.

Stastny, Charles, and Gabrielle Tyrnauer. *Who Rules the Joint?* Lexington, Mass.: Lexington Books, 1982.

Taylor, Charles. *Sources of the Self: The Making of the Modern Identity.* Cambridge: Harvard University Press, 1989.

Thompson, Leon (Whitey). *Last Train to Alcatraz.* Fiddletown, Calif.: Leon Thompson, 1995.

Tithecott, Richard. *Of Men and Monsters: Jeffrey Dahmer and the Construction of the Serial Killer.* Madison: University of Wisconsin Press, 1997.

Toch, Hans. *Corrections: A Humanistic Approach.* Albany, N.Y.: Harrow & Heston, 1997.

———. "The Future of Supermax Confinement." *Prison Journal* 81 (2001): 376–88.

———. "The Life of Lifers: Wolfgang's Inquiry into the Prison Adjustment of Homicide Offenders." In Marvin E. Wolfgang, *Crime and Justice at the Millennium: Essays by and in Honor of Marvin E. Wolfgang,* ed. R. A. Silverman. Boston: Kluwer, 2001.

———. *Living in Prison: The Ecology of Survival.* New York: Free Press, 1977.

———. *Mosaic of Despair: Human Breakdowns in Prison.* Washington, D.C.: American Psychological Association, 1992.

———. "Psychopathy or Antisocial Personality in Forensic Settings." In *Psychopathy: Antisocial, Criminal, and Violent Behavior,* ed. Theodore Millon et al. New York: Guilford Press, 1998.

Toch, Hans, and Kenneth Adams. *Coping: Maladaptation in the Prison*. New Brunswick, N.J.: Transaction Books, 1989.

———. *The Disturbed Violent Offender*. Washington, D.C.: American Psychological Association, 1994.

Tonry, Michael. *Malign Neglect: Race, Crime and Punishment in America*. New York: Oxford University Press, 1995.

———. "Prediction and Classification: Legal and Ethical Issues." In *Prediction and Classification in Criminal Justice Decision-Making*, ed. Don M. Gottfredson and Michael Tonry. Vol. 7. *Crime and Justice: A Review of Research*. Chicago: University of Chicago, 1987.

Topham, James. "The Sting: Anatomy of a Set-Up." *Corrections Technology and Management* (September/October 1999): 20–26.

Torrey, E. Fuller. *Out of the Shadows: Confronting America's Mental Illness Crisis*. New York: John Wiley and Sons, 1997.

Tsing, Anna. "The Global Situation." *Cultural Anthropology* 15.3 (2000): 327–60.

Tucker, Gary. "Putting *DSM*-IV in Perspective." *American Journal of Psychiatry* 155.2 (1998): 159–61.

Unseem, Bert, and Peter Kimball. *States of Siege: U.S. Prison Riots, 1971–1986*. New York: Oxford University Press, 1989.

Ward, David A. "Supermaximum Custody Prisons in the United States: Why Successful Regimes Remain Controversial." *Prison Service Journal* 97 (1995): 27–34.

Webb, Lonny R. "Addressing Severe Behavioral Problems in a 'Super-Max' Prison Setting." Unpublished paper.

Wicker, Tom. *A Time to Die*. New York: Quadrangle/New York Times Books, 1975.

Wilson, Mitchell. "*DSM*-III and the Transformation of American Psychiatry: A History." *American Journal of Psychiatry* 150 (1993): 3, 399–410.

Winerip, Michael. "Bedlam on the Streets: Increasingly, the Mentally Ill Have Nowhere to Go." *New York Times Magazine*, May 23, 1999, 42–70.

Winner, Langdon. *The Whale and the Reactor: A Search for Limits in an Age of High Technology*. Chicago: University of Chicago Press, 1986.

Yochelson, Samuel, and Stanton Samenow. *The Criminal Personality*. New York: Jason Aronson, 1976.

Young, Allan. *The Harmony of Illusions: Inventing Post-Traumatic Stress Disorder*. Princeton: Princeton University Press, 1995.

Young, Iris Marion. *Justice and the Politics of Difference*. Princeton: Princeton University Press, 1990.

Zimmer, Lynn E. *Women Guarding Men.* Chicago: University of Chicago Press, 1986.

Zinger, Ivan, Cherami Wichmann, and D. A. Andrews. "The Psychological Effects of 60 Days in Administrative Segregation." *Canadian Journal of Criminology* (January 2001): 47–83.

ACKNOWLEDGMENTS

Many people have contributed to the creation of this book. My first debt is to the prisoners, prison staff, and correctional officials who appear anonymously in these pages. I am also deeply indebted to my colleagues on the Correctional Mental Health Collaboration. The collaboration, and my part in it, would not have happened without the work and vision of David Allen, who has been a faithful friend, generous colleague, and patient reader throughout these years. David Lovell has been a constant presence, never faltering in his good-humored willingness to read, listen, and attend to details at all levels. I am grateful to Kristin Cloyes and Cheryl Cooke for their interviewing skills and much rewarding conversation, and to Susan Lewis Graham, who held the whole thing together. The support provided by the Washington Department of Corrections was crucial to this project, and I thank Secretary Joseph Lehman and Deputy Secretary Eldon Vail for making it possible.

I could not have written this book without the friendship of many people who work in prisons and who have been extraordinarily generous in everything, from assisting my first tentative steps into their world to commenting on the manuscript. I am especially grateful to Mike Wall, Ron Wineinger, Linda Gaffney, Willy Hamby, Vicky Beckmeyer, Jack Uglick, Tracy Johnson, James Tucker, and Jay Rothrock. I am deeply indebted to Gary Jones for his encouragement and care; to Ella Ray Sigmund Deacon for her friendship and support throughout this project; and to Marianne McNabb for her generosity and kindness.

I thank all the prisoners who responded to our study by extending us the benefit of the doubt and offering their perspectives. I particularly thank those prisoners to whom I have given names in this book and those who kindly allowed me to reproduce their drawings. I am also grateful to Bonnie Kerness for her warm words at moments of doubt; to Hans Toch for helpful suggestions on the manuscript; and to members of the Critical Resistance to Prisons Project at the University of California Humanities Center for important comments at an early stage of writing. For much-appreciated help with the illustrations, I thank Phyllis Kornfeld, Bonnie Kerness, Bruce Porter, Andrei Moskowitz, David Montero, KMB Justice Facilities, and everyone who made it possible to include photographs.

Many friends and colleagues encouraged me to write about prisons in the first place and have been remarkably tolerant of my long preoccupation with this work. Colleagues in the University of Washington Department of Anthropology gave me much support; I thank Janelle Taylor for being such a willing and thoughtful reader, Celia Lowe for keeping me on track, and Ann Anagnost for many years of collegial friendship. Mimi Kahn, Steve Harrell, Gene Hunn, and Devon Pena were helpful at crucial moments. The Robert Wood Johnson Clinical Scholars Program at the University of Washington was an important source of collegial and material support. Many students in anthropology, public health, nursing, and medicine contributed to my thinking. And I am deeply grateful for the friendship and comments of Emily Martin, Carey Jackson, George Callan, and Jim Hardman. Michelle Barry's amazingly patient assistance made it possible to deal with the details of library research and illustration preparation. My editor at the University of California Press, Naomi Schneider, was as responsive and careful a reader as anyone could hope for, and Sierra Filucci helped with many production details.

Finally, I thank my husband, Jerry Weatherman, with deep appreciation for his love and kindness through all the years of this project. This book is dedicated to my daughter Lila, with much gratitude and love.

LIST OF ILLUSTRATIONS

Page references followed by *fig* indicate an illustration or photograph.

history, 136–37; role of DSM diagnosis in, 140–41, 142–43

Cleckley, Hervey, 185

Cohen, Stanley, 197

Cold Storage, 29

Conover, Ted, 12

control booth, 24 *fig*

control prison technology: application to meals/mealtime, 41–42 *fig*; contemporary preoccupation with, 39–40; used to control violence, 86–87; described, 7; stun belts, 92–95, 253n.32–54n.33; on stun guns/electrical demobilization devices, 90–92, 254n.37

control unit cells: behavioral model basis of formal system of release from, 54; loss of control during removal from, 50–55; untitled drawing of cell extraction, 53 *fig*; visit to empty, 49–50

control unit plans: architect's oval prison, 39 *fig*; architect's preliminary, 28 *fig*; comparison of contemporary with early experiments in, 39–40; questioning real purpose served by, 59–60; relationship between larger institutional system and, 58; "Self-Sufficient Isolation" vision of, 36, 37 *fig*, 241n.14–42n.14

control units: assignments to, 13; characteristics of, 237n.1; governmental approaches to behavior and, 252n.26; historical roots of dream of perfect, 36, 38–39; interior of cell in, 31 *fig*; "level" or step system operation of, 30; literature on, 240n.9; "lockdown" system of, 23; logic of volitional criminology

supporting, 84–85; "machineries of the system" of, 173; noise/sensory stimulation in, 240n.11–41n.11; officers' description of work in, 26–27; prisoner description of life in, 24–26; reputation enhanced by assignment to, 78; similarity between silent system and, 40–41; terminology of, 23–24; described, 21–23. *See also* prison system

control unit tiers: photograph of, 22 *fig*, 23; reform of "tier walk", 200, 201–9, 279n.18–80n.18

Correctional Mental Health Collaboration, 235n.23

correctional trade journal advertisements: "The Best Design Implementation", 25 *fig*; "Do You Know Who This Is?", 178 *fig*; "Identify and Classify Inmates", 135; "They Won't Get Past Your S.T.A.R.", 89 *fig*; "The Toughest Tray on the Block", 42 *fig*; "The Violent Prisoner Chair", 50, 51 *fig*; "When It Comes to Choices, They Should Be Yours Not Theirs", 87 *fig*; "When You Can't Trust What's behind the Bars", 167 *fig*; "Your Worst Nightmare", 86 *fig*

Corrections: A Humanistic Approach (Toch), 108

corrections bureaucracy: local level of, 11–12; prison management by, 10–14

Corrections Forum, 36

crackdowns, 239n.7

crime: fascination of public with, 8–9; harm from, 6; perceived as central social problem, 234n.16

"The Criminal Mind: A Challenge to Corrections" (Gondles), 177

criminals: fascination of public with, 8–9; perceived as central social problem, 234n.16

Critchef Panopticon (Bentham), 38 *fig*

Crowds and Power (Canetti), 99

"cultural anesthesia", 8

custodial (security) staff: abuse of authority by, 57, 246n.45; accountability of, 59; on capacity for inmate violence, 88–90; on decision making function of infraction system, 81–85; description of control unit work by, 26–27; disconnection between mental health staff and, 11, 132–34, 154–57, 265n.26–66n.26; "dog on a chain" expectations of, 170–71; emotional responses to throwing behavior by, 45–47; excessive use of force by, 246n.45; frustrations expressed by, 220–21; guns carried by, 238n.3; on impact of isolation on prisoners, 30–31; institutional methods for dealing with antisocial prisoners, 185–87; perspective on potential of change, 277n.6; psychiatric treatment and alignment of mental health staff and, 152–54; regarding "stupid" inmates, 145–47; relationship between legitimate/illegitimate force by, 62–63; specialized emotional stance required of, 27–28; throwing behavior as mark of affiliation and, 47–48

custodial (security) staff training: on handling disturbed prisoner, 105–7; legitimacy of intensive coercion element in, 64–65; mock scenes of throwing behavior during, 48; on opportunistic orientation of inmates, 85–88; point of cautionary lessons in, 267n.7; rule-oriented "security mindset" emphasized during, 57–58; on use of stun belts, 92–95, 253n.32–54n.33; on using restraints, 61–64; on "verbal tactics", 166–70, 266n.3

"custody" organizational hierarchy, 11

"The Dangerous Individual" (Foucault), 270n.18

Davis, Angela, 60

death penalty, 272n.30

decompensation, 258n.26

Delano, Sam, (pseudonym) 145, 147–48

"Derek Janson" (untitled self-portrait drawing), 73 *fig*

Derrida, Jacques, 248n.4

developmental approach: mental health treatment using, 124–26, 147; on psychopathy, 183, 272n.29

diagnosis: assessment of delusional prisoners, 104–5; Axis I (DSM-IV) diagnosis, 141; Axis II (DSM-IV) diagnosis of, 141, 143, 158, 177, 269n.16–70n.16; Axis I/II distinction in, 142; connecting inmate behavior to identity, 157–59; DSM-IV used in, 140–41, 142–43, 263n.12, 264n.16; early orientations of, 263n.15–64n.15; screening of new prisoners as part of, 99–101, 102–3; various approaches to personality typing/criminal thinking, 268n.13–69n.13. *See also* mental health staff

Kramer, William (pseudonym), 109–10, 114, 150, 257n.16

Larson, John (pseudonym): doubt regarding category of psychopathy, 216; education booths reform by, 200–201, 209–19; frustrations expressed by, 220–21; on need for change, 195–96, 198; regarding Janson's transfer from control unit, 95, 203–4, 205; on struggling it out, 191–92; "tier walk" reform by, 201–9

Lawes, Lewis, 134

"lockdown" system, 23

long-term control unit confinement: dangers of antisocial behavior/psychopathy during, 176–87; desire for respect during, 174–75; elements that maintain, 164–65; issues of reinclusion following, 187–90; lack of nationwide information on, 266n.1; systemic compulsions making up, 164

Lynds, Elam, 40, 41, 43, 51

McGowan, Randall, 134

"machineries of the system," 173

McKinley, Bill (pseudonym), 191–92, 195, 197, 202, 219–20, 221

"mad" and "bad" as used to distinguish prisoners, 4

The Mask of Sanity (Cleckley), 185

Masters, Jarvis Jay, 44, 48

Mattingly, David (pseudonym), 78, 79, 91–92

maximum security prisons. *See* control units

maximum security in relation to rationality, 5

meals/mealtime: example of power struggle during, 42–43; prisoner complaints regarding, 41–42; special technologies used for, 41, 42 *fig*

Melossi, Dario, 43

mental health facilities: debate over prisoner transfer to, 165–66; description of, 116–17

mental health staff: assessment of delusional prisoners by, 104–5; attitude toward intentions of prisoners by, 120–21; counter transference reactions to psychopathy by, 274n.35; debate over emotional detachment by, 132; disconnection between custody staff and, 11, 132–34, 154–57, 265n.26–66n.26; DSM-IV diagnosis used to assess/negotiate by, 140–41, 142–43, 177, 263n.12, 264n.16; facilities housing, 116–17; feelings of incompletion by, 129–30; listening to inmates by, 119–20; parenting response by, 123–24, 259n.34–60n.34; perspective on future of charges by, 119; prisoner screening by, 99–101, 102–3. *See also* diagnosis

mental health treatment: alignment of custody/mental health staff during, 152–54; behaviorism perspective of, 126–28; conflict between custodial/mental health staff during, 154–57; developmental perspective of, 124–26, 147; examined as alternative to punishment, 5; inconclusive nature of, 129–30; inmate's reflections on, 122–23; limited nature of supplied, 263n.11; medication given during, 153, 258n.28, 259n.30, 265n.24; parenting orientation of, 123–24, 259n.34–60n.34

269n.16–70n.16; assumptions made regarding, 6; behaviorism focus on modifying, 126–28; classification/diagnosis connecting identity to, 157–59; defiant use/throwing of body products, 43–49; frustration over failure to reward good, 70; "guarded", 35; positive impact of change on, 196–97; staff assessment of delusional, 104–5. *See also* "choice to be bad"; infraction system; psychopathy; rational decisions

prisoners: arrival/receiving/screening of new, 99–103; demographics of, 9; description of isolation by, 29–34; expressions regarding "loss of control" by, 54–55; impact of prison environment on, 83; institutionalized referring to, 240n.10; issue of rational decision making by, 5; narratives and perspectives of, 236n.27; niche created by, 236n.25; silent system goal of "tame", 43; straight behavior accountability of, 59–60; stun belts used when transporting, 92–95, 253n.32–54n.32; "stupid" as designation for, 144–49; survival techniques used by, 34–35; terminology referring to, 9, 232n.8; treated as rational actors, 5. *See also* long-term control unit confinement; mentally ill prisoners

The Prison and the Factory (Melossi and Pavarini), 43

prison riots: recollections by prisoners, 50–52; undermining authority element in, 280n.20

prison system: classification system used in, 134–39; conflicts between intersecting authorities in, 11; corrections bureaucracy management of, 10–14; custody as central function of, 75–76; debates over power, self, or personhood formation and, 7; differences between early 20th century and contemporary, 278n.10–79n.10; examining existence of "give" or hope in, 6–7; examining rationality of, 5–6; Foucault on power/containment and knowledge/normalization dynamic of, 210; frustration over failure to reward good behavior, 70; historic aspect of, 14–15; incapacitation/punishment over rehabilitation in, 139–40; as industry, 9–10; modernity of, 267n.5; shifting patterns of expansion of, 10; terminology of, 9, 231n.3–32nn.3, 8, 238n.5–39n.5; utilitarian theory of motivation of 19th century, 198; warehouse model of, 198–99, 200; women incarcerated in, 233n.10. *See also* control prison technology; control units; infraction system

prison system environment: capacity for violence in "secure", 88–90; effect on inmates, 83; mentally ill prisoner's perception of, 112–14; punishment through, 5

prison system population, 232n.9–33n.9, 234n.17, 237n.2–38n.2, 246n.46–47n.46

"Prison Torture" (drawing by Tarselli), 111 *fig*

prison workers, 231n.3. *See also* custodial (security) staff; mental health staff

Psychiatry Inside Out (Basaglia), 131

throwing behavior: alienation of custody workers due to, 45–46; "conversation" produced by chronic, 48–49; described, 43–44; emotional responses of prison workers to, 45–47; HIV/AIDS and hepatitis contamination element of, 46; meaning of, 45; prison workers and mark of affiliation from, 47–48; as social act, 44–45; social boundary effect of, 46–47

"tier walk" reform, 200, 201–9, 279n.18–80n.18

Tillich, Stephen (pseudonym), 112, 114, 115, 116, 122, 123, 257n.20–58n.20, 259n.32

A Time to Die (Wicker), 248

Toch, Hans, 108, 110

Tocqueville, Alexis de, 36, 40

Topham, James, 165

"The Toughest Tray on the Block" (advertisement), 42 *fig*

training. *See* custodial (security) staff training

Trumble, Rick (pseudonym), 82, 83

truth: power struggle over deception and, 176–77; prisoner's desire to be believed when telling the, 173–74

Tucker, Gary, 139

Turner, Willie, 44

Tuttle, Carl (pseudonym), 73–75, 81

Twenty Thousand Years in Sing Sing (Lawes), 134

Tyrnauer, Gabrielle, 75

untitled drawing (Tarselli), 175 *fig*

utilitarian theory of motivation, 198

"verbal tactics" strategies, 166–70, 266n.3

victim awareness class, 212–15, 281nn.26, 28

Vincent, Thomas (pseudonym), 2, 3, 4, 231n.2

violence: during application of restraints to prisoner, 62; by and upon individual inmates, 52, 54, 232n.4, 236n.26; opportunistic orientation of inmate, 85–88; prison riot, 50–52; prison technology to control opportunistic, 86–87, 90–95; during removal from control unit cells, 50–55, 53 *fig*; respect theme in prisoners' descriptions of own, 55–56; "secure" environment and capacity for, 88–90; self-control by prison workers to prevent, 57–58; threat to "coherence of the self" as central to, 56–57; "verbal tactics" strategies to defuse, 166–70, 266n.3. *See also* force

"The Violent Prisoner Chair" (advertisement), 50, 51 *fig*

Viridiana (film), 261n.41

volitional criminology: control units supported by logic of, 84–85; emphasis on the individual by, 84

walk-arounds ("tier walk") reform, 200, 201–9

warehouse model, 198–99, 200

weapons: guards on finding inmate, 88; made by prisoners, 52

"The Well-Ordered Prison: England, 1780–1865" (McGowan), 134

The Whale and the Reactor (Winner), 85

"When It Comes to Choices, They Should Be Yours Not Theirs" (advertisement), 87 *fig*

Compositor: BookMatters, Berkeley
Text: 11/14 Adobe Garamond
Display: Gill Sans Book
Printer and binder: Thomson-Shore, Inc.